Psyche and Demos

Deety
Davis
4 Oct 77

RECONSTRUCTION OF SOCIETY SERIES

General Editors
Robert E. Lana   Ralph L. Rosnow

JEFFREY H. GOLDSTEIN
Aggression and Crimes of Violence

ROBERT SOMMER
The End of Imprisonment

BERNARD RUBIN
Media, Politics, and Democracy

WARREN B. MILLER and R. KENNETH GODWIN
Psyche and Demos: Individual Psychology and the Issues of Population

PSYCHE AND DEMOS

Individual Psychology and the Issues of Population

Warren B. Miller
American Institutes for Research

and

R. Kenneth Godwin
Oregon State University

New York
Oxford University Press
1977

Library of Congress Cataloging in Publication Data

Miller, Warren B   1935–
   Psyche and demos.

   (Reconstruction of society series)
   Bibliography: p.
   Includes index.
   1. Population. 2. Population policy. I. Godwin,
R. Kenneth, joint author. II. Title. III. Series.
HB885.M53   301.32   76-42618
ISBN 0-19-502200-9
ISBN 0-19-502199-1 pbk.

To our wives, children and parents,
To continuity,
And to the demos within us all

INTRODUCTION TO THE SERIES

> When society requires to be rebuilt, there is no use in attempting to rebuild it on the old plan.
>
> —John Stuart Mill, *1858*

The problems of society are many and complex, and sound plans for revitalizing it are few. Institutions that once seemed to work quite well no longer do so; and many new programs, hastily conceived, have failed or just faded into oblivion. Therefore, it is time now to determine what has and has not been accomplished, to analyze and challenge our assumptions, and to offer new and carefully conceived blueprints for rebuilding society. At the same time that we examine the problems of society, we must also consider the institutions that function as agents of change.

That is the purpose of this book and the others in the Reconstruction of Society series. Knowledgeable social scientists have been asked to direct their expertise toward solving some of the problems of society—to develop plans that are specific enough to form the basis of policy discussions and decisions. In the end, of course, even the best blueprint can be no more than a technical exercise if the means and the will are lacking. As Justice Felix Frankfurter observed, "In a democratic society such as ours, relief must come through an aroused popular conscience that sears the conscience of the people's representatives." The ideas presented in this series may be a step in that direction.

This fourth volume in the series, by Warren B. Miller, M.D., and R. Kenneth Godwin, Ph.D., explicates a basic dilemma of a multitude of social ills: There are too many people and too many new people being born. Estimates are that in merely two generations the world population will be more than double the current astounding figure of four billion—double the number of people alive in 1930. The social problems rooted in this simple fact can only be exacerbated when the population prophecy is fulfilled. Miller and Godwin elucidate the complex interaction of individual and social variables affecting population growth. Further, they carefully analyze the psychology of population policies in order to develop specific recommendations for beneficial social actions, ranging from information and consciousness-raising programs to the preparation of population impact statements.

Radnor, Pennsylvania   Robert E. Lana
August, 1976   Ralph L. Rosnow

CONTENTS

Preface xi

1. An Introduction to the Issues 3
2. Evolutionary and Historical Perspective 30
3. The Psychology of Decision Making and Adaptation 64
4. Psychodemography and Demopsychology 114
5. Culture, Institutions, and Population Psychology 171
6. Types of Governmental Policies 206
7. Potential Population Policy Actions 233

Notes 287
Suggested Readings 311
Author Index 317
Subject Index 322

PREFACE

The authors of this book come to the writing of it from entirely different disciplinary and professional backgrounds. One of us (WBM) is a psychiatrist who has moved from an academic setting, which included teaching and clinical practice, into a full-time research career. The other (RKG) is a political scientist who has moved from governmental work to an academic career of research and teaching in the fields of political behavior and policy analysis. In spite of these disciplinary differences, both authors have been captivated professionally and personally by the practical urgency and intellectual challenge found within the population field. We hope that the combination of our training and experience will ensure that a balanced discussion of decision making at both the individual and the societal level will be incorporated in this book in a manner that accomplishes the objectives of the Reconstruction of Society Series: the development of intellectual frameworks that can be used to solve problems in the real world. In the collaborative writing of this book, both of us have learned much about population phenomena by sharing and attempting to integrate our respective disciplinary perspectives. We hope that the reader will share equally in the profit of this joint venture.

For whom has this book been written? We intend that this book serve a broad and diverse readership. It should appeal to persons outside of as well as within the academic community who are interested in expanding their understanding of the problems of population and in developing some solutions. It should be of value to administrators, policy makers, and professionals whose work impinges on the population field. It should interest behavioral and social scientists who want to explore the population field in some depth, especially through a nondemographic perspective that puts an emphasis on psychology and public policy. Finally, this book should meet the needs of students who wish to acquire knowledge and develop understanding of the psychological and political science aspects of population problems.

What is the primary purpose of this book? It serves as a detailed and integrated introduction to the study of human population. It does not do this by presenting the standard demographic material available through a number of excellent textbooks; rather it represents an alternative, perhaps complementary, approach to the subject of human population, focusing on individual psychology and introducing a general model that ties individual behavior to other levels of analysis. Throughout, emphasis is placed upon individual decision making as it affects fertility, mortality, and mobility, with primary emphasis on fertility. Other aspects of individual psychology will be discussed, in particular, patterns of adaptation and coping. Our emphasis is also primarily on material drawn from the United States, although we believe our general framework is applicable to other cultures. These emphases have been made for specific, practical reasons. On the one hand, they help to keep the task of writing manageable and the volume of subsequent material within reasonable limits. On the other, they enable us to write primarily within the limits of our expertise.

Chapter 1 makes a general statement of the problems we will address. It introduces the model we propose for analyzing these problems and it discusses the psychological and social issues fundamental to that analysis. It begins with a consideration of the nature of population problems, with an emphasis on their complexity and interrelatedness. A general systems model is then introduced in order to clarify the dynamic interaction among the factors of individual behavior, population phenomena, and the influence of social institutions. Since individual decision making is a key element in the model, the discussion then focuses on freedom in decision making and the potential conflict between individual and social interests. The chapter concludes with a brief treatment of the types of public policies that affect individual decision making in distinct ways and the particular characteristics of these policies that make them effective.

Chapter 2 begins with a discussion of individuals and populations from the perspective of evolutionary biology. It then turns to a discussion of primate species and their populations, which leads in turn to a treatment of humans and their populations at three distinct stages of cultural and technological development. The central themes of the chapter are the continuity and the increasing complexity across evolutionary and historical time of the interactions and interdependences between the individual organism and the population within which it is located.

Chapters 3 and 4 examine individual decision making and adaptation in connection with the domains of individual behavior that collectively affect the size and distribution of populations. Chapter 3 is concerned primarily with the processes and sequences that occur during population-related decision making and adaptation and that affect the outcomes of those decisions and the results of adaptation. Chapter 4 is concerned with the substance of population-related decision making and adaptation, that is, with what the individual decides and what he or she adapts to. Throughout this chapter behavior at the individual level is linked to concepts and measurements appropriate to the aggregate level and to current social issues.

Chapter 5 discusses a number of different social institutions affecting individual population-related decision making and adaptation. Included in these institutions are the family, educational and counseling institutions, the media, and government. Chapter 6 then focuses more closely upon government and governmental policy as factors affecting individual decision making and adaptation. After an examination of the problems inherent in evaluating and selecting from amongst policy alternatives, a social-justice criterion is proposed and then developed. This chapter concludes with the exposition of a fourfold policy typology designed to help evaluate the different policies' ability to affect different types of population problems.

Chapter 7 draws upon all of the material in the preceding chapters to suggest both general public policies and specific policy actions for dealing with the variety of population problems. These problems are categorized according to whether they result from ineffective decisions, conflicts between competing interests, or conflicts between individual and social interests. The policy typology presented in Chapter 6 is utilized to suggest specific ways for dealing with specific types of problems. Although Chapter 7 is systematic, it is not comprehensive in the sense of discussing all or even most of the potentially important population-related policy actions. Rather, it serves to illustrate the application of our general systems model and our other analytic frameworks to a variety of actual population problems.

For those who are interested in using this book as part of a college or university course, we envision several types of usage. *Psyche and Demos* may be used as a supplementary text in a standard, introductory demography course; as one of several basic texts in a general course on population or on population and the environment; or as a basic text, together with supplementary readings or with a companion text presenting a complementary viewpoint, in higher-level undergraduate courses in social psychology, political science, sociology, and anthropology—whenever there is a special focus or interest in population.

The reader should keep in mind that the field of population study is rapidly developing. The increase of knowledge during the last decade makes this book both possible and necessary. However, the material that we present here and discuss in terms of various stages, dimensions, and factors must be seen as subject to refinement and modification as our knowledge increases further during the next few decades, as inevitably it will.

This book owes many things to many people. In particular, we would like to express our great appreciation to Henry David, Richard Clinton, and Bruce Shepard for their enlightening critical reviews of the text and to Alice Levine and Kristy Sprinker for their invaluable help with the manuscript.

February 1977   W.B.M., Palo Alto, California
                                                   R.K.G., Corvallis, Oregon

Psyche and Demos

AN INTRODUCTION TO THE ISSUES

1

During the last two decades, there has been an increasing public awareness of the "problems of population," highlighted by events such as the publication of Ehrlich's book, *The Population Bomb* (1), the development of the popular movement Zero Population Growth, and the formation and deliberation of the President's Commission on Population Growth and the American Future (2). The very rapid growth of both the United States and the world population during this century has had a great deal to do with the development of this popular awareness and concern, but other events closely related to population growth have also played an important role. For example, parallel social movements have developed with philosophies that are resonant with and sympathetic to the concern about overpopulation. Two of the most important of these parallel movements have been the women's movement and the ecology movement; the former because of its concern, among other things, with women's roles and with family planning, and the latter because of its concern with the impact of man and society, especially contemporary mass society, on the environment. In association with the women's movement, there have been major technological innovations in the field of contraception and related changes in social values regarding the acceptability of abortion and of sexuality independent of reproduction. These latter changes have brought the prospect that "something can be done" about population growth much closer to being a reality.

A number of social, economic, and technological developments less directly related to population problems have also played roles in the recent growth of popular concern. Fuel and economic crises have highlighted the interdependence of all peoples and the need for coordinated social planning in the contemporary world. Also, there has been a noticeable increase of violence in the United States, epitomized by the occurrence of a number of political assassinations, and apparently stimulated by the existence of several conventional wars and by the constant threat of nuclear war. Such an ascendence of violence, together with the growth of the impersonal factors in society, has served to remind us of our mutual vulnerability and to increase our sense of helplessness. The threatened and, in some cases, actual social and economic breakdown of the greatly expanding urban centers adds considerable impetus to these feelings. Another important factor during the last several decades has been the growth of humanitarian concern in the United States and a greater recognition of the discrepancies between our ideals and social realities. The landmark Supreme Court desegregation decision of 1954 seems to represent the crucial turning point in this development. Since then, policy makers, law makers, and the courts have increased their efforts to protect and promote the individual, the minority group, and the socially and economically deprived from the potential injustices of a mass society. Finally, all of these events and developments have been promoted in the public consciousness and, at times, even overexposed through the mass media. This pervasive and powerful influence has been made possible by the rapid growth and improvement of communication technology and abetted by the development of new concepts and catch phrases for understanding ourselves and our world, such as "the population explosion" and "spaceship earth." (3)

THE PROBLEMS OF POPULATION

The common image of the contemporary problem of population seems to be based upon the problem of size. In other words, many persons believe that there are too many people, that too many new people are being born, and that the number of people is increasing too rapidly. A look at the long- and short-term trends in population size for the world as a whole, and for this country in particular, certainly confirms this image. The worldwide pattern is well illustrated by Figure 1.1. As will be discussed further in Chapter 2, most of human history has been characterized by alternating periods of pop-

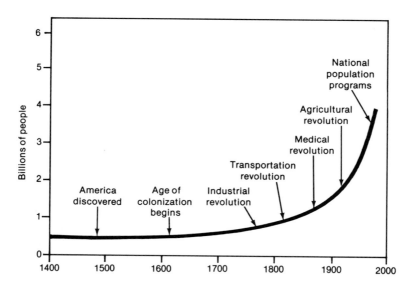

SOURCE: U.S. Bureau of the Census Population Reference Bureau 75-18

Figure 1.1. World Population Growth, 1400–1975.

ulation standstill, loss, and gain. Overall, a very gradual net increase in worldwide population has taken place, until recently when growth has accelerated. It took many thousands of years for the human population of the world to reach a half billion in 1650. By 1930 it had reached two billion. In 1976 it was four billion. Projecting ahead, in about one generation at the beginning of the twenty-first century the world's population will have reached approximately seven billion (4). The same kind of escalation has occurred in the United States. In 1790, at the time of the first census, the U.S. population was less than four million. By 1860, it was 31 million; by 1900, it was 76 million; and by 1950, it was more than 150 million (5). Projecting into the future again, it is estimated that the population of the United States will reach 300 million shortly after the beginning of the twenty-first century. One hundred years from now, depending in large part upon whether American families maintain a two- or three-child average, the population will lie somewhere between 340 million and almost one billion persons (6, 7). These figures dramatize well the exponential growth that populations are capable of achieving when the number of individuals entering a population is in excess of those leaving. A convenient way of determining how rapidly an increase is being achieved is by calculating the "doubling time," that is, the amount of time it takes for a population to double in size. A good rule of thumb is that the doubling time is equal to 70 divided by the constant annual growth rate (8). With the annual growth rate in the United States approximately 1 percent, it can be seen that the United States will double its population approximately every seventy years. For the world as a whole, the annual growth rate is a little more than 2 percent. (9). This means that the entire world is doubling its population every 35 years. For some countries in Southeast Asia, North Africa, and tropical South America, where the annual growth rate is approximately 3 percent, there is a doubling of their population every 23 years, or approximately with each generation.

Is Size A Problem?

It is certainly true that population growth is of major and perhaps unsurpassed importance among the issues facing the world today and that, as a result of it, humankind may be said to be ''at the hinge of history.'' Nevertheless, the common perception that population growth and size constitute a problem deserves closer examination and analysis. There are at least three reasons for doing this. First of all, to say that there are too many people, or that the size or the growth of a particular population constitutes a problem is to place a value on the number of people in a population and its size and growth. Such values are the outgrowth of personal experience and preference. They may be studied scientifically but they may not be validated or demonstrated as true by scientific method (10). For example, some people may feel that the existence of 200 million people in the United States is about the right number. (Indeed, it can be predicted with reasonable certainty that most people, at any given time, will react with that sentiment to whatever the existing number is, whether it is 50 or 400 million.) However, some persons may feel that 200 million is far too many people and some may feel that it is far too few. In general, such disagreements about the relative merits of different population sizes rest on several different issues relating to the quality and quantity of life. One issue is whether the quality of life for individuals increases or decreases with different population sizes. A related but distinct issue is whether the population size should be allowed to increase as long as there is an increase in the total quality of life for all people. Since the total quality of life is equivalent to the product of the average quality of life and the total number in the population, when the population grows it is possible for the average quality of life to decrease at the same time that the *total* quality of life is increasing. For this reason some may argue that population size should be allowed to increase, even while diminishing the average individual quality of life, as long as more people are getting at least a balance of enjoyment out of life.

The second reason for questioning the perception that population growth and size constitute a problem relates to our limited scientific understanding of population phenomena and our limited ability to predict the long-term and even the short-term demographic course of events. Anyone reviewing the comments of behavioral scientists and politicians in the middle and late 1930s (11) realizes that many

of them had the same sense of urgency and imminent danger
regarding demographic trends as are heard today. At that time,
however, the target of concern was decreased population growth
and size. The reason for concern was that the birthrate during the
previous ten years was at its lowest in American history and threatened to persist at a level below replacement. For this reason major
efforts were initiated toward gaining a better understanding of the
behavioral aspects of reproduction (12). No one foresaw the "baby
boom" that was to be launched during the next decade. Now, in
the mid 1970s, after experiencing a wave-like rise and fall of births
in the 1940s, 1950s and 1960s, we are again approximating the
birthrates of the 1930s and reproducing at about replacement level.
To be sure, our scientific understanding of fertility and population
growth rates has increased significantly (13). Nevertheless, there
continues to be uncertainty, with conflicting predictions about the
immediate and long-term demographic future (14, 15).

The third reason for analyzing the perception that population
growth and size constitute a problem is the complexity of the population phenomena and the fact that the size of the population is in-
tricately tied to other highly valued aspects of a population's life in
ways that are as yet poorly understood. Perhaps the best way to
explicate this point about the complexity and interrelatedness of
population phenomena is with an historical review and discussion
of demography and population study.

Demography, the science of population, grew out of the bureaucratic needs of government. Once a society had grown to a certain
level of complexity and hierarchical development, some central
body for administrating, regulating, and planning had to evolve. In
order to meet the bureaucratic needs of such a body, it was important to keep track of people within administrative units. Especially
important was knowing how many people there were and where
each one of them was located. Hence, the origin of the term demography from *demos* for "people" and *graphy* for "writing" or
"record." Administrators not only needed information which could
identify the size and distribution of a population at a particular
time, but they also needed to record change over time; hence their

interest in vital statistics and recording events such as births and deaths. It was this plus the registration of moves within or between administrative, social, or political units that enabled the government to account for all its people. With the development of greater complexity and interdependency within society, administrative needs were not sufficiently met by knowing the numbers and locations of people. Information was also needed about age and sex, for example, so that plans could be made regarding family formation, school construction, labor-force activity, military recruitment, and care for the aged. For similar reasons, knowledge about the educational, occupational, racial, and religious characteristics of a population was necessary. As society grew more complex, it needed more precise population projections into the future. It is for this reason that demography in the United States during the twentieth century moved from being largely a descriptive science to one which relied heavily upon mathematics. New analytic tools have been developed and complex mathematical models constructed. In many cases these have greatly improved the ability to estimate the rates of population change and to project the future characteristics of a population. Many of these more precise methods have become important for both the determination and the application of government policies.

THE POPULATION SYSTEM

We see, then, that the development of the science of population has been based on much more than simply a concern with population size: the geographic distribution of a population is also important. Both of these factors are structural. They describe the structure of a population in space at a given time. A third structural factor of importance to demographers is "population composition." This term refers to the social status structure of a population or, in other words, the distribution of people within a population across different social statuses. These three structural factors change in time as a function of the dynamic factors such as fertility, mortality, in- and out-migration, and status mobility. In- and out-migration are perhaps better encompassed by the general term "geographic mobility," with the recognition that the latter also includes spatial movement within a population system as well as movement in and out of it. Recently, demographers have emphasized the interdependence of the various aspects of population structure and of the changes in that structure which take place over time (16). This view leads to a more dynamic appreciation of population phenomena and also sets the stage for a systems approach to understanding them.

A Systems Model

A specific population may be conceptualized as a system (17, 18, 19, 20). It is composed of components (people and associations of people) that act and interact in regular ways to maintain the integrity of the whole system. Through feedback and the mutual adjustment of these components, homeostasis, or balance within the system, is preserved and its goals are achieved. A central goal for any group consists of the balanced regulation of its population over time within the adaptive limits of its internal and environmental resources. This is achieved by the dynamic interaction of those factors within it which constitute the population regulation system. Those factors which appear to be of fundamental importance for the current U.S. population are schematically represented in Figure 1.2.

At the aggregate level a population may be described in terms of the three demographic structural factors which change as a function of the four demographic dynamic factors. The latter are themselves simply a function of the collective decisions being made at the individual level by the people within a population with regard to the various vital and other demographically relevant events in their lives. These relations are depicted in Figure 1.2 by arrows. It can also be seen that many of the decisions made at the individual level are strongly influenced and/or constrained by a variety of social institutions that exist at a level intermediate between the aggregate and the individual level. The figure also indicates that individual patterns of adaptation are influenced by both the aggregate structural factors and by social institutions and they in turn have a direct

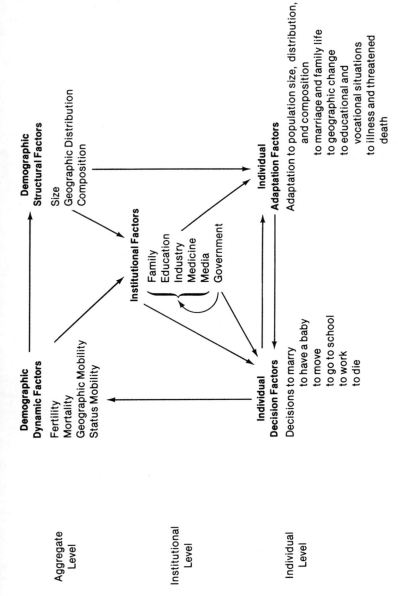

Figure 1.2. A schematic representation of the major factors that constitute the U.S. population regulation system and the key relationships between these factors.

influence on individual decisions. Individual adaptation is further influenced by various decisions, such as having a baby, that create a whole set of new conditions the individual must adapt to. Social institutions themselves are affected by the aggregate dynamic and structural factors and thus serve as mediators of the feedback effects of aggregate level factors upon individual decision making and adaptation. It will be noted that the figure indicates that governmental institutions have a direct effect on other institutions and on individual decision making. One of the chief ways in which these effects are accomplished is through policy formation and implementation.

Not all of the possible connections have been indicated by arrows in Figure 1.2. For example, it is possible for both the dynamic and the structural factors at the aggregate level to have a direct effect on individual decision making. This is the case when the decision maker's perceptions of infant mortality or the population density of the community enter directly into the decision about whether or not to have a baby. As another example, both individual voting behavior and institutional influences provide major feedback effects upon governmental policy activities at the institutional level. Thus, the arrows included in Figure 1.2 should not be interpreted as indicating exclusive relations. Rather, they should be seen as calling attention to relations which will be emphasized in our treatment of the general model or paradigm which is presented in this book.*

Each of the subsequent chapters will treat specific features or elements within the model represented by Figure 1.2. Chapter 2 discusses the evolution and history of the overall population regulation system. It describes some of the biological, natural selective, and historical origins of various components of the system. Chapter 3 discusses the various and sometimes complicated behavioral processes involved in making demographically relevant decisions and

---

* Throughout this book we use the term "model" in the general rather than the strict scientific sense. In the general scientific sense a model is a simplified but analytically useful representation of reality. In the strict scientific sense a model is a logically consistent, precise set of propositions which represent reality.

adapting to various demographic conditions. Chapter 4 relates individual decisions to the demographic dynamic factors and demographic structural factors to individual adaptation. We call these two areas of interest "psychodemography" and "demopsychology," respectively. They are depicted in Figure 1.2 by the arrows forming the left- and right-hand sides of the box-shaped model.

Chapter 5 deals with a number of the more important institutions that directly affect individual decisions and adaptations of demographic significance. Chapter 6 focuses on one of those institutions—the government—and discusses different types of policies by which it can influence other social institutions and individuals. Finally, Chapter 7 analyzes a series of population-related policies which might be implemented by government at the present time. In order to limit the amount of material that must be given consideration and thus keep the scope of the book within manageable limits, the discussion in this book, with the exception of that in Chapter 2, will deal with the application of this general model primarily within the context of the contemporary United States.

Other Systems And Factors

There are some other important societal systems and factors that influence and interact with the various demographic factors, and thus with the population regulation system, but which are not explicitly included in Figure 1.2. Little direct attention is paid to these in the subsequent chapters and therefore some mention is due at this point. For example, there is the link between population growth and economic growth. This link has many sources (21, 22, 23), but fundamental to all of them is the pressure within a capitalistic economy for social-economic units to expand production in order to increase profits and to meet the threat of competition. The expansion of production tends both to be facilitated by and to stimulate population growth.

There is also the link between the size of a community's population and the relative costs of production and services. Fundamental to this is the relationship between population size or density or both and the complexity of individual interaction. As size or density increase, individual interactions become more complex; as a result, the laws of organizational efficiency and economy of scale make it possible for managers to decrease the costs of production and services.

There are also important links between community organization and various population factors. For example, many school systems around the nation have recently experienced an excess of schools as a result of children from the "baby boom" of the 1950s moving out of the school-age groups. As another example, there is a link between community organization and geographic mobility (24). As a community becomes more differentiated and complex, the increased emphasis on job-specific role behavior makes it feasible for individuals to move in and out of roles and, thus, in and out of the community. This development, along with the increase in information exchange and improvement of transportation that takes place between such a differentiating community and its neighboring areas, makes geographic mobility both easier and more desirable.

There is also the link between group politics and group demography. For example, in the eyes of minority group members there is an important relation between the numbers in their subpopulation and their power vis-à-vis the majority. Ultimately this may manifest itself in a concern with racial or ethnic genocide and in conscious efforts to increase population size (25).

Finally, there is the link between population size and the resource-carrying capacity of the environment (26, 27). In general, as the population size and/or density increases, there is a corresponding increase in demand upon environmental resources and the subsequent production of potential environmental contaminants. At what level these effects begin to occur, how rapidly they increase, and what may be done to prevent, attenuate, or compensate for them, depends upon both the level of relevant technology, upon human values, and upon the relative priorities of both the public and those directly responsible for doing something about actual or potential ecological problems. All these specific examples demonstrate how closely the population regulation system is interlocked with economic, community, political, and ecological systems. A full understanding of the population regulation system of a nation such as the United States can only come about through simultaneous consideration of these other interlocked systems.

INDIVIDUAL DECISION MAKING
AND FREEDOM OF CHOICE

As we have indicated, the dynamic population factors represent the aggregate effects of a large number of individual decisions. For example, each couple regularly makes a number of decisions about sexuality, fertility regulation, and childbearing. Out of millions of such decisions, the generations of Americans are born. Each individual decides matters of life style, where to live and for how long, how much education to achieve, what occupation to pursue, and what type of health care to utilize. Out of these countless decisions, society develops its needs for schools, colleges, and universities, for jobs, for space and housing, for transportation and communication systems, and for health delivery systems. In other words, the aggregation of individual decisions shapes the educational, occupational, housing, and other institutional systems of society. The status of any one of these provides feedback which then influences ongoing individual decisions as they are made. This type of interaction is fundamental to the balance that is achieved in the United States between the needs and desires of the individual and the overall allocation of resources by society between individual and social interests.

In the United States, great emphasis is placed upon individual free choice in all decision-making spheres up to the point where such free choice conflicts with the social interests. When the social interest is sufficiently compromised by individual decisions, institutions within American society act to impose limits on individual behavior through the establishment of regulations, punishment, and the like. In general, however, because of the high value placed on individual liberty in the American social philosophy, such intervention is limited wherever and to whatever degree is possible.

This American social philosophy of laissez-faire individual liberty is ultimately founded on a belief that the interests of the individual are, to a significant degree, in conflict with those of society, and that the interaction between the individual and society is characterized by the tendency for society, unless checked, to impose costs and restrictions on the individual to a greater degree than it provides benefits and opportunities. Discussions of possible United States population policies have tended to make the same assumption about the inherent opposition of the individual and society. For example, discussions of fertility-control policy are commonly organized according to the degree to which planned interventions interfere with voluntary individual choice (28, 29), beginning with a consideration of nonintervention, progressing through voluntary methods that involve the provision of information and/or service, to those that involve the suggestion of attitudes and the inducement of behavior, and concluding ultimately with those that require and coerce behavior. Most of the policies actually in use have placed emphasis on voluntary individual fertility regulation through the development of contraceptive technology and the distribution of this technology and information to the public. Although some individuals have argued persuasively that more active intervention by policy makers is necessary in order to change social institutions that have strong pronatalist effects (30), the counter-argument has been that the large portion of United States fertility that is above replacement is due to unwanted children and this would largely disappear if more effective contraceptive methods were widely available (31). Thus, in this country fertility-regulating policies have been drawn almost exclusively from the voluntary end of the policy spectrum. Even the most coercive policies which have been suggested have a major voluntary component built in. For example, it has been suggested that with continued population growth it may be advisable to issue each individual a marketable license to have a child. Since such licenses could be bought or sold, they would be subject to the mechanisms of the marketplace, and would thus preserve, within severe constraints, a certain amount of free choice (32).

The emphasis upon the potential conflict between the individual and the social interest and upon individual freedom of choice is by no means limited to the area of fertility regulation. For example, in the area of geographic mobility important questions have been raised about the collective effects on the public interest of private mobility decisions (33). Further, it has been argued that a central objective of geographic mobility policy should be the enablement, socially and economically, of the disadvantaged members of the population to act freely on their mobility preferences (34). In the area of occupational mobility a recent request for contract proposals from the National Institute of Education cited the current limitations for women and ethnic minorities and sought the development of a new television series that would expand the occupational awareness of these groups and increase their freedom of choice in connection with occupation selection (35).

Three Levels of Freedom

Given the social philosophy of this country, which emphasizes free choice, it is important to examine and understand the implications of this philosophy as it relates to the problems of population. In doing this, it is useful to identify three types of freedom: biological and technological freedom, psychological freedom, and social freedom. In each of these what we shall mean by freedom is the relative absence of constraint of any form upon the individual's behavior. Thus, biological and technological freedom means the absence of constraints that are biological or technological in nature. For example, one is not free to reproduce if one is not biologically able to conceive. Similarly, one's freedom to regulate conception and childbearing is relatively limited if contraceptive technology remains undeveloped. Psychological freedom means the relative absence of internal, psychological constraints. The latter occur when an individual lacks information about a matter of concern or when the information that he or she has is incorrect. Restraint of choice also occurs when disruptive or excessive emotionality, conflicting motivations or attitudes, or weak and inadequate decision-making skills interfere with an individual's development and execution of a decision which reflects his or her true interests. For example, someone is not free to make family-planning decisions if that person's information about the costs of childbearing or about the timing of the fertile period is inaccurate. Similarly, someone is not free in making such decisions if anxiety or extreme passion overcome a well-reasoned choice, or if that person is so full of conflict or so ineffective in decision making that the choice made does not represent his or her true and lasting interests. Social freedom is based on the absence of social constraints and limitations. The latter include systematic restrictions on access to information, on achieving desired objectives, or restrictions on the desired objectives themselves. Restrictions also include the systematic application of influences such as social pressure, suggestion, positive or negative incentives, and physical force of a kind that coerces individuals to act outside their own long-term interests. For example, individuals are not free with regard to reproduction if the services of a family-planning program are not available in their community, if social disapproval or ridicule follows utilization of that program, or if coercive or punitive measures are applied should they have more than some number of children determined by the state.

The Meaning of Freedom

Several qualifying comments will clarify the meaning of the term "freedom" as we have been using it here. First, it must be kept in mind that in talking about freedom as the absence of constraint, we are talking in a very general sense. In actuality, we measure freedom in terms of particular situations and particular options with respect to which we may be constrained. Thus, it may be said that our overall freedom is really composed of many smaller freedoms. Put in somewhat different terms, our macrofreedom is the sum total of the entire set of our microfreedoms (36), each of the latter involving specific situations with specific options and constraints. This type of multiple option-multiple constraint account of freedom seems to us to do better justice to psychological reality and to what we usually mean by the term when we speak in a general sense.

Second, in real life, constraints tend not to operate in an all-or-nothing way. In other words, they do not operate to completely close off an option but rather, to reduce its availability and/or increase the cost of selecting it. For example, the absence of child-care opportunities for a woman with young children who desires to go to work does not so much eliminate her option to work as it makes difficulties for her in terms of time, energy, or money.

Third, it is important to appreciate that freedom is a function of both the number of options available to a person and the degree of constraint on those options. In other words, one's macrofreedom may decrease either with a loss of options or with an increase in the degree of constraint on available options. For example, the government could pursue a fertility limitation policy in two different ways: in one, individuals would lose the option to have more than two children; in the other, they would retain that option but experience a very severe increase in constraints if they selected it. In the latter case it is very likely that the costs which they incur by selecting that option, be they in terms of money, energy, time, or whatever, would severely constrain their selection of other options. In the United States, it appears that the more significant, although perhaps less obvious, limitations on freedom have derived from an increase in the degree of constraint on options rather than from their complete loss. Comparatively speaking, individuals have many options in this country. The important question becomes, what will each cost. It also appears that the number of options available has increased in direct proportion to the growth of social complexity. Although some authors have argued that our freedoms have "peaked" in American society (37), it does not seem true that our options are decreasing. If anything, they are greatly expanding. It does appear true, however, that Americans should anticipate increasing constraints on their options. In other words, in the foreseeable future, the total pool of options will be greater but the number of choices among them for the average individual will remain unchanged or might even diminish. Thus, it will become increasingly important for each individual to establish a priority of choices.

A fourth qualifying consideration with regard to the meaning of freedom is that options and constraints may be judged from two very different vantage points—that of the individual making the choice and that of the observer. While the individual may consider

him or herself to be making a free or unconstrained choice, the observer may judge the individual to be biologically, psychologically,
or socially unfree. For example, someone who is either unaware of
the existence of effective methods of birth control or whose community does not provide access to such methods may, as a result of lack of
knowledge or interest, not perceive him or herself as unfree. However, by some general standard, that individual does lack a degree
of freedom. This difference between perceived and actual freedom
has been called "potential freedom" (38). Its importance lies in the
fact that large degrees of potential freedom tend to stimulate policy
responses, with policy makers intervening largely on the basis of
their own values. For example, the policy to promote the distribution of contraceptive methods in a community where such methods
are not available and where the unplanned pregnancy rate is very
high rests on a number of assumptions about the goodness of
planned pregnancies and the relative benefits and costs of contraceptive use.

A fifth and final qualifying consideration is that many of the
social constraints on individual action derive directly from the
needs and rights of other people. This is the meaning of the maxim,
"Freedom necessitates responsibility." In a society where everyone
is supposed to be equally free, everyone's freedom is limited by the
degree to which his or her behavior impinges upon someone else's
freedom of action. Thus, freedom can only be understood in a general social context where it is bound and shaped by the rights and
duties which the people of that society accept and value.

The Problems of Free Decision Making

If, as we have argued, the social system in the United States depends heavily upon a social philosophy that places the greatest emphasis on free individual decision making, then it will be helpful to
identify the types of problems which result from such an emphasis
and how these problems manifest themselves in the area of population before selecting population-relevant policies. The chief problems appear to separate into two broad categories, those associated
with ineffective decisions and those associated with decisions that

lead to conflicts of interest. Ineffective decisions are those that do not achieve the results desired by the individual decision maker. In these decisions, there is some factor which either prevents effective decision making or leads to an undesired outcome in spite of effective decision making. On the other hand, decisions that lead to conflict of interest are those in which there is some conflict between the interests of the individual decision maker and the interests of other members of society. Such conflicts assume two primary forms: either the decision maker is in conflict with another individual or group of individuals, or with society as a whole. The classical illustration of the latter type of conflict, which is of particular importance in the area of population, is the overgrazing of the common land by individual herdsmen in England during previous centuries (39).

Let us examine some specific examples of these problems. The problem of making an ineffective decision occurs, for example, when an individual lacks information or possesses inaccurate information about some area of interest. Misinformation about the chances of getting pregnant, lack of information about the dangers of abortion or the costs of bearing a child, misinformation concerning employment opportunities in another city, or lack of information about available medical-care facilities are all illustrations of informational limitations potentially leading to ineffective decisions. Lack of decision-making skills may result in a failure to consider alternative courses of action, the development of indecisiveness or ambivalence, or failure to consider the long-term implications of a decision. As a result, such lack of skills may also interfere with making effective decisions. Finally, situational factors may interfere with an individual's making an effective decision. This may be because the situation is stressful and decision-making skills are disrupted. Or it may occur as a result of the normative or opportunity structure of the community. For example, a sexually active teenage girl from a small community may avoid seeking information about oral contraception because she believes her family physician will disapprove and because there is no other community resource to which she can turn.

Decisions lead to the first type of conflict of interest when an individual or a group of individuals gains at the expense of another individual or group. This is the case, for example, when the citizens of a town pass an ordinance setting an annual quota on new house construction and thus limiting the number of individuals who may immigrate to the town. Another example is where one individual wants an abortion and another individual (such as the sexual partner and presumptive father of the fetus), or a group (such as a community hospital), are opposed. These problems are fundamentally a question of the appropriate distribution of human and legal rights. Do the citizens have a right to restrict immigration, or do those who wish to immigrate have a right to do so? Does the woman who wants an abortion have the right to it, does the sexual partner have the right to prevent it, or does the hospital have the right to refuse service? Since in such conflicts of interest what is one person's right is necessarily another person's duty and what is one person's gain is another person's loss, there is no simple solution. The problem becomes, then, a question of the proper ordering of rights, or a question of which individual's or which group's rights should be given priority. The history of decisions regarding the various priorities of a single community are reflected in the rights structure of that community or the distribution and ordering of rights within the community. Such a structure is established by convention, public sentiment, the various branches of government, and ultimately by that community's sense of and system of justice (40).

The second or "commons" conflict of interest arises when individual decisions impinge upon the common interest. The best example of such a conflict in the field of population is the overproduction of children in a community or in a society where individual families pursue their own family-size desires without regard to the public good. This commons type of problem is made possible by three social conditions. The first occurs when a significant portion of the negative effects of an individual's decisions do not return to that person but are conferred either upon contemporary and helpless (or unknowing) others or upon someone in the future. This is possible when the incentive structure of the community within which the decision maker lives does not reflect the costs to the whole community of that person's actions. For example, the costs to a community of its public school system is commonly not distributed among the citizens through taxes in proportion to the number of children they have. The second social condition which makes commons problems possible is the relative absence in people of those two qualities that protect a community from exploitation by its own members, namely their tendency to become involved in their community and their future orientation. The presence of both of these qualities in an individual or in a group strongly promotes decisions leading to long-term community gain as opposed to short-term individual gain. It is only when individuals perceive the community's loss as their own loss that self-interested actions reinforce the community's interests. Further, the perception of the community's loss must include what happens in one year, one decade, and in one generation or else the community's future interest is sacrificed to its present interest. The third and final social condition leading to commons-type problems is the presence of "free riders" in a community. Even if most of the people of a community follow the long-term social interest, if there is a large enough percentage who do not but take advantage of the other's good will and act as free riders, then the latter's actions tend to cost the "common" all that has been saved by the majority. At the same time, they demoralize the majority and discourage them from acting in the common good.

Free Decision Making and Public Policies

What means are available for dealing with these three problems derived from the American social philosophy emphasizing free, individual choice? In particular, what public policies will be responsive to the sources of these problems? There are a number of different qualities or dimensions according to which public policies may be described or evaluated. In the remaining paragraphs of this chapter we will discuss some of these qualities or dimensions briefly, leaving a more substantial treatment of them for the last two chapters. The two qualities of paramount political importance for public policy are the degree to which public policy distributes or redistributes public monies and the degree to which it requires the regulation or self-regulation of behavior (41, 42, 43). For example, policies may act by distributing general public monies for the research and development of new contraceptive technology or for the establishment of widespread sex-education programs. On the other hand, policies may act by redistributing the money of those with large families to those with small ones via a special tax measure, or by establishing special scholarships or vocational-training programs for unemployed women at the expense of working individuals through an income tax. As examples of regulatory policies, we may cite those which provide for self-regulation in family size by promoting the dissemination of contraceptive information and methods, and a hypothetical policy which directly regulates family size through the licensing of childbearing.

Policies also vary in the extent to which they are symbolic as opposed to material. Symbolic policies achieve their objectives by conveying status and recognition. They tend to encounter low political resistance and operate at a relatively low cost. Examples of these in the population area include those with pronatalist effects such as the distribution of motherhood awards and those with antinatalist effects such as giving patriotic buttons to individuals with small families or publicly acclaiming achievement-oriented and successful women. Material policies generally involve the distribution of material goods, most commonly money. Therefore, they are generally included in the distributive policies described above.

Policies may act at the biological, psychological, or social level. An example of a biological-level policy would be one which promoted the development of medical technology. Examples of psychological-level policies would include one that promoted the discovery of knowledge about the motivations for geographic mobility through a behavioral-science research program, one that sought to expand career awareness among primary-school-age children through T.V. programming, and one that sought to alter individual attitudes toward health care through a massive propaganda program. At the social level, policies may be designed to alter the opportunity, incentive, rights, or normative structure of a community. With respect to shaping community opportunity structure, an example would be a policy providing financial support to those community institutions that help individuals and families during the process of geographic mobility. An example of a policy directed toward the incentive structure of a community would be one which subsidized children's health care, day care, and education in an effort to remove some of the disincentives for having children. An example of a policy designed to alter a community's rights structure would be one that granted individuals the right to sterilization or that granted communities the right to limit growth. Finally, examples of policies aimed at the normative structure of a community would be those using the mass media in an effort to alter a community's prevailing attitudes toward contraceptive services for teenagers or the acceptability of smoking cigarettes.

Given the complexity of population problems and the diversity of potential population policies, how are specific policies to be judged and selected? There is, in fact, a large set of criteria for judging such policies (44). Some are based upon a policy's efficiency, its effectiveness, and upon the equity of its outcome. Additional criteria include the administrative, financial, and political feasibility of the policy. One particularly helpful way of judging population-related policies—a way actually incorporating most of the above criteria—is to assess the degree to which it is responsive to the three problems resulting from the American emphasis on free choice. First, it should be asked, does the policy facilitate individuals making effective decisions, either by improving their decision-making ability or by changing situational aspects of their decision? Second, does the policy order or give priority to certain rights in some standard or just way? In doing this, it is important that the policy not infringe upon certain individual rights that the consensus of public sentiment indicates are fundamental and inalienable. Although a complete list of such rights relevant to the issue of population would be difficult to formulate without some controversy, consensus probably exists about the fundamental importance of the right of reproduction, of health maintenance, and of geographic,

educational, occupational, and social mobility. Third and finally
does the policy promote the internalization of externalities? In other
words, does the policy change those consequences of a decision
that ordinarily do not have a significant incentive value for the
decision maker so that they do, in fact, have an incentive value and
therefore become a part of the decision-making deliberations? It is
desirable that a policy act to alter the incentive structure of society
and return all the significant costs (and benefits) of individuals' actions to those persons themselves. To the extent that this type of incentive structure is achieved by a policy, to that extent the policy
ensures the establishment of a market mechanism that, through its
invisible hand, can conduct the statistical aggregate of individual
decisions in concert with the general social interest.

However, the internalization of externalities is extremely difficult
to achieve in reality. To a large degree, this is because such a step
depends upon the existence of one or more common denominators
or "universal exchange media" into which most people's utilities*
can be translated. Money is of course the most obvious medium,
yet its usefulness is sharply curtailed. In part this is because money
is very unevenly distributed throughout populations and subpopulations; but there are two even more fundamental reasons. First, people's utilities do not translate easily into dollars and cents. How can
one express the value of a geographic move or of an additional two
years of education, much less the value of a child or of an abortion,
in monetary terms so as to capture fully and accurately the worth
of these objects or events? Second, different people's utilities are
usually noncomparable on complex matters. The value of a child to
one person will usually be totally different in kind from the value of
a child to another. In such cases there is no satisfactory way to
choose a monetary value approximating the value of the object or
the course of action in question to two different people, much less
to an entire population.

There are other types of universal exchange media. One of these

---

* A "utility" is anything that meets the need or satisfies the desire of a person.

is political behavior. To the extent that individuals are able to influence government actions, political behavior becomes an expression of individual values and the priorities among those values. In the bargaining and compromising that occurs during the political process, individual political behavior becomes a medium of exchange between interested parties. Again, however, there are drawbacks to the use of this medium, especially in view of the grossly uneven distribution of political influence within the population and various subpopulations. If externalities are to be internalized, it seems inevitable that multiple universal exchange media be utilized and that society constantly take active measures to redistribute the supply of these media to the deprived sectors.

In conclusion, it should be emphasized that our presentation and analysis of the problems of population and of the possible solutions to them is ethnocentric and chronocentric. In other words, the discussion in this book is based upon assumptions and perceptions which are specific to our culture and our time. In spite of these limitations, we believe we are dealing with generic issues which are relevant to most societies at most times, past, present, and future. Paramount among these issues are the complexity of population problems, the connection of these problems with a wide variety of other individual and societal problems, the basic evaluational nature of these problems, their fundamental dependence on aggregate individual decision making, and the constant struggle necessary to bridge the gap between individual and social interests. In this first chapter, we have attempted to develop a model which discusses and explores various aspects of these issues. In the remainder of the book, we shall treat in more detail a number of specific features of this model, some of which have only been adumbrated during this initial discussion.

SUMMARY

In this chapter we make a general statement about the analysis to be conducted throughout the remainder of the book. After reviewing many recent events and developments that have focused popular concern on the population problem, we discuss how personal values, uncertainty about future population trends, and the complex connections between population and other societal phenomena all influence the way in which people perceive and evaluate population problems. Having indicated the complexity of population problems and the multiplicity of factors upon which they are based, we then discuss the major demographic, institutional, and individual psychological factors serving to regulate dynamically the population of a specific group of people. This leads to the presentation and elaboration of a general systems model of these three groups of factors and their interaction within and across their three respective levels of organization. We suggest that this model, although by no means comprehensive, is useful for analyzing and understanding the population regulation system of specific groups of people, especially those within the United States.

Because of the importance of individual decision making in this model and because of the potential conflict between the individual and social interests that may develop when a culture places a high priority upon individual freedom, we examine individual decision making and freedom of choice. First, we describe how individual freedom may be constrained at the biological or technological level, at the psychological level, or at the social level. This leads us to consider the different meanings of freedom and to emphasize the difference between macrofreedom and microfreedom, the various ways in which constraints operate to curtail freedom, and the relation between freedom and responsibility. Next we discuss the problems generated by the emphasis placed on free decision making in the political philosophy of the people of the United States. These problems are separated into two groups: those associated with the making of decisions that do not achieve the results desired by the decision maker, and those associated with conflicts of interest between the decision maker and others. The latter type of problem is further categorized into conflicts of interest between individuals or between groups and conflicts of interest between individuals (or groups) and society in general (the so-called "commons" conflict).

Finally we analyze public policies and their ability to deal with and be responsive to these problems and conflicts. Public policies are analyzed in terms of the degree to which they distribute or redistribute public monies and the degree to which they require the regulation or self-regulation of behavior. These and other analytic categories of public policy are discussed with reference to how well they address the different types of population problems that emerge in a cultural context which places high priority upon free decision making. We argue that those policies which either improve the effectiveness of decisions, rank rights, or internalize externalities would be most responsive to the population problems that are associated with the type of population regulation system that has developed within the United States.

EVOLUTIONARY AND HISTORICAL PERSPECTIVE

2

In the contemporary world with all its special social problems, it is only too easy to forget humanity's biological and evolutionary heritage and its acquired capacity for different forms of individual and cultural adaptation. This is especially true in the population field, where the immensity of the present problems may blind us to the lessons intrinsic in our biological and evolutionary past and in our cultural history. The evolutionary and historical perspective, however, is vitally important in that it helps to clarify the nature and origin of various population issues, while at the same time suggesting important psychological and social mechanisms and causal relationships that are important for population regulation. In short, such a perspective allows us to use the past in order to understand the present and to plan for the future.

THE INDIVIDUAL AND THE POPULATION
IN EVOLUTION

In Chapter 1 we outlined and discussed in a preliminary way the tension existing in society between the individual and the social interest. This tension exists also in a closely parallel form in nature because for all biological organisms, including humans, the individual is a member of a local population of similar organisms with which it regularly interacts. Its interests and those of the population are related not just in the ecological sense that an individual organism is dependent to some degree for its development and survival upon other similar organisms in its immediate community, but also in the larger, evolutionary sense that each individual organism is a product of the forces and pressures of natural selection acting upon a population of similar organisms and, at the same time, participates with that population of similar organisms in the formation of future generations.

Evolution is the central unifying theory in biology. Through it we can understand the origin, the diversity, and the complexity of living organisms, including humans. Central to the theory of evolution is the principle that organisms survive through adaptation. The principle actually applies to both the individual organism and to the population of closely similar organisms (the "species") to which the individual belongs. At the individual level, it means that each organism survives by adapting to its environment. At the population level, it means that the species survives by adapting or modifying itself across generations in accordance with the forces and pressures of the environment. Hence, all those individuals who are best adapted to the environment survive to reproduce themselves and thereby contribute their genetic material to the next generation. In this way, the genetically determined structures and behaviors of the ongoing generations of a population are most influenced by those individuals who survive and reproduce. In other words, adaptation for a species comes about as a result of the reproductive success of its individual members.

For all organisms, there is a local population of closely similar organisms which is known as a "deme" (1). This term generally refers to a local, interbreeding population of individuals, such as a forest of pine trees or a field of grasshoppers. Local populations tend to replace themselves or part of themselves with each generation. When such replacement is reasonably balanced with respect to numbers, the population has a life of its own across time, with all individuals maintaining close similarity due to interbreeding and their common genetic background. The pool of genes located within such local populations serves to maintain the basic structure and behavior of each individual organism within a narrow set of limits. Some variation of individual structure and behavior does, of course, occur due to various recombinations of genetic material from the gene pool through sexual reproduction and due also to various mutations in the genetic material. This variation in structure and behavior plays a vital role in evolution because it allows the local population to change its modal structure and behavior across generations in response to changes in local environment.

The process of natural selection depends to a large extent upon the differential reproduction of those individual organisms which are most fit in the ever-changing environment. Differential reproduction takes place through three primary means: nonrandom mating, nonrandom fecundity,* and nonrandom survival to reproduce. The great evolutionary advantage of sexual reproduction is that it combines the genetic material from two separate individuals and thus greatly increases the structural and behavioral variation in their offspring. This in turn increases the capacity of the local population to respond to the environment's selective pressures. Nonrandom mating—including all of its components such as courtship, pair-bonding, copulation, and fertilization—maximizes this advantage of sexual reproduction. Nonrandom fecundity means the differential production of offspring. Some species, and within some species certain individuals, produce comparatively more or fewer offspring. Although the concept of differential fecundity suggests that natural selection might favor those individuals and species with a large production of offspring, there is, in fact, a trade-off between fecun-

---

* The terms ''fecundity'' and ''fertility'' are used in opposite ways by biologists and demographers. With one exception, we follow the demographic usage in this book: fecundity meaning the capacity to bear children, fertility meaning the number of children born to an individual or population. The exception occurs in the first (the biological) section of this chapter, where we use fecundity to mean the number of offspring.

dity and survival of offspring to maturity. If the chances of individual survival to the age of reproduction are low, there will be considerable selective advantage in high fecundity. This is the case, for example, in fish like the sturgeon which annually lays large numbers of eggs. If these chances are high, on the other hand, high fecundity has no selective advantage. In fact, with the evolution of elaborate child-care systems which demand high levels of time and energy investment from parents, selective pressure favors low fecundity because of the practical limitations on the amount of parenting behavior by adult organisms. The third factor involved in differential reproduction—nonrandom survival to reproduce—is based on the variable success of individual organisms in surviving the period of development, growth, and maturation which follows birth and ends in the reproduction of the next generation. During this period, mortality or any form of morbidity which interferes with the individual's achieving reproductive success, results in nonrandom survival to reproduce.

Reproduction, Mortality, and Migration

The evolutionary advantages of sexual reproduction will be achieved only if the species has evolved a reliable set of mechanisms for ensuring that the gamete (sperm or egg) of an individual of one sex will find and join the gamete of an individual of the other to produce a zygote and, eventually, a new individual. In many lower forms of life, this process of bringing gametes together is essentially random. For example, the oyster simply releases the eggs and sperm into the water in very large numbers. Fertilization depends on the high probability that viable sperm will encounter a viable egg. Through evolution biological organisms have developed a number of mechanisms for bringing opposite-sexed gametes in close proximity at the appropriate time, thus improving the chances of fertilization over the largely random method. For a great many species there is a synchronization of the release of gametes according to the time of the season, month, or day. In those species of animals which have become adapted to life on dry land, fertilization is ensured through copulation and takes place internally in one of the individual organisms. This type of fertilization depends upon anatomical alterations which make possible the internal deposition of sperm and upon physiological processes which enhance the transport and union of sperm and egg. Behavioral processes also make major contributions toward ensuring the union of gametes. Such processes include a wide range of behavior varying from patterns of courtship to patterns of copulation.

All three of the factors of anatomy, physiology, and behavior work together in the typical estrus cycle of mammals. As a result of coordinated sex-hormone changes within the female mammal, anatomical, physiological, and behavioral changes take place during the estrus cycle, most prominently in association with ovulation. The female genetalia may become more prominent, vaginal lubrication may increase, the female may emit sexually stimulating odors through pheromones, and in the presence of a male, she may assume postures and emit sequences of behavior which are sexually stimulating to him. These anatomical, physiological, and behavioral changes in the female elicit responses on the part of the male which include approach and courtship behavior, attempts at sexual mounting and intromission, and pelvic thrusting and ejaculation. The female, in her turn, responds to these specific patterns in the male's behavior with sexual responsiveness, copulatory receptiveness, and, in some cases, ovulation. In some species, the patterns of behavior just described are so specific that the patterns of copulatory behavior of the species may provide a more reliable identification than its anatomy does (2).

Among all mammals, individual sexual behavior is to some extent determined by social factors above and beyond innate patterning. This is particularly true among the higher mammals such as carnivores and monkeys, where group life forms the basis of existence for many. For example, the social system of the lion consists of units called prides, made up of a group of three to twelve females, a smaller group of males, and cubs of various ages. Each pride has its own territory from which nomadic males are excluded by the dominant males of the pride. Hunting is cooperative. The females of the pride are often in heat synchronously and mate with any of the males in the pride. The synchrony of the estrus cycle among females presumably has the evolutionary advantage of reducing competition among the males for sexual gratification, thus allowing them to develop larger teeth, claws, and more powerful muscles for hunting purposes. Synchronous estrus also leads to the synchronous birth of litters. This, in turn, improves the survival chances of the cubs through the opportunity for communal suckling by synchronously lactating mothers. This latter arrangement not only increases the amount of milk available for all cubs but also allows more nursing mothers to participate in communal hunting (3).

In some mammals pair-bonding becomes another important social regulator of individual sexual behavior. Wolves and foxes often mate for life and, as with the lion pride, this pattern of social regulation of reproduction among canines is closely tied to all other major aspects of group life. Among monkeys, there are several different patterns of mating, depending upon the species. Again, the patterns of mating are highly integrated with the overall pattern of life in the monkey troop. A few monkeys are monogamous and live in single families. In others, a dominant male controls a harem of females. More commonly, however, monkeys live in large, mixed-sex groups. Although in the latter the males appear to be promiscuous, close examination reveals that there are definite constraints on mating and reproductive behaviors. These constraints include the dominance position of the individual monkey, whether or not there is a kinship relationship in the potential dyad (mother-son matings appear to have the lowest frequency), and the existence of particular affiliative or affectional relationships which have developed spontaneously between a monkey pair. These considerations suggest that among primates under natural conditions, social factors have assumed new importance in the regulation of sexuality relative to hormonal and other biological factors (4).

As we have indicated, natural selection works in part through the differential survival of individuals from their birth until the next generation has been successfully reproduced. In the simpler organisms, this survival depends upon the ability of the individual organism to obtain subsistence and escape disease and predation. Once the individual has reproduced sufficiently, there is no adaptive advantage in continued survival. Therefore, there is no natural selection for longevity beyond the reproductive period, and all species appear to have a maximal age limit, determined by an aging process inherent in their own biological systems, extending their lives only a little beyond the period of reproduction. Of course, most individuals die long before they have obtained their potential age limit under the most favorable conditions. In mammals, mortality, like reproduction, is subject to important and major influences from group life. This is perhaps best illustrated by the crucial importance of parental behavior for survival of the young until they have achieved a certain level of independence (5).

The reproduction of individuals and the growth of interbreeding populations always occurs within a specific environment. There are, however, many factors which tend to expand a population outside of its particular niche. Virtually all organisms are equipped with mechanisms for individual or intergenerational migration and dispersal (6). In some organisms, dispersal is simply a function of random factors such as the distribution of seeds by the wind or the undirected spread of animals as the result of an innate tendency to move. In many animals, movement comes about as a result of competition for resources. In the higher vertebrates, especially in the mammals, social factors again assume an important regulatory role in dispersal and migration. Territoriality is perhaps the most important of these factors. As a result of it, individual organisms drive competitors—including their own offspring—out of their territory. Those individuals who are driven out in this manner either remain marginal to the original group or establish a new territory in a slightly different environment. In this way, populations push out from the point of origin and test the suitability of new niches, many ultimately adapting themselves to the new conditions.

POPULATION REGULATION

When the local population or deme does not reproduce itself in a way that is balanced over time by both mortality and migration in and out of the local area, then it tends either to increase or decrease in size progressively. In the case of population increase the result is an increase in density that, in turn, leads either to an outstripping of the local resources and a dying back of the population, or to a movement out of the local area in proportion to the excess population. In the case of a progressive decrease in overall population size, the result is a decrease in density that, in turn, leads either to a slowing of decrease as resources become more abundant in proportion to numbers, or to an eventual dying out and extinction of the local population.

Charles Darwin discussed the tendency of organisms to increase their numbers and the "checks to increase" which prevented such population growth (7). He indicated that there were four types of checks on increase: the amount of food available locally, the amount of predation by other animals, the effects of physical factors such as climate, and the effects of disease. The discoveries of population biologists in the last hundred years have indicated that there are, in addition to these four factors, important behavioral and social factors that act as sources of population regulation. It has been demonstrated that many vertebrates, as a result of the action of these additional factors, do not tend toward a natural increase in population, but rather toward an optimum population—one which is specific for each species in each environment. For example, if several breeding pairs of guppies are placed in an aquarium, they will reproduce until the population of the aquarium reaches a stable level. If members of that population are then systematically removed, the remaining guppies will compenstate by producing more young that survive to the age of reproduction. When the systematic removal is terminated, the excess young will be cannibalized by the adults and the aquarium population will maintain its previous stable level.

A general principle of evolution is that all organisms tend to be hyperadapted to their environment (8). This means that each species has considerably more adaptive capability than is required for living in its modal or typical environment. Hyperadaptiveness is a characteristic promoted and maintained in any successful organism by natural selection. It occurs because the wide natural variations that occur in all environments tend to eliminate those organisms not having this adaptive reserve. One form of hyperadaptiveness is reproductive reserve. This is manifested by the fact that most higher organisms reproduce at a rate significantly below their maximum capacity, only achieving the maximum under certain infrequently occurring environmental conditions that favor the rapid expansion of a population. The advantage to the species of having this population regulatory device is obvious. It acts to prevent the species from exhausting the resources of a niche and, at the same time, allows for rapid expansion of the local population under appropriate conditions.

In general, mechanisms for the regulation of population tend to be density dependent (9, 10). These density-dependent factors have been classified as follows: enemies, such as predators, parasites, or pathogens; required resources, such as food; and self-limiting systems. A primary example of the latter is the territorial behavior of birds that acts to spread out members of a similar species, limiting access of selective individuals to food or to mates or interfering with their normal mating and reproduction. It has been shown, for example, that when two pairs of robins are confined to a space adequate for only one pair, only the dominant pair will mate and reproduce. In such cases, dominance as well as territoriality plays an important role in the self-limiting system.

As we have indicated, the mechanism of population regulation may occur through alteration of the patterns of reproduction. It may also occur through differential mortality, especially infant mortality. Each of these mechanisms may occur in closely similar species, or even in the same species, becoming functional under somewhat different conditions. For example, in one population of house mice, growth of the population was slowed and eventually stopped through a decline in birthrate, while in another population, a decline in the survival of nurslings was responsible for the same type of slowing and eventual stoppage of population growth (11). In some cases it appears that these alterations in reproduction and mortality result from psychosomatic processes (12), including especially the effects of stress due to crowding on adrenal, pituitary, and gonadal hormone function (10). In addition, in mammals, where the development of parental and caretaking behavior has achieved its peak development, alterations of these latter behaviors in response to population density appear to seriously affect survival of the young (13). This effect is the direct result of behavioral alterations which vary from decreased infant care up to and including cannibalism.

Another density-dependent factor affecting population growth is migration. Lemmings and locusts are well-known examples of animal species that respond to a critical population density with a sudden surge of out-migration behavior. In both of these cases, the surge seems to occur spontaneously. In the lemmings' case, it occurs following a period of increased irritability and fighting among all members of the population. In some cases, however, out-migration results from intraspecies competition and forced expulsion of the less agressive individuals by the more dominant ones. This has been illustrated by the Scottish red grouse. The outcast birds of this species do not reproduce and tend to have a relatively high mortality because they fall easy prey to predators and starvation. This example demonstrates a response to population density characterized by dominance and territorial behavior in association with differential migration, differential reproduction, and differential mortality. We see in this what may be less apparent but nevertheless true for all species—namely that all of the density-dependent factors interact in a summative and often complex way to produce an equilibrium size which is optimum for each particular species in a particular environment (14).

It is clear that there are many physiological and behavioral mechanisms which affect population size and distribution. The total set of those mechanisms that jointly acts to maintain the numbers of a specific population in balance in a specific environment constitutes a population regulation system. Such a system is homeostatic in that it responds to environmental change in a way tending to return a population to its range of optimum size and density. It is adaptive in that it promotes population survival. As we have indicated, it includes mechanisms at all levels of biological and social organization—an important consideration as we turn to a discussion of primates and humans.

PRIMATE POPULATION REGULATION

Before examining what is known about the history of human population growth, we turn to a brief review of primate population-related behaviors and a discussion of how the evolutionary transition from ape to human appears to have affected humans' capacities and methods for regulating their population. There are several features of primates that distinguish them from other animal orders. These features include the primacy and complexity of the social group, the rich development of auditory and visual communication, the greatly expanded capacity for both observational and trial-and-error learning, and the long period of dependency and immaturity of the infant and young primate (15, 16, 17). The net result of these features is that primate species have evolved highly complex, variable, and adaptable patterns of behavior. Not only do these patterns vary between species, but there is considerable variation within a particular species, depending upon the particular ecological conditions confronted by the troop or local group. Specifically, this means that all of the behaviors influencing the population dynamics of a local group are subject to considerable variation, depending upon the environment, the adaptive capacities of the species, the history of the local group and its accumulated "culture," and the personal traits of individual members. As a result, population regulation in primate society is a uniquely complex process, with many sources of variation and feedback. Compared with other animal orders, primates are relatively more strongly influenced in population regulation by group and individual factors than by biological factors.

Patterns of heterosexual dyad formation and mating among primate species are highly variable. Although the general pattern is one of varying levels of promiscuity in conjunction with the development of relatively short-term stable pair bonds, there are a number of important exceptions. The male hamadryas baboon establishes for himself a harem of females which he protects and guards jealously and with which he forages and feeds cooperatively (18, 19). Monogamy is practiced by the gibbons and South American callicebus. In the latter, a variety of behaviors demonstrates the closeness and intensity of the mated pair bond, including the assumption by the male of a large portion of the parental labor (apart from suckling) and great distress on forced separation. (20). The variations in heterosexual bonding and mating behavior between monkey species appears to be highly related to the resources of the environment and to the local group structure, especially as this is influenced by dominance and territoriality.

In all primate societies, females form the center around which the entire society is structured. This is seen among baboons, where the females tend to cluster around the graphic center of the moving troop (21), and where in comparison with the adult males they rarely leave their troop. This central role for the female is not particularly a function of her being the object of sexual interest. In fact, most of her life—prior to adolescence, during each pregnancy, and during each period of lactation—she is of relatively little sexual interest to males. Rather, this central position she occupies is a function of her reproductive role and her association with infants and young.

Some primates have definite breeding seasons, while others have peaks during particular seasons. In chimpanzees, matings and births occur throughout the year. Field observations indicate that sexual behavior among primate varies considerably from a point where repeated copulations may occur in the space of a few hours to one where, as with the gorilla (22), several troops were observed over a period of more than a year with the recording of only two or three copulations. Thus, it does not appear that sex is a primary bonding force in primate societies. Individual, group, and species factors account for much of the wide variation in sexual behavior observable among primates.

As a rule, females produce one infant at a time (23). Birth intervals tend to be somewhat over one year for the smaller primates, and may vary between three to five years for the great apes. The primate mother nurses and socializes her infant child through a comparatively long period of dependency. As a consequence, the mother-infant relationship is probably the most intense one among all primates. Males demonstrate a varying pattern of interest in and tolerance of infants and young, depending upon different social and personal factors (4). In those primates where the social group is characterized by the presence of a single adult male, paternal behavior is likely to become highly developed (24). In most species, however, the adult male tends not to have enduring relationships with his own offspring or with other infants and young members of the troop. Rather, his function seems to be that of the "generalized father" (25), whose concern is with protection of the troop from predation, with movement of the troop, and with dominance interactions within the troop.

Predators act as an important source of mortality for primate groups. Other major sources of mortality include diseases— especially viruses, bacteria, and parasites—and accidents. Relatively little information is available regarding rates of infant mortality. However, in at least some species, the percentage of infants dying before adolescence appears to approach 50 percent (26, 27).

The degree of geographic mobility of primates varies considerably, depending on whether they are arboreal or terrestrial. In general, primate troops have home ranges which vary in size from a few acres up to 50 or 75 square miles. In some species, such as the gibbon, the home range is well defined and highly territorial. In others, it is much more loosely defined, with large areas of overlap between adjacent troops. Troop size tends to vary considerably from the single "family" unit of the gibbon to the large troops of baboons which may be composed of well over 100 members. In general, the terrestrial troops are larger than the arboreal ones. In some species of primates there is considerable geographic mobility of males from one troop to an adjacent troop. In addition, males may migrate away from a particular troop and become peripheral to it for a period of time (26).

THE APE SYSTEMS

A clear understanding of how a complex population regulation system works in primates can only be achieved through a consideration of specific species. For this reason we shall discuss the four species of apes, examining within the limits of our current knowledge the system of behaviors that interacts at the individual and aggregate levels to influence and, ultimately, to regulate population size and distribution. Perhaps the clearest example can be found in the gibbon (28). The gibbon troop consists of an adult male, an adult female, and their offspring, which usually number from one to four. The gibbons are a predominantly arboreal species, living in the Malayan forest. Each troop has a well-defined territory and the adult male of the troop spends approximately 6 percent of his waking hours directly engaged in ritualized border disputes at the edge of his territory. To some extent, he is supported in these daily confrontations with neighboring troops by other members of his own troop, but the primary burden falls on him. The daily conflicts consist of chases and challenges principally between the adult males of troops along the common border of adjacent territories. It is through these conflicts that the borders of the different troops' respective territories are defined and maintained. The chief functional significance of the territory is the food that it provides for the gibbon troop. Food is far from abundant, and at times may even be extremely scarce. Territorial size appears to some extent to be a function of troop size, but it also varies with the fluctuation of food supply. Typically, a mated adult pair of gibbons lives within a territory feeding themselves and caring for their children. As a subadult male approaches adulthood, he is forcibly kept out of fruiting trees by his parents, the mated adult pair in the troop. As a result, he comes to spend more and more time foraging on the periphery of the troop and eventually becomes fully "peripheralized." At about the time he moves out of the troop he is replaced by a newborn gibbon. In summary, then, through behavioral patterns involving strong pair-bonding, close "family" life with active parenting by both males and females, strong intratroop dominance patterns, and strong intertroop territorial patterns, the size of a gibbon troop is maintained below an upward limit of six and the troop territory is maintained within a more or less constant acreage.

The orangutan system of population regulation is based upon an entirely different style of life (29, 30). Adult orangutan males live solitary lives. Adult females live similar lives except that they associate with their own children during the latter's period of dependency. Each adult occupies a large range which coexists with the ranges of a number of other adults. Although solitary animals, the adult males give periodic long and loud vocalizations that may be heard for more than a kilometer. These calls probably function both to maintain spacing between adult males and to attract sexually receptive females. The long calls may also have other important functions relative to population regulation (29). The long calls of an older, well-established male seem to serve as a signal to the females and younger males within his territory, many of whom are genetically related to him, about where the food sources are. The calls may also serve to protect this ''genetic family'' by warning off other old males, and the younger adults who are related to them, from the local territory. Other observations within forest areas of different population density suggest that as the density of orangutans increases, there is a greater need for males to involve themselves in protecting their range and status. Such competitive territorial behavior is associated with a decrease in both long calling and in sexual and reproductive behavior. In summary, then, the population regulatory system of the orangutan is similar to that of the gibbon in its reliance upon territorial mechanisms, but the pair-bonding and the form of family life is entirely different. Moreover, in contrast to the gibbons, the orangutans appear to have a form of cooperation between older males and younger adults who are genetically related. The total effect of this new combination of behaviors is to make reproduction responsive to the density of the orangutan population.

Little is known about the population regulation system of gorillas and chimpanzees. In part this is due to the relatively short period during which field observations have been taking place and the relatively long period necessary to draw conclusions relative to population. In part it may also be due to the complex and loosely organized social system within which these two great apes live. Such a system makes it difficult, without long and careful study, to identify anything more than the proximate factors affecting population size. The very limited data available suggest that for both the chimpanzee and the gorilla the two most important proximate factors are childbearing frequency and infant mortality. For example, evidence indicates that a very large majority of females are usually either pregnant or taking care of an infant or juvenile under the age of three years (22, 31). This fact, combined with the age of sexual maturity being seven to ten, longevity being twenty-five to thirty years, and birth intervals being three to four and one-half years, suggests that five is the maximal number of young that the average female will bear and raise in a lifetime. In fact, the true average is probably considerably below that. Given these figures, it is easy to see that infant mortality, which has been estimated as high as 50 percent in the gorilla (22), could play a significant role in determining whether a local population increased or decreased.

Given the current state of our knowledge, we can only speculate regarding what intermediate mechanisms might be influencing these proximate factors of childbearing frequency and infant mortality. In the gorilla, it is possible that childbearing frequency is influenced by this primate's apparently low level of sexual activity. In both the gorilla and the chimpanzee, infant mortality rates might be influenced by geographic movement into a less optimal niche, the introduction of endemic disease, or the development of crowding in the troop. Whatever the intermediate mechanisms may be, it is certain that they are regulated through the complex social structure of these great apes, which close observation indicates is richly patterned, subtle, and highly individual, especially in the chimpanzee (32). It is the presence of this type of social structure, the flexibility of which is undoubtedly a major adaptive resource for the chimpanzee, that makes the latter of such potential importance for shedding light on the evolution of population regulation systems at the time of humanity's emergence as a species. Clearly the trend in the evolution of population-regulation systems from the lower animals to humans is in the direction of a larger set of interacting mechanisms, more of which are at the behavioral and the social level, and more of which are the subject to individual variation. The chimpanzee, most closely related to humans of all the great apes through descent from a common ancestral population, is an important source for developing a greater understanding of this transition.

THE EVOLUTIONARY TRANSITION
FROM APE TO HUMAN

The evolutionary transition from ape to human began some time during the late Pliocene and early Pleistocene over three million years ago (33). The most significant anatomical changes involved the bones of the limbs and the hip and were associated with the shift to bipedalism. This shift was crucial in that it freed the arms and hands from locomotor activity, making them available for greater use of tools, and committing humans to a terrestrial life with the opportunity for extensive geographic mobility. By two million years ago, evolution had produced a progressive increase in brain size, probably as a result of the selective advantage a larger brain provided in conjunction with the new adaptive strategy made possible by the earlier anatomical changes. This new adaptive strategy included the extensive use of tools, the gathering, hunting, and sharing of food, the use of language, and the construction of shelters (33, 34). Somewhat more than half-a-million years ago, this series of evolutionary changes culminated in the emergence of various early human forms closely approximating Homo sapiens of today. From that time forward, until the emergence of agriculture six to ten thousand years ago (35), humans lived as gatherer-hunters (36, 37). During this period, they lived in small local groups probably averaging about twenty-five in number (38). They mastered a life style that included ranging over large areas, gathering plant food, hunting game in cooperative groups, using complex tools and fire, preparing of food cooperatively, using water for fishing and transportation, and domesticating the dog (39). Although there is some uncertainty, this life style seems to have included a family structure consisting of a basic male-female unit, with the women assuming the majority of child-rearing functions and the men protecting and providing. Although there have been many behavioral changes for humans during the last 6,000 years, these are largely a result of the growth, development, and alteration of culture rather than of further biological evolution (40). Thus, the biological given of humankind today evolved through natural selection during that 99 percent of history when humans lived as gatherer-hunters.

The new adaptive strategy made possible by the evolutionary transition from ape to human represents a culmination of evolutionary trends already apparent in the primate order. As a result of a fourfold increase in brain size, learning and memory systems played a far more important role in individual behavior, and group culture vastly increased in complexity. Associated with this was a comparative freeing of behavior from biological determination, with greater regulation by the social structure and by individual psychology. The development of extensive use of tools and of complex language elevated humans to an entirely new level of environmental control, greatly improved communication with fellow humans, and promoted understanding of nature itself. What was the impact of these changes upon those behaviors involved in population regulation? In the next few paragraphs we discuss the possible impact on a number of specific behaviors.

In the evolutionary transition from ape to human, sexual behavior was further freed from cyclic biological controls. This is evidenced by the relative absence of a period of "heat" in women, the greater prevalence of sexual activity during pregnancy and lactation, the extension of the period of adult sexual activity beyond the limits of the period of reproduction, and the greater role of learning in sexual behavior. All of these factors, together with the increased tendency toward sexual play and the predominance of the ventral coital position in humans, tend to increase the personal meaning of sexual behavior, give it a more important role in bonding between mated pairs, and increase its inclusion in the social fabric (41).

With the emergence of humans, heterosexual pair-bonding and mating took on an added importance. With the development of marriage, lifelong commitments were made, not only to another adult but to that adult's family. Whether one married and when one married became important determinants of one's adult status and had important social, economic, and political consequences for one's own family and for the local group.

The effect of the evolutionary transition from ape to human was to change reproduction from an event to which individuals responded and adapted to an event that individuals and couples could decide upon, plan, and anticipate. This change depended, of course, on a correct perception of the relation between sexual intercourse and the occurrence of conception and pregnancy. Although there is some small evidence from contemporary examples of gathering-hunting humans that early humans may have only partially understood this relation (42), it seems likely that an accurate perception of it has been highly adaptive in most societies in view of the markedly increased control of conception that it would provide and in view of the universal importance of the childbearing function.

The evolutionary transition from ape to human affected childbearing and child rearing as well. As with all primates, women have been universally involved in the child-rearing process (43). However, the introduction of lifelong mating through marriage and the recognition of the relation between sexual intercourse and pregnancy helped to make paternity an important feature of human societies. In monkeys, systems of behavior which serve to establish and maintain the psychological attachment of an infant to its mother have been described (26, 44). Bowlby has described in humans a series of five behavioral systems that operate for the infant to achieve and maintain a relationship with its mother (45). These five systems include sucking, clinging, following, crying, and smiling. They function by cuing certain maternal care-giving behavior and thus control the infant's environment in the direction of the closeness and interest of a protective adult. The net effect in humans, one which is abetted and shaped by learning and social custom, is the establishment of a strong love bond between the mother and child. It is this bond that, in humans, forms the foundation of later interpersonal relationships and is so essential when the child itself becomes an adult and has the opportunity to develop and express parental behavior. These behavior systems and the processes they generate enable us to understand why human males, although they may never have been involved to a significant degree in child-caring activities, are fully capable, with the help of learning and cultural sanctions, of expressing the full range of parenting and child-rearing behaviors.

The evolutionary transition from ape to human resulted in a great increase of self-awareness and self-knowledge. This, in turn, led to the identification and anticipation of one's own death. Because this was feared and rejected, humans increasingly turned their skills to environmental manipulation and to attempts to control and deal with this problem. Inevitably humans have come to devote considerable attention and resources to disease and death control.

As we discussed above, the geographic mobility of a local population of organisms is essential to its adaptation. Movement allows invasion of more favorable niches and the escape from intolerable local conditions. The transition from ape to human produced an organism whose bipedalism provided great migratory capacity. This was enhanced by the human ability to master nature through technology and to adapt to various environmental conditions through culture. These factors, together with curiosity and desire for self-improvement, led early humans beyond the simple wanderings and rangings associated with the gathering-hunting way of life (46) to intercontinental migration, with the result that they had inhabited every continent on the globe with the exception of Antarctica 20,000 years ago (47).

The growth of civilization and the development of various forms of culture represent an extension and refinement of the adaptiveness of humans (48), and these broad changes have coincided with different population sizes and patterns of growth (49, 50). It has been estimated that the rate of annual increase among gathering-hunting humans was roughly .015 per 1000 until the year 8000 B.C. at which time humans numbered from three to five million. The population growth rate appears to have made its largest historical jump with the development of agriculture and the more or less sedentary life style associated with it. This is reflected by an annual growth rate of .36 per 1000 beginning about 8000 B.C. and continuing until the beginning of the Christian era. Around the time of Christ, the numbers of humankind approximated 300 million. From then until the beginning of the industrial revolution around 1750, the annual growth rate was approximately .56 per 1000. Around 1750 the numbers of humankind approximated 800 million. It was at this point that the great modern acceleration of population growth began. From 1750 to 1850 the population of the world increased to 1.3 billion with an overall average annual increase of approximately five per 1000. By 1950 the world population was 2.5 billion as a result of an annual growth rate during the previous 100 years of almost eight per 1000. From 1950 to 1975, the annual growth rate more than doubled to somewhat less than twenty per 1000, resulting in a world population of approximately four billion.

These trends make it apparent that the growth rate for human kind was modest until the industrial-colonial period. In fact, other evidence indicates that prior to that period, fluctuations in population size were common, there were many examples of sustained periods of population decrease, and such changes in population size were dynamically responsive to local environmental conditions and social structure (51, 52, 53). Contemporary world-population problems seem to be associated with a logarithmic surge of population growth during the last two centuries. In fact, there appear to be two main transitions in size and growth patterns, the first at the beginning of the agricultural period and the second at the beginning of the industrial-colonial period. These two transitions divide human history into three convenient stages for discussion, each stage being characterized by different modal patterns of technological development, economic organization, and institutional complexity. To a degree, each of these stages represents in its modal form a new adaptive strategy for the human populations involved. Since the people in each of these stages create a new environment for themselves through their technology and culture, each stage also represents a different set of modal conditions to which individuals must adapt. Therefore, it seems reasonable to assume that each of these stages was associated with a different population regulation system. For an examination of these three systems we will discuss some of the behavioral and demographic patterns among gathering-hunting populations, preindustrial agricultural populations, and industrial populations.

THE GATHERING-HUNTING SYSTEM

Local group size for gathering-hunting humans seems to have approximated twenty-five individuals (38). Such groups were composed of several families, consisting generally of an adult male and female and their children. Average completed family size was probably between four and five children, with the range between none and seven (54). Subsistence for these groups was achieved through daily gathering of fruits, seeds, vegetables, and insects and hunting small and in some cases large animals. This subsistence pattern generally required that the local group range over a large territory, the size varying according to local climate, flora, and fauna but often reaching several hundred square miles (39). Several of these local groups tended to live and to interact within a larger community of groups called the "dialectic tribe." As the name suggests, the common denominator of such a tribe was its common language, which promoted the frequency of exchange between the constituent local groups. It appears that the size of the dialectic tribe was commonly about 500 persons, with a breeding population of approximately 175 (38).

Marriage patterns in the gatherer-hunters were typified by exogamy, that is, marriage to someone outside of the local group. There were several adaptive advantages to this pattern. For one thing, marriage ties between local groups tended to protect any single group from a subsistence crisis during a period of drought or some other environmental extreme, by providing it with a potential ally and support system from outside the local area. A second advantage of exogamy was that, with local group size averaging around twenty-five, chance factors operated to make it unlikely for an individual to find an age and sex appropriate marriage partner within his or her own local group. Exogamy is one example of the way that gathering-hunting man regulated reproductive behavior in order to bring individual and group interests together. The incest taboo is another example of this type of regulation. It forbids sex, and therefore prevents reproduction, under conditions where one or both individuals are unlikely to be able to provide care for a child and where the burden of care would therefore fall, at least in part, on the group.

The relatively small average completed family size of the gatherer-hunter, compared with the possible maximum of around eleven which has been observed among certain sedentary populations (55), meant that there was spacing of births averaging, much as in the anthropoid apes, about three to four and one-half years. Birth spacing would have the adaptive advantage of decreasing the limits pregnancy and young children necessarily placed upon the mother during the normal nomadic existence. The existence of three or four child-free years between births allows the woman in the gathering-hunting society to transport belongings, care for older children, and gather food. The presence of two closely spaced children would virtually preclude these activities. There were several additional compelling reasons for spacing births. One was the relative lack of foods appropriate for weaning an infant at ages of less than two and one-half or three years. The second was the degree of responsibility and burden assumed by the natural parents in socialization and child care. Although child rearing was to some extent shared generally by all members of the local group, it appears that children actually lived with their natural parents and that the latter were most invested in the care of their children.

The mechanism of birth spacing, to the degree that it was intentional, was guided by social custom and norm, and appears to have been achieved primarily through four means: lactation, abstinence, abortion, and infanticide. Although the prevention of ovulation by lactation is inconsistent in humans, it is clear that breast-feeding for a two- or three-year period significantly reduces the chances of conception (56). Undoubtedly, this effect was supplemented in many cases by a varying period of postpartum sexual abstinence. Abortion has been shown to be widespread in human societies (57) and was probably also used in many gathering-hunting societies to help in the spacing of births. Probably of greater importance, however, was infanticide. For example, there is some evidence that as much as 15 percent of the children born to some aboriginal women are eliminated by infanticide, especially female infanticide (38).

The health of individuals among gathering-hunting groups was probably moderately good. For example, life expectancy among a contemporary gathering-hunting group has been calculated as 32.5 years, with 60 percent of all children born surviving to age fifteen (58). This general pattern of survival was probably also true in early human history due to the general availability of food, the relative absence of predators, and the fact that the small group basis of social life protected against epidemics and the spread of contagious diseases.

In general, then, gathering-hunting humans appear to have had a population regulation system that greatly depended upon the social regulation of reproduction for the purpose of moderating the impact that childbearing and child-rearing had on individual and group survival. In addition, reproduction was balanced by an infant mortality rate adjusted through infanticide, and by a moderate life expectancy. Under appropriate environmental conditions, however, it appears that the net reproductive rate of gathering-hunting humans could increase rapidly from one to two in order to fill a new and favorable niche (54). Such a rate would lead to the doubling of a population in one generation. It was probably this capacity to change from a steady to a rapidly expanding state that was so important in the spread of gathering-hunting groups across the globe.

THE AGRICULTURAL SYSTEM

With the advent of agriculture six to ten thousand years ago, humans had created and developed an entirely new adaptive strat-

egy. Fundamental to this new strategy was a sedentary life associated with the intense use of local resources and with increases
in population density. Whether the growth of local populations itself caused the development of new forms of agricultural and other
technology, whether it was the result of such development, or
whether it represented a combination of cause and effect, is currently uncertain. There is, however, general agreement that population growth and the adoption of the agricultural adaptive strategy
went hand in hand (51, 53, 54, 59).

In association with the sedentary way of life, holding property
became far more important and group membership tended to stabi-
lize. More value was placed on the relation between generations
and lines of descent. In conjunction with these changes, the extended family became the modal form of family life and formal ties
between families assumed greater importance. In this context, marriage became a way of establishing bonds of allegiance, cooperation, and obligation between family groups. As a result, the selection of a marriage partner was subject to considerable influence by
parents and other elder family members.

In agricultural societies, several factors acted to increase fertility
levels in comparison with gathering and hunting societies. One of
these was the prominence of the family labor system. In this system, all members of the family participated in the farm work and,
as a result, there was a direct incentive for married couples to
produce large numbers of children who could help with this labor.
A second incentive came from the social importance of lineage and
the desire among reproducing couples to have a sufficient number
of children to guarantee the parents' support when they grew too
old to work. Also, agricultural peoples were relatively less affected
by several disincentives important in gathering-hunting society. For
example, the extended agricultural family provided a built-in child-
care system not available in the nomadic local groups of gatherer-
hunters. In addition, the sedentary form of life eliminated child
transport as a major role activity, one which was highly incompatible with the close spacing of children. Finally, although the percent
who married and the age of marriage have varied from one agricul-

tural society to another, in most such societies the great majority of individuals did marry and at a young age. This was another set of factors conducive to high rates of reproduction.

There were also several factors that tended to depress the size of families and rates of reproduction in agricultural societies. One of these was the inheritance system. If it was so organized that land was passed on to the oldest son, then there often was no economic base for the younger sons to build on. As a result, they tended not to marry and take on family obligations. A second antinatal factor was the strenuous, demanding role of women. Commonly they not only had domestic, childbearing and child-rearing responsibilities but were expected to work in the fields as well. However, no methods of fertility control were available for putting the antinatal sentiments into effect except the same methods found in gathering-hunting societies, and those methods were either unreliable or unacceptable.

In association with the formation of agricultural societies, new forces developed that acted both to increase and to decrease mortality. With the agricultural form of subsistence came a generally improved and constant food supply that tended to result in improved nutrition and health. However, this improvement could be offset if a people relied primarily on one type of agricultural product, thus producing vitamin and other nutritional deficiencies. Nutritional improvements could also be offset by periodic famines secondary to drought or flooding, conditions the sedentary agricultural societies were particularly vulnerable to. Further, the greater sedentary life and the presence of domestic animals which could serve as hosts for new pathogenic organisms encouraged the development of new bacterial and parasitic diseases (60). In the dense and sometimes crowded towns and cities, new epidemiological factors came into play giving ascendency to infectious diseases such as smallpox. In addition, rats, which acted as carriers for plagues and other diseases, tended to multiply in the accumulated garbage and human waste associated with urban conditions. Finally, with the increased size and organization of political units that was characteristic of agricultural societies came increased competition and struggle between those units, frequently resulting in war and slavery. These, too, tended to increase mortality. The net result of these effects upon mortality levels in agricultural societies was to make the levels comparable to or somewhat higher than those of gathering-hunting societies.

With the development of agriculture, the small local group of the gatherer-hunter was transformed into the village, town, and small city. The sedentary life markedly increased the density of people so that thousands of individuals might live together in a few square miles of land. In some instances, the preindustrial city grew to the point where several hundreds of thousands of people lived in one location (61). In situations where small independent villages were the dominant pattern of life, geographic mobility was limited by family ties and political allegiances. As agricultural societies became more complex, with the centralization of power and the increased density of population, they developed various forms of feudal states and preindustrial cities. The latter attracted people like magnets, drawing them over great distances from the rural countryside. Greater degrees of social stratification and social-role differentiation occurred. In spite of these changes, family lineages continued to be the focus of individual life, social organization remained centered around local sources of agricultural production, and the feudal state and preindustrial city remained essentially agricultural in their mode of organization, in their value systems, and in the inhabitants' patterns of behavior (61, 62).

In general, the population regulation system of agricultural societies involved mechanisms greatly influenced by the new methods of subsistence, the sedentary life style, and the importance of the extended family. Technological developments introduced greater human control in some areas such as in nutrition, but brought with them new adaptational challenges, especially those resulting from high-density living and the increase of epidemics. In other areas, such as fertility control, technological advances had not occurred. The overall role of free choice with respect to population-related behaviors was increased only a little in an agricultural society because technological developments, in balance, did not substantially increase the human control factor, and freedom of choice was substantially limited by the strong normative regulation exerted through the extended family system and by the pressing exigencies of daily life. Behavior based on individual choice was perhaps most significantly affected by the increased institutional and role complexity characteristic of the densely populated areas.

THE INDUSTRIAL SYSTEM

The industrial revolution began in England and western Europe about two hundred years ago. It had multiple technological and social origins, including the development of new methods for increasing agricultural productivity, the invention and development of ingenious laborsaving machines, the discovery of important new sources of power (especially coal), the development through international trade of the capital necessary for industrial development, and the enclosure movement. The latter promoted the industrial revolution by driving large portions of the labor force from the manors, freeing them to migrate and to work in the developing industrial centers. The industrial society that grew out of these changes represented an entirely new adaptive strategy for humans. Society became far more complex and the occupational and social roles within it became far more diverse. Much of the power and influence previously invested in the lineage systems and in the royal aristocracy was transferred to the state. Less credence was given to tradition and religious authority and more to rationality and scientific understanding. Individualism grew in strength and with it an emphasis on competence, performance, and achievement.

In the wake of these fundamental societal changes, marriage came to be more a matter of individual choice. This meant that the decision to marry allowed individuals to regulate if and when they would assume family responsibilities and begin having children. In short, the timing of marriage became an important method of individual fertility regulation. As a result, although many agricultural societies had practiced early and nearly universal marriage, during the eighteenth century in western Europe marriage tended to be late, frequently in the mid- and late twenties, and nonmarriage was common. The role of women was also profoundly affected by industrial development and the movement away from the extended family system. One trend was for women to become more involved in the home and in raising children. Another was to extend their activities outside the home before, during, and after childbearing through labor-force participation. This latter trend was made possible by women's higher educational achievements, the improvement of conception control, smaller families, humanitarian pressures for equal opportunity and better child-care facilities.

There were no improvements in methods of conception control early in the period of industrial development, so that childbearing and family size continued to be regulated by the traditional methods, especially by abstinence and infanticide (63, 64), and by delay in the age of marriage. In the present century, major developments in the field of medical contraception have greatly improved the capability of conception control, with the result that individuals have had far greater freedom in choosing the timing and number of children. The most important developments in the field of contraception and of birth control have included the development of oral contraception, the IUD, and surgical procedures for induced abortion and sterilization. Concurrent with these developments in contraceptive technology has been a general liberalization of sexual norms during the past 50 to 75 years. The interaction of these two developments has resulted not only in greater freedom of choice in childbearing but also in the psychological separation of sexuality from reproduction and thus the growth of recreational sexuality within marriage and other lasting relationships.

With industrialization came a steady and progressive decrease in average family size. A number of different social, psychological, and technological factors played a role in this development. One of the most important of these was the decrease in child mortality making it unnecessary for couples to overproduce children in order to have a certain number survive to adulthood. A second important factor was that the state in industrial society assumed many of the functions that the local group and the family group assumed in other societal forms, especially the care of aging individuals. This trend decreased the pressure on reproducing couples to have many children in order to ensure that they would be provided for in later life. A third general factor important in reducing family size was the opportunity in industrial society for more people to provide all of their children with the material necessities and some of the luxuries of life, an opportunity which was difficult to pursue with a large family.

Scientific and medical knowledge expanded the capability of industrial societies to control and prevent disease. During the early nineteenth century, many of the first changes were related to hygiene. Large-scale immunization programs also made a significant contribution. Finally, with the introduction and rapid development of surgery, antibiotics, and other chemical forms of treatment, disease and death control began to have a major impact on the length and quality of life in industrial society.

Industrialization was associated with a surge of what has been called free migration (46). Technology increased the capacity to transport food and material, with the result that many individuals and groups of people migrated from the western European countries to the rest of the world. Some of this migration was stimulated by the need, within the governmental and industrial sectors of the colonialized nations, for people trained in business, administration, and certain crafts. Much of it, however, was the result of undesirable conditions in the countries of origin, and a wish on the part of migrants to find or create a better life. With the growth of urbanization, a new geographic mobility occurred with increased frequency. This was characterized by the movement of individuals and to some extent families within or between areas or states of one nation. These local or regional moves commonly occurred several times in a lifetime and were associated with individual milestones or transition points, such as the completion of education, marriage, and the search for a new job.

The net effect upon population-related behaviors of the changes introduced by industrialization was to move the population of preindustrial Europe from comparatively high levels of fertility and mortality through what has been called the demographic transition (65, 66) to comparatively low levels of fertility and mortality, as is now the case. The historical pattern was very different for the nonwestern, nonindustrialized countries (51, 62). At the time of contact with and colonialization by the western European nations, mortality commonly increased considerably as a result of war and the spread of epidemic diseases introduced by the Europeans. Later, during the period of colonial rule, birthrates frequently increased in response to the demand for agricultural labor, the latter being stimulated and controlled by the western colonial powers. In recent decades, mortality has dropped dramatically as a result of the systematic importation of western medical techniques to treat and prevent common diseases. To a lesser extent, and only more recently, the importation of western contraceptive techniques has lowered birthrates in many areas. At the present time, the nonwestern nations seem to be going through an accelerated demographic transition, with different linguistic and cultural groups following different patterns (67) but with the general trend somewhat similar to that followed during the western European transition (68).

In general, the system of population regulation in industrial societies has become highly complex. The various behaviors relevant to population are subject to the influences of many levels of organization within society beyond the family, including the state and those institutions intermediate between the state and the family. With the advent of the numerous technological advances that have impinged upon many areas of population-related behavior and with the decrease of normative regulation in these same areas of behavior that is characteristic of technological nontraditional societies, most of these behaviors have become to a great degree, subject to individual decision making. As a result, market-type mechanisms are central to their regulation.

PAST TRENDS AND THE FUTURE

At the beginning of this chapter we described how the interests of the individual organism and of the local population of similar organisms, or deme, are linked through the processes of evolution. Thus, the individual who survives to produce offspring, who themselves survive, contributes to the future population of the deme. In this way, the adaptive qualities of that individual organism are passed on and distributed within subsequent generations of the local population, increasing its total adaptive potential. The interests of the individual organism and the local population are also linked through the effect of the deme on the individual organism's environment. This environment has both physical and social features. Through the cumulative effect of individual actions, a local population changes the physical environment for an individual organism, thereby affecting its chances of survival. In addition, the other members of an organism's local population make up that organism's social environment. The latter is an important regulator of the individual organism's behavior.

We have described how population regulation appears to be based on a system that involves interactions between different levels of organization, one that is different for each species. The evolutionary significance of a population regulation system is that it maintains the adaptiveness of a population to its current environment and simultaneously allows continuing evolution of the population to a new or changing environment. The population regulation system utilizes biological, psychological, and social mechanisms in virtually all animal species. However, in higher animals and particularly in vertebrates, mammals, primates, and humans there are increasing degrees of population regulation by psychological and social mechanisms. A different set of factors operates to regulate population within each species, and in humans, within each system of technological and organizational development. In the apes, the population regulation system involves primarily the individual and the troop or local group. In gathering-hunting humans, it involves the individual, the couple, the local group, and the tribe. In agricultural humans, it typically involves the individual, the couple, the extended family or lineage system, the village, and the feudal state. In industrial humans, it appears to involve the individual, the couple, the family, various religious, ethnic, social class, and occupational reference groups, the community of residence, and the nation-state. On the basis of this description and the material presented earlier in the chapter, there appear to be three important historical trends in the development of human population regulation systems: an increasing size and complexity of the interacting systems; an increasing number of psychological and social factors that are a part of the system; and an increasing degree of individual decision making affecting system-related behavior.

What trends can be expected in the future? First, it seems likely that the national population regulation system will become increasingly linked to the worldwide system. In this book, we focus on the current system in the United States. To the degree that the system in this country is linked with other national systems our account is incomplete and it will tend to become progressively incomplete if the prediction of a growing worldwide population regulation system is accurate.

What changes can we expect within the United States system in the future? Most likely there will be increased complexity and diversity, made possible by the new electronic technology and other features of postindustrial society. As a result of increased technological control of nature, it can be expected that new factors and new mechanisms will enter into the population regulation system. For example, it is interesting to imagine the consequences for population regulation if and when we are able to control the genetic outcomes of reproduction, substantially extend the duration of life, or migrate from the planet earth. Finally, as a result of developments at many different levels within U.S. society that will increase the degrees of biological, psychological, and social freedom of its members, it can be expected that the U.S. population regulation system will be even more subject to individual preference and choice. It is the importance of individual decision making in the current U.S. population regulation system and in our vision of the future system that leads us to the next two chapters.

SUMMARY

This chapter reviews the evolutionary and historical development of the dynamic relation between the individual and the population within which she or he is located, beginning with a consideration of biological organisms in general and then moving up the phylogenetic scale to concentrate ultimately on primates and humans. First, we discuss the survival of the individual organism and the local group or deme by means of adaptation to and alteration of local environmental conditions and by means of differential reproduction. This leads us to consider the three factors of reproduction, mortality, and migration as basic determinants of the size of a local population and as the most important factors whose interactions form the local population regulation system. We describe some of the mechanisms in such systems and discuss how such systems are largely density dependent.

Next, we move to a consideration of the various mechanisms of primate population regulation, illustrating our discussion with material from the four apes, which are closest to humans in evolutionary terms. We then move into a discussion of the transition from ape to human, focusing upon the new adaptive strategy involved in this change, and the new lifestyles this transition made possible. In particular the transition had profound implications for behaviors involved in marriage and reproduction, mortality, and geographic mobility. It is these varied behaviors and their interactive population regulative function to which we turn our attention in the next three sections of this chapter. Each section deals with three different levels of human cultural and technological development, discussing in turn the gathering-hunting, agricultural, and industrial population regulation systems. Since one of the main functions of such regulation is to keep a population prepared for adaptation to any one of the most likely worlds of tomorrow, the chapter concludes with a few brief speculations about the future of the population regulation system in the world as a whole and in the United States in particular.

THE PSYCHOLOGY OF DECISION MAKING AND ADAPTATION

3

We will begin this chapter with a general discussion of the psychological and behavioral territory encompassed by the concepts of decision making and adaptation. Both these terms are very broad in their meaning. Generally speaking, decision making has to do with choosing a course of action, although under certain circumstances it is possible to talk about deciding upon an attitude or even a feeling. There may or may not be more than one course of action from which to choose. Thus, both choosing whether or not to follow a course of action and choosing which of several courses of action to follow involve making a decision. The scope of the behavior and the consequences of the course of action resulting from a decision vary considerably, as does the amount of conscious deliberation that goes into the decision. The behavior may be very simple in scope, limited in the importance and magnitude of its consequences, and characteristically performed without much thought. Examples are taking a vitamin pill upon arising each morning or driving a particular route to work. These types of behavior tend to be routinized and habitual, without any subjectively obvious decision being made except when the habit or behavior is first being learned, and in specific situations which call for omission of the behavior. On the other hand, the behavior that follows a decision may be highly complex and extended over long periods of time, great in the importance and magnitude of its consequences, and one involving lengthy intrapsychic and interpersonal consideration. Such is typically the case when an individual decides about getting married, having a baby, or pursuing an occupation. The behavior required in making such decisions is decidedly unroutinized precisely because it is pursued so infrequently during the course of a lifetime. In spite of this great variability in the scope of decision behaviors and in the consequences that follow from decision making, what all hold in common is that they are, at least potentially, subject to conscious, self-aware choice by the individual.

The concept of decision making is often used in a manner very similar to the concept of problem solving (1). Generally, however, decision making refers to a situation where a choice depends upon the individual's goals or objectives, whereas problem solving implies that there is a solution and a right course of action. Related to both of these is the concept of psychological adaptation. This concept implies a response to some internal or external situation or development. The response involves the whole organism in an effort to maintain or establish the best possible level of satisfaction and integration under given environmental conditions. Adaptation includes both an intrapsychic aspect and an aspect reflecting interaction between the person and the environment. This latter interaction includes adjustment to the environmental demands, compromise with the environment, and alteration of the environment to suit individual needs and desires. There are three additional concepts closely related to that of adaptation (2): psychological defense, mastery, and coping. The first of these refers to protection of the ego from excessive or intolerable levels of anxiety, fear, and other distressful affects. Mastery refers to the ability of an organism to understand and successfully manipulate a complex problem area through the organism's own behavior. Finally, coping refers to the adaptive behavior that occurs under unfamiliar, difficult, or stressful conditions. All these three concepts refer to aspects of behavior covered by the more generic concept, adaptation.

Much of the discussion of individual psychology in this and the next chapter focuses on decision making and adaptation. As the general model or paradigm introduced in Chapter 1 suggests, decision making is especially important in considering the psychological antecedents to demographic behavior, and adaptation is especially important in considering the psychological or behavioral responses to the demographic characteristics of a community or area. This may be illustrated through a series of examples from the population field. The decisions that may be made within the domain of reproduction are numerous. Most obvious, of course, is the decision to have a child. In many cases, this decision is separate from the decision about when to have that child. In connection with the timing of children, a decision must be made on methods of proception.* Also, in cases where an individual or couple may risk bearing a child with a genetic or congenital condition, part of the decision to bear that child involves a decision regarding what to do to prevent or decrease the chances of a genetic or congenital condition. This may involve, for example, a decision to seek amniocentesis† in order to make a prenatal diagnosis, or it may involve a decision to seek a certain type of antenatal medical care, or to have a certain type of childbirth. A related decision, on the verge of becoming a significant social reality, involves predetermining and, through selective abortion, preselecting the sex of a baby. There are also a whole set of decisions to be made with respect to problems of infertility, especially how far to pursue medical investigation and whether to attempt adoption.

Another very important group of reproductive decisions includes those resulting from the occurrence of an unplanned pregnancy. These include decisions about whether or not to seek an abor-

---

* "Proception" is the opposite of contraception. It is the attempt to achieve conception.

† "Amniocentesis" is the drawing off of small amount of the fluid surrounding the fetus in the amniotic sac for the purpose of examining some of the skin and other cells that have come from the fetus and collected in the fluid. These cells may allow a prenatal diagnosis of certain congenital conditions in the fetus that, if present, may cause a couple to seek elective abortion.

tion and whether or not to place a child for adoption following birth. If an unplanned conception has occurred prior to marriage, it frequently leads to a decision regarding marriage. When an unplanned conception occurs within marriage, it may necessitate decisions regarding the type and amount of work that will be possible or necessary for one or both spouses.

Many decisions made before a conception and birth are directly or indirectly important in determining its occurrence. For example, decisions regarding engagement in sexual activity with a particular partner or with a given frequency, decisions regarding the selection of a particular contraceptive method, and the repeated decisions involved in the utilization of a particular contraceptive method all have an important effect on whether or not conception occurs. So also do decisions regarding cohabitation, marriage, separation, and divorce. Finally, since employment and life style have a direct bearing on the desire for children, decisions regarding these factors will have an important bearing on subsequent childbearing decisions.

It would be possible to present a similar outline of the subset of decisions operating in the behavior domains related to mortality, geographic mobility, educational selection and achievement, and occupational selection and achievement. Further, the same behavior domains could be discussed with respect to the psychology of adaptation. Thus, patterns of adaptation that share common elements occur in response to reproduction-related events such as the birth of a planned child, the occurrence of an unplanned conception, the manifestation of an infertility problem, the occurrence of a genetic or congenital condition in a child, and the simultaneous pursuit of child rearing and work. Further, there are similarities across behavior domains in the adaptation of individuals to illness, geographic mobility, divorce, occupational changes, population densities, aging, and even to their own gender.

It is well for the reader to keep in mind that the distinction between decision making and adaptation, while intuitively obvious and analytically convenient, is also somewhat arbitrary and dependent upon one's viewpoint. For example, decision making is an important ingredient in adaptation to new or difficult conditions. Creating change may also be a way of adapting to the sameness of conditions or to the lack of stimulation. Similarly, depending to some degree upon the scope of the decision and the magnitude of its consequences, various degrees of adaptation are necessary as part of any given decision. With the differences and similarities of these two concepts in mind, we turn now to a more detailed discussion of the psychology of individual decision making and adaptation. Our emphasis will be on the former, although many themes in our discussion apply equally well to both types of behavior.

FIVE ASPECTS OF DECISION MAKING

Further clarification of decision making may be achieved by discussing some of the variations in individual subjective states and behavior and in situational conditions that characterize it. For this purpose, we have selected five fundamental features of decision making for further examination. These include the temporal feature, the probabilistic feature, the rational feature, the active-passive feature, and the dyadic feature of decision making.

Decision Making and Time

People often think of decisions as taking place at a single point in time. Scientists often propose decision-making models that describe the push-and-pull forces acting upon a person with regard to a given course of action and they assume that the decision itself is an instantaneous calculation of the resultant forces at the decision juncture. In actuality, decision making is extended over various degrees of time and is made up of a series of overt acts and covert psychological states. It is true that someone may be able to identify a very specific point in time when a particular decision is made, but in most cases it would be a mistake to assert that some of the intrapsychic and interpersonal processes that led up to that point and followed from it were not a part of the decision making itself. People do not simply make a decision. They work toward it with observation, fantasy, discussion, and other forms of exploration, often making a number of minidecisions along the way. Once the decision has been made, they continue their observations, fantasy, and discussion in order to review and modify their objectives and even to reconsider the decision itself. Thus, it is not surprising to find many decisions that do not have a clear decisional point. For example, if married individuals are asked when they decided to marry, many report that there was not an identifiable time when they made their specific decision, but rather that they developed it—or it occurred—over a period of weeks, months, or years. This extended temporal characteristic of decision making is of such fundamental importance that it is useful to distinguish between the decision-making process and the decision-making content. The process refers to the series of steps or the sequence of psychological states and behaviors determining how the decision was made over a period of time. The content of a decision, on the other hand, refers to what decision is made and, more specifically, what motivational and other forces acting for and against the possible courses of action enter into the personal equation. Much of the discussion in this chapter will focus on the decision-making process. In Chapter 4 we will turn to an extended discussion of the content of those decisions bearing on the issues of population and the population regulation system.

There are three temporal aspects of the decision-making process that deserve special mention. The first and most obvious is time duration. As we have already indicated, decisions are made over varying periods of time. This variation occurs not only with different types of decisions, but also with the same decision as approached by different individuals. One couple may decide to have a child in a matter of days and another may take years to decide. A second important temporal aspect is that of time constraint. Some decisions must be made within a limited time period. A good example is the abortion decision. Although it is possible to prepare for such a decision, the fact that an unwanted pregnancy is so commonly unanticipated necessarily limits the degree of preparation possible. On the other hand, once conception has occurred, the decision to abort must be made within a limited time period, depending on local abortion laws and practices. After that period, an abortion is no longer possible. A third important temporal aspect of decision making is its degree of reversibility. For example, the selection of an intrauterine device for long-term contraception is a different matter from the selection of a vasectomy or a tubal ligation. If the decision maker changes his or her mind about not having any more children, the IUD may be removed, while for all practical purposes, surgical sterilization cannot be routinely reversed.

Decision Making and Probability

A second important feature of decision making is that it is directed toward outcomes that are only probabilistic. Probability is a constant companion in daily life and the behavior of most people is based upon assumptions that account for its effects. For example, it is obvious that probability affects our lives in such matters as the purchase of life insurance, planning for a weekend at the beach, voting, and playing cards. In these and other matters the psychology of probability is subtle, complex, and difficult to analyze scientifically (4, 5, 6, 7).

Probability enters into virtually all of the population-related decision-making areas, in different ways and to different degrees. One obviously important area is procreation. Both the successful achievement of conception through proception and the successful avoidance of conception by contraception are dependent upon the probabilistic relationship between sexual intercourse and conception, with a large number of behavioral factors influencing the probabilities either upward toward one or downward toward zero (3). Contraception in particular is a matter of balancing probabilities or risks (8, 9, 10). Not only are both its use and its nonuse associated with outcomes which are only probabilistic, but the outcomes have features which themselves are only probabilistic if the outcome is achieved. Let us take for an example the young, unmarried woman who is making a decision regarding the use of oral contraception. She has to consider the probability that she is going to be sexually active. This probability may depend upon whether or not she obtains oral contraception. She must also consider the probability of getting pregnant if she is sexually active without using a contraceptive method or while using a contraceptive method other than oral contraception, and the probability of pregnancy while using oral contraception. In addition, she has to consider the probability of such diverse outcomes as contracting venereal disease, damaging her reputation or her relationship with her boyfriend, developing high blood pressure, amenorrhea, thrombophlebitis, or painful breasts if she does use oral contraception, and not being able to obtain an abortion if she does become pregnant. Thoroughly complex as this example may seem, it does not fully describe the complexity likely to exist in a real situation because we have mentioned only the probabilities of the most important primary consequences and of the most important secondary consequences (those that occur only if the primary consequences occur). However, the probability of tertiary consequences may also be important. For example, there would be a certain probability of abortion complication (a tertiary consequence) if the woman did become pregnant and if she did obtain an abortion. The complexity of a real situation is also greater than we have described because this example utilizes only negative consequences. Clearly there are many positive primary, secondary, and tertiary consequences in this illustrative situation, each associated with its own probabilities.

It is useful to distinguish between decision making under conditions of uncertainty and decision making under conditions of risk (11). The former generally refers to situations where it is impossible to tell with any accuracy what outcomes will occur or what the probabilities are that they will occur. On the other hand, conditions of risk generally refer to situations where there is a known probability that certain outcomes will occur. For example, if a person decides to bear a child, it is an uncertainty as to what that child will be like in, say, five years. On the other hand, the risk of pregnancy with any single unprotected act of intercourse or while using a particular contraceptive method over a one-year period can be calculated with reasonable accuracy. The former, for example, is 4 percent and the latter is around 1 percent for oral contraception and 2 to 3 percent for the IUD. The distinction between uncertainty and risk is important because with the latter the decision maker may be more adequately prepared through prior information about probabilities and the final decision may be more realistically based.

In many cases important differences may exist between the objective probabilities or risk figures that are based on the actual relationships between events observed in nature and society and the subjective probabilities or perceived risks existing in the mind of the individual decision maker. The latter are especially susceptible to distortion by the decision maker's needs and desires (9). For example, in a recent research project 642 women, each having an abortion for an unwanted pregnancy, were asked what psychological or behavioral factors played a role in their getting pregnant (12). Thirty-five percent indicated that they had thought it was during the safe period, 21 percent indicated that they had put the possibility of pregnancy out of their minds, 14 percent indicated that they had not thought pregnancy was likely because they had infrequent intercourse, and 14 percent indicated that they had thought they would not get pregnant since they had often had intercourse without precautions and had never gotten pregnant before. These interviews made it clear that a large proportion of the responses were based on inaccurate subjective estimates of the probability of conception distorted by the women's own wishes.

The uncertainty or risk factors in decision making induce individuals to develop strategies for dealing with the probabilities (13). There are three strategies covering most common situations: the wish strategy, the safe strategy, and the combination strategy. The wish strategy may be called the maxigain strategy. In it individuals strive for what they desire most or for a maximization of their gain, regardless of risk or possible cost. The safe strategy may be called the miniloss strategy. Individuals seek to avoid or minimize their loss, regardless of the risk or possible gain. In the combination strategy, decision makers base their choice on a combination of probability and utility. Their choice depends on the net of probability of gain and probability of loss, or what has been called subjective expected utility (11). In order to illustrate these strategies, let us imagine a situation where an individual has an opportunity for sexual intercourse but has no contraceptive method. He or she might feel that the sexual act itself would almost certainly be highly gratifying but that the occurrence of a conception would be extremely undesirable. The person choosing the wish strategy would have sexual intercourse whatever the risk of conception and no matter what the cost. The person choosing the safe strategy would decide to avoid sexual intercourse no matter how small the chances of conception were and no matter how rewarding the sexual experience would be. The person selecting the combination strategy would consider the chances of sexual gratification and the degree of its desirability, and compare that with the chance of conception and the degree of its undesirability. Two aspects of this illustration deserve further comment. First, it is clear that virtually everyone in life uses some form of combination strategy. In fact, it is more accurate to say that the wish and the safe strategies represent the extreme forms of a wide range of intermediate combination strategies and are rarely used as such. However, most people do tend to fall toward one end of the range or the other in their use of combination strategy. To the extent that this is consistently true for them across a variety of decision-making situations, they may be said to have a decision-making style. Second, decisions infrequently involve courses of action with only high gain or high cost. Usually there is some intermediate course of action. For example, in the above illustration, the decision maker might have elected a course of action between one of having no sexual intercourse and one of having unprotected sexual intercourse. Such a course of action might involve utilizing a contraceptive method that slightly compromised the level of sexual satisfaction (as many men feel the condom does) or carried costs of its own for the user (as many women feel oral contraception does) but that significantly decreased the probabilities of conception.

Decision Making and Rationality

A third important feature of decision making is the degree to which it involves rationality. Models of decision making have been generated in order to optimize the making of decisions by politicians, businessmen, and managers in general. These models have been highly rational in the sense that they rely upon quantifiable information and mathematical formulas. In addition, psychologists who construct theories and models for understanding everyday types of decision making make assumptions about "rational man" (11, 14). These assumptions posit that humans act rationally in decision making when they know what they want or like and act to maximize their gain. This type of assumption greatly simplifies the construction of mathematical theories of decision making and game playing. Although some of these theories have proved useful in understanding behavior under highly specified and controlled conditions, they offer very little for understanding the individual decision maker in an everyday life situation. Perhaps this is because it is just in such situations that decisions are most highly influenced by nonrational factors.

What are some of these factors that prevent decisions from being primarily a matter of choosing courses of actions with the greatest net value for the individual? First of all, they include attitudinal and motivational forces that influence behavior and decision making but that are poorly controlled or poorly integrated by the decision maker. This lack of integration often occurs because the decision maker has not acquired a conscious appreciation of the forces or has defensively excluded them from consciousness. Second, these factors include decision-making processes that are either self-defeating for the decision maker or that lead to action inconsistent with decisions made at other points in time. Examples here are impulsive decision making or the use of an unrealistic decision-making style. Third, these factors include psychological changes which produce inconsistencies over time in the evaluation of different courses of action. These changes may be brought about by growth and development, by social field interactions, or simply by day-to-day alterations in mood and outlook. Finally, these factors include emotional and other psychological states and stressful environmental events that alter and disrupt the usual and consistent functioning of the decision maker. Considering the many nonrational factors that can affect decision making, a useful and accurate definition of rationality would involve a well-integrated and balanced expression of self by the individual ego in a realistic way within the given decision context. In this sense, the decision not to pursue one's education due to an unconscious fear of success, an impulsive decision to marry, an uninformed decision to undergo surgery, and a decision to get pregnant made while partly intoxicated, all represent forms of nonrational decision making.

Active and Passive Decision Making

A fourth feature of decision making is the degree to which it is actively or passively entered into by the decision maker. In active decision making the ego takes the initiative. In passive decision making the ego accepts the decision after it has been instigated by some external factor. The factor can be a person, as, for example, when someone decides to quit smoking after the doctor strongly suggests it for reasons of health. It can also be an event as when a person decides to move after being fired from a job or to seek an effective contraceptive method after a pregnancy scare. The presence of an instigating event does not by itself make a decision a passive one. In fact, there are probably instigating factors in most decision making and everyone is familiar with the type of decision that is simply cued by or precipitated by an external event or opportunity, the ego having been actively involved well before the instigation. Thus, the activity or passivity of a decision depends primarily on the degree of influence of the external or instigating factor.

A common type of decision making that falls close to the passive end of the continuum is decision making by default. This type of decision making is well captured by the familiar expression "not to make a decision is to decide." In such a decision, the individual involved often feels that none has been made and that he or she was, in fact, powerless to make one. Although it may appear that no specific decision was made, an implicit one actually was made. A good example of decision by default is when someone does not seek diagnosis or treatment for a physical condition and thereby makes a decision about his or her health, or even his or her life. Another example is when an unwanted pregnancy occurs following an instance of unprotected sexual intercourse. To the person involved it may have appeared that the only decision was to have sexual intercourse; however, implicit in the decision not to seek contraception prior to intercourse and/or not to use contraception at the time of intercourse lay the decision to take a chance on having an unwanted pregnancy. It is probabilistic situations like these that are particularly susceptible to passive decision making.

A common phenomenon in the United States involves having a baby within marriage through the nonuse of contraception but without any specific intent of conceiving. Couples interviewed following such a conception frequently state that they had not personally made any decision about having a baby and were leaving the occurrence of pregnancy to God or fate. Although it may seem somewhat inappropriate to say that such couples have decided to have a baby, in fact, by virtue of deciding to expose themselves consistently to the chance of conception and, simultaneously, by deciding not to take any action to prevent conception, they have made such a decision, albeit an indirect and passive one.

It should be apparent from the above discussion and examples that decision making is not limited to being either active or passive. Rather it falls at different points along an active-passive continuum. Where it falls depends to some degree upon the amount of instigation in the situation. It also depends upon the individual. As we observed in connection with strategies dealing with risk, each individual tends to develop and utilize a characteristic decision-making style. In many cases, this style has an active or a passive quality about it, and this will determine the degree to which a particular instance of decision making is itself active or passive.

Dyadic Decision Making
The fifth and final feature of decision making is the degree to which it is made as a member of a dyad. In actuality, dyadic decision making is a special instance of decision making involving two or more people. However, because so much everyday decision making of relevance to population regulation is made in a couple context,

particularly a marital-couple context, our comments will focus primarily on dyadic issues and examples.

When thinking about dyadic decision making, it is tempting to assume that the decision represents the wishes of the two particular individuals summed or totaled in some simple or complex way. However, dyadic decision making is not just the summation of two individual decisions because the decision is made in the total context of the particular dyadic relationship and is influenced by all aspects of that relationship. Two of these aspects of special importance are communication and dominance. Patterns of communication will determine how aware one member of a couple is of the other's desires and attitudes. These patterns will also determine how much information is shared. Perhaps most important of all, these patterns will determine how much working together and back-and-forth exchange of thoughts and feelings goes into the actual decision-making process. There are several important factors affecting the patterns of communication. Beyond the ability to express oneself either verbally or nonverbally, there is the factor of trust and confidence in the dyadic relationship. These latter qualities are necessary if individuals are to fully explore their doubts and to expose some of their more private perceptions and feelings to each other during the decision-making process.

Dominance patterns in couple relationships act in complex ways to affect decision making. Only rarely does one member of a couple totally dominate the other and take over all decision making. More typically, there is a dominance of one member in one domain, such as child rearing or social life, and a dominance of the other member in a different domain such as financial management or leisure time. Which one assumes the dominance, and in which area, depends on a variety of factors, including the personalities, personal values, and gender role orientations of each individual, their relative ages and education, their relative employment status, and the presence or absence of children (15). In most marriages, couples tend to be more or less egalitarian at the beginning, with a later trend toward increasing role specialization and separate decision making for both members. Apart from these general patterns, it is important to appreciate that decision making involves bargaining and exchanges in dominance. Thus, a wife may agree to her husband's decision to accept a job promotion that involves their moving to another part of the country only with the understanding that she will choose the type and location of the house that they buy. An agreement negotiated at a less overt and explicit level might be one where the husband agrees to allow inconsistency in the use of contraception—an implicit decision to have a baby—while the wife agrees to be more responsive to his sexual advances.

Dyadic decision making has both advantages and disadvantages. A major advantage lies in the enrichment of individual experience. Intimate interaction over a decision matter, including challenge and resistance from one partner, can lead to the discovery of new aspects of oneself and to the development of new values. In addition, sharing with or yielding to a trusted partner in a decision matter can lead to results that would never have been experienced had the individual made the decision alone. A major disadvantage of dyadic decision making lies in its potential for generating or reactivating serious and painful conflict. This is more likely to happen if two individuals do not agree that there is a decision to be made, do not share some common values, or do not have a minimal degree of initial cohesion.

BEHAVIORAL SCIENCE MODELS OF DECISION MAKING

At this point we turn to examine some of the models that behavioral scientists have developed in order to understand decision making, especially in those behavior domains relevant to population regulation. It should be noted that many of these models were not intended to be comprehensive or fully detailed in their original presentation. In addition, each was originally presented in a specific context, with special purposes related to that context. We have selected each one for inclusion here because, in common with several or all of the other models, it deals with features of decision making that we wish to emphasize, or because it highlights a particular feature of decision making that the other models ignore. Our general purpose in reviewing them here is to set the stage for the presentation and discussion of our own comprehensive model of decision making presented in the next section.

We begin with several models that attempt to explain decision making in the domain of family planning and contraceptive use. One of the more popular of these models involves an expectancy–times–evaluation approach (16, 17, 18, 19). In this approach, decision making is assumed to be a function of the product of expectancy and evaluation, where expectancy is the perceived probability of certain outcomes occurring and evaluation is the value placed upon those outcomes. In a refined version of this approach, decision making is additionally assumed to be a function of perceived social norms regarding the possible outcome weighted by the motivation to comply with those norms. In illustration, let us consider the decision to use oral contraception. The simple expectancy–times–evaluation model could be used to predict the decision for a particular individual if one knew the following: the decision maker's perception of the consequences of oral contraceptive use such as increasing the frequency of sexual pleasure, producing specific side effects, being highly reliable, and being moderately expensive; the decision maker's perception of the probability that each of these consequences would follow; and, the value placed upon these consequences by the decision maker. Using the more refined model, greater accuracy of prediction could presumably be achieved by knowing the following as well: the decision maker's perception of the attitudes regarding oral-contraceptive use held by various important people in her or his life, such as parents, spouse, friends, siblings; and, the strength of the decision maker's wish to conform with these people's attitudes. This group of expectancy–times–evaluation models, emphasizing as it does the perceived probabilities and values of consequences and the perceived normative pressures, is highly substantive in nature, and, as such, tells us little if anything with regard to the decision-making process.

Another popular model for investigating the psychology of contraceptive use focuses on the sequential contraception-adoption process (20, 21). Such models are based on the assumption that there are stages through which an adopter moves. Although the naming and categorization of these stages varies, four are commonly mentioned: a) the stage of awareness and interest, when the individual learns that contraception is possible and acceptable, becomes interested in it, and wants to learn more about it; b) the stage of information gathering, evaluation, and deciding to adopt the method; c) the stage of implementation and trial, when the individual seeks the method, obtains it, and begins to use it; and d) the stage of adoption and continuation, when the individual feels that the choice is a good one and plans continued use of the method.

A somewhat different account of the decision-making process has been developed with the use of Janice's conflict theory and Festinger's dissonance theory (22). In this model, the decision-making process begins when an individual's usual course of action is challenged. This occurs when that person is exposed to information calling attention to important losses that will occur if he or she continues to follow the same course of action. This information is inconsistent with the individual's preexisting cognitions about his or her present behavioral policy, and it generates a temporary personal crisis. Attempts may be made by the individual to dismiss the conflicting information as untrue, irrelevant, or relatively unimportant. If this is not possible, however, the individual experiences anticipatory regret for the potential losses and accepts the challenge. The second stage of decision making consists of an appraisal of the possible or available alternative courses of action. This process includes the soliciting of more information about possible ways of resolving the situation. In the third stage, a tentative decision is made regarding the best behavioral policy by means of a thorough evaluation of the best alternatives. The best choice is tentatively selected but without commitment. During the fourth decision-making stage, the individual commits him or herself to the behavioral policy selected by revealing it to others. The fifth and final stage of the decision-making process consists of the individual's adherence to the new behavioral policy in spite of negative feedback from others and a certain amount of negative information generated by his or her own behavior.

Fawcett has developed a model of marital decision making, one that is designed to deal with whether to marry as distinct from when to marry or whom to marry (23). In this model, the final common pathway is an unspecified decision process that involves some type of "weighing" of the various influences acting upon the individual, although not necessarily at a conscious level or in a rational fashion. The result is a decision to marry or to pursue an alternative to marriage, most commonly to remain single. There are four types of influences leading to the final decision process. First, there are the perceived benefits and costs of marriage and of its alternatives. For example, an individual might perceive marriage as beneficial because of the affectional ties, companionship, or sexual gratification it provides, but costly because of the loss of personal freedom and the assumption of economic obligation involved. Second, there are the social facilitators or barriers to marriage and its alternatives. These include facilitators such as social norms that encourage marriage, unrestricted divorce laws or customs, and tax and welfare provisions that reduce the cost of marriage. These also include barriers such as laws or customs restricting the choice of a spouse, normative requirements for a dowry, and the social availability of alternatives to marriage. Third, there are the immediate situational factors that influence an individual's marriage decision. These include such factors as the decision maker's economic status, the availability of potential marriage partners in the immediate locale, and the existence of social pressure from significant others. Fourth, there are the psychological traits of the individual that are likely to affect perceptions of all three of the previous influences, as well as the decision-making process.

A similar model of decision making that deals with a different behavioral domain and that is equally silent regarding the process of decision making has been developed by Lee for explaining the decision to migrate (24). In this model, there are positive, negative, and neutral factors at both the point of origin and the point of destination for the potential migrator. Only the positive and negative factors operate to incline the individual toward or away from migration. These factors, traditionally called "push" and "pull" factors by demographers, include such considerations as the presence of high levels of unemployment or close family ties in the home area and a promising job opportunity or an undesirable climate in another area. In this model, the decision to migrate is not conceived solely to be a function of pushes and pulls. There are also assumed to be intervening factors serving as obstacles or facilitators to geographic mobility. These include such considerations as the distance between the two areas, geographical characteristics intervening between them, types of intervening transportation, and the costs of moving from one area to the other.

Rosenstock, Becker, and others have developed a model of individual decision making in relation to preventive health behavior (25). In this model there are three main components. The first is the individual's "readiness to take action" relative to a particular health condition, such as influenza or obesity. This readiness to act is itself determined by the person's perception of his or her susceptibility or vulnerability to the particular condition, by his or her perception of the consequences of developing the condition, and by his or her evaluation of those consequences. The second component is the person's evaluation of the preventive health behavior that is required in terms of its potential for reducing his or her susceptibility to the condition or the severity of the condition itself, and his or her perception of the psychological and other barriers or costs of the proposed behavior. The third component is a cue to action which serves to trigger the appropriate preventive behavior. Such a stimulus may be either internal, such as the perception of changed bodily states, or external, such as being personally acquainted with someone affected by the condition, or interacting with people or the mass media in connection with the condition. Although this model is presented here in terms of health behavior, it has also been developed in relation to illness behavior and sick-role behavior (25).

The final decision model selected from the behavioral-science literature for review is that developed by Blau and others with regard to occupational choice (26). This decision has elements that make it similar to the decision to marry in that there are actually two distinct decisions being made—one by an individual and one by an agency or organization. It is for this reason that, in Blau's model, occupational choice by individuals can only be understood in conjunction with occupational selection. The final determinants of an individual's decision regarding which job to apply for are his evaluations of the available job opportunities and appraisal of the probability of being selected for the job. The evaluation is a function of the individual's preference hierarchy, and the perceived probability of selection is a function of the individual's expectancy hierarchy. Actual decision making involves combining these two hierarchies to create a rank order of choices. The latter, then, results in a series of decisions regarding which jobs to apply for and in what order. Whether or not the individual is selected depends upon the ideal standards regarding the available occupational position on the part of the selectors and their estimate of the chances that a better qualified candidate is available and will apply. An important characteristic of the decision-making process suggested by this model is the searching process individuals go through until they are selected and accepted for a job position. This search process involves frequent reevaluations and reassessments of expectancies as well as a number of intermediate decisions such as the decision to apply for job X or turn down an offer for job Y. As we have explained this model here, it is applicable primarily to the later stages of occupational decision making and does not apply to the earlier stages when decisions are being made about whether to work, when to start work, and what general type of work to pursue.

A COMPREHENSIVE DECISION-MAKING MODEL

We turn now to a more detailed and comprehensive account of individual decision making including the development and discussion of a general model that synthesizes the material discussed in this chapter up to this point, together with some observations and conclusions drawn from our own research. This account will proceed through the discussion of five topics of relevance to individual decision making and its psychology. These topics include the following:

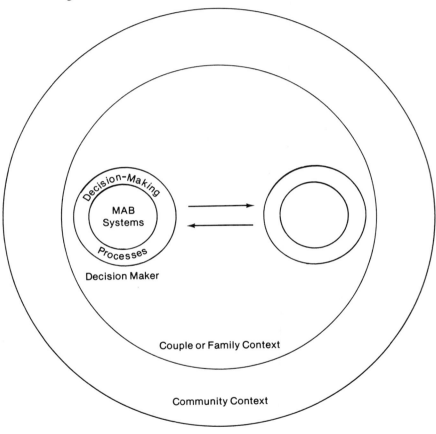

Figure 3.1. A schematic representation of the elements of the comprehensive decision-making model developed in this chapter. These elements include the motivational, attitudinal, and belief systems and the decision-making processes of the decision maker. The decision maker is located within two concentric decision contexts.

(a) the motivational, attitudinal, and belief systems of the individual involved in the decision making;

(b) the hierarchical and sequential organization of goal-directed behavior;

(c) the process of motivational and behavioral integration by the ego;

(d) the stages of the decision-making process;

(e) and the contextual or situational influences on decision making.

Following a full exposition of the model, we shall examine some of the factors involved in effective decision making and the occurrence of decision outcome failures.

Motivational, Attitudinal, and Belief Systems

The motivational, attitudinal, and belief systems of the decision makers are what determine the directions their decisions take. It is these systems that give substance to what people want and do not want, what they approve and do not approve of, what they understand about the world and how it operates. These systems strongly influence and give shape to the perceptions, expectations, and interpretations of decision makers, what objects or goals they seek, and the feelings and emotions they experience. For example, these systems determine people's desire for children, their feelings about women who have a career, and their beliefs about the chances of contracting a particular disease or the usefulness of a particular type of education. These systems are of such crucial importance in decision making that we will deal with them in far greater detail within the next chapter. For the purposes of this chapter their central importance in our general model is indicated by their position in Figure 3.1. There they have been located at the core of the decision maker, surrounded by the process factors of decision making through which their valences are translated into choice and behavior. The process factors themselves will be discussed in the next three sections. In the figure, the individual decision maker is located within two of the important decision-making contexts discussed in the final section of model exposition.

The Hierarchical and Sequential Organization
of Goal-Directed Behavior

An understanding of the hierarchical and sequential organization of goal-directed behavior is necessary in order to appreciate the full complexity of decision making and the rich interconnections between different specific decisions. It is self-evident that human behavior is highly goal directed and that it is organized according to the many goals of the individual. These goals may be short or long term, involving plans for tomorrow or next year. They may also be specific or general, calling for particular behavior or broad trends in behavior. In other words, the objectives governing individual behavior are organized within that individual on superordinate and subordinate levels. A person may want to have a large number of children or to be president of a company, but these are broad, long-term goals and many short-term, more specific ones, such as maintaining health through a pregnancy or negotiating a specific business deal, are component parts of the superordinate goals. In the examples given, the subordinate goals themselves may be further subdivided on more specific, even shorter-term levels. Thus, at a descriptive level we may talk about broad trends of behavior within which are nested subordinate behaviors with increasing specificity, down to where we are describing specific behavioral acts. As we move in our description down such a hierarchy from the general to the specific, the time frame will change from years to seconds. And as we move in our description along the time frame, the general or specific behaviors with which we are concerned appear in sequences which are determined by the broad goals and specific subgoals of the individual. It is in these ways that goal-directed behavior is hierarchically and sequentially organized.

Because decision making is a specific aspect or form of goal-directed behavior, the same kind of hierarchical and sequential organization applies to it as well. This is illustrated in the following example which is depicted in Figure 3.2. The example involves an

Figure 3.2. A schematic representation of the hierarchically and sequentially organized decisions faced in a hypothetical situation by a sexually active female teenager.

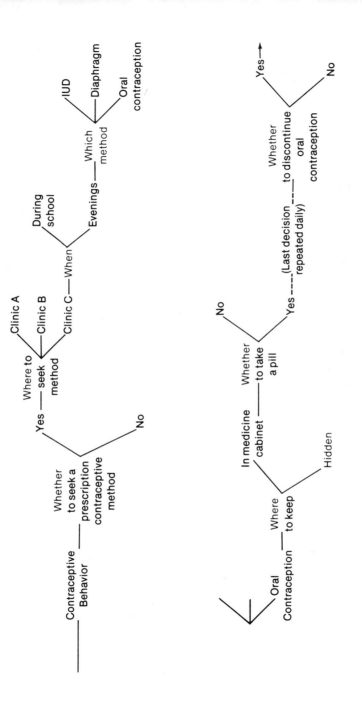

hypothetical young woman in late adolescence who is a senior in high school and living at home with her parents. She has been sexually active for the best part of a year while relying on ad hoc methods of contraception, such as withdrawal and "rhythm." She meets a young man whom she dates for six months and with whom she then falls in love. Until this time, they have been sexually involved only to a limited degree. After some thought and discussion, she decides that she cares enough about this young man to become involved with him on a regular basis. Having made this decision, she must then cope with the possibility of pregnancy and is, therefore, faced with a new decision regarding the use of contraception. She considers whether or not to seek a prescription contraceptive method and, after thinking this over and talking with her boyfriend, decides that she will. In implementing this decision she must decide where to seek the contraceptive method. Nested within that decision may be subordinate ones such as whether to attend the contraceptive methods lecture and rap session prior to the clinic and whether to attend the clinic during school hours or in the evening. The latter decision may be related to that of telling or not telling her parents her intentions. Once she arrives at the clinic of her choice, she will be faced with a decision about which contraceptive method to select. During her consideration of this decision, she may have to make another about where she is going to keep her contraceptive device when she has obtained it. She may then have to reconsider her previous decision about informing her parents. Once she has selected her contraceptive method, unless it is one which requires only one decision, such as the insertion of an intrauterine device, she will have to make repeated decisions while using it, either immediately prior to intercourse itself or, in the case of oral contraception, on a daily basis independent of sexual activity. Finally, after using her contraceptive method over a period of time, she may be subsequently faced with another decision: whether to discontinue using it. For example, if the method she is using is oral contraception and she happens to terminate her relationship with her boyfriend, or if there is considerable negative material in the local newspaper regarding the potentially dangerous side effects of oral contraception, she may decide that the costs or risks to her of continued use outweigh the potential benefits and she may decide to discontinue use. If she does make that decision, then she will almost certainly soon be faced again with a whole new sequence of decisions regarding the securing and utilization of contraceptive protection.

This example illustrates both the way in which decisions are nested hierarchically within higher-level decisions and the way that one decision leads to a series of secondary ones in a time sequence. Many observers have described these hierarchical and sequential aspects of sexual, contraceptive, and procreative behavior in essentially similar terms (9, 10, 27). This example also demonstrates that part of the sequential arrangement and temporal dependency of decisions results from the fact that many decisions are constantly reevaluated and frequently remade. Sometimes the objective behavior associated with this process of reevaluation and remaking of decisions may give the impression to an observer that the decision maker is uncertain about his or her goals or unstable in the pursuit of them. In actuality, the observed changes are often a function of the normal response to changing or uncertain conditions. There have been a whole series of investigations regarding contraceptive method utilization which assumed that significant rates of discontinuation represented failure on the part of the clients. However, if these investigations looked beyond the single decision to discontinue at superordinate and subordinate decisions and antecedent and consequent decisions, the single decision on discontinuing contraception could be far more easily understood. As a result, the clinic programs could be judged more positively and could be modified to fit more appropriately with the specific set of goal-directed behaviors of their particular client population.

Ego Integration

The complexity of the task faced by an individual ego is apparent from the previous illustration of contraceptive decision making by an adolescent woman. In that illustration the ego had to integrate a set of decisions within the contraceptive behavior domain across

levels and over time in order to achieve its goals in a consistent and
satisfactory way. For any single decision, the ego may also face an
equally difficult integrative task. A good example is the case where
someone is trying to decide whether or not to have a child. Let us
say that there are six procreational motives influencing the decision,
three inclining the decision maker toward having a child and three
acting in the opposite direction. We depict this situation in Figure
3.3. For the purposes of this example we say that the decision
maker wants to have a child because there is a strong wish for an
object of nurturance, a desire for some of the social gains of parenthood such as approval by family and friends, and a wish to have a
male heir. Counterbalancing these motives are the decision maker's
concern that another child would create marital strain, a feeling that
the firstborn child of the decision maker was still too young, and

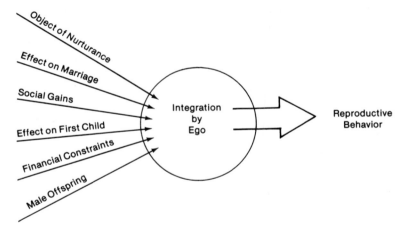

Figure 3.3. A schematic representation of the way the ego must integrate multiple
procreational motives and express them over time during the relevant behaviors. The
motives, arbitrarily selected for purposes of illustration, include: the wish for an object of nurturance; concern that another child will create marital strain; a desire for
some of the social gains of parenthood; feeling that the first child is still too young;
concern over a limited budget; and a desire for a male child.

great concern over a limited family budget. All six of these procreational motives enter the ego independently as derivatives of different motivational, attitudinal, and belief systems. In the ego they are integrated. At any one point this integration is likely to manifest itself as a complex mixture of procreational feelings and wishes. In addition, since each of these motives is likely to assert itself with a different intensity in different contexts, this mixture will often reveal a variable profile across time. When this variability results in either an inability to make a decision or a frequent changing back and forth of the decision, then we speak of ambivalence. The latter may result from the low integrative capacity of the ego, unconscious symbolic (neurotic) conflicts, or strong conscious conflicts among competing motives. Low integrative capacity of the ego may be partially determined by constitutional and genetic factors, but it is commonly a function of psychological stress or physical disrupters such as fatigue, drugs, or disease.

It is not simply within one behavioral domain that the ego must integrate. There are multiple domains, each with their own hierarchies and sequences. It is arguable and somewhat arbitrary how many behavioral domains there are and where to draw the line between them. Nevertheless, a large number of different domains do exist in the sense that people's goals and behaviors are differentially associated with each other in clusters within which they are organized in hierarchies and sequences in the way that we have discussed. Often a decision in one domain is in conflict with a decision in another. For example, the decision of the previously described adolescent to tell her parents about obtaining oral contraception may be in conflict with her decision to do everything possible to bolster their confidence in her so that they will support her living away from home while she attends college. Motives or goals from different behavior domains may also be in conflict. At any one point, there is likely to be a mixture of sexual, contraceptive, abortion, and procreational motives available to the ego. Because sexual, contraceptive, abortion, and procreational behaviors are potentially all separate from each other in time, it is likely that the mixture of motives generating these behaviors will vary in its

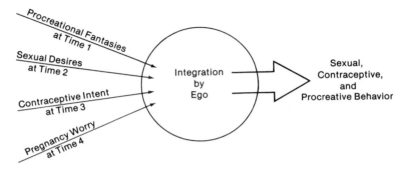

Figure 3.4. A schematic representation of the way the ego must integrate motivational influences from different behavior domains and express them over time through the appropriate behaviors.

relative proportions across time. This principle is depicted in Figure 3.4. In illustration we cite an unmarried young woman who takes her contraceptive pills each morning, has sexual intercourse with her boyfriend at night on the weekends, has fantasies about having a baby while visiting her married friends during occasional weekday evenings, and experiences release from the fear of an unwanted pregnancy each month with the onset of her menstrual period. Another example would be the married woman who talks with her husband during dinner about when they might have their next baby, routinely inserts her diaphragm several hours later while getting undressed for the night, and has sexual intercourse with her husband an hour later after they have gone to bed. Such separation over time of motives and behaviors which are clearly distinct, yet strongly interactive, further challenges the integrative capacity of the ego.

Throughout this complexity, the ego serves to integrate the ongoing stream of motivation and behavior into a goal-achieving, adaptive process. Generally this integration occurs across four dimensions: the integration of internally generated and externally generated (i.e., by the environment) motives and behaviors; the integration of motives and behaviors oriented to the achievement of pleasure, happiness, and success with those oriented to the avoidance of pain, unhappiness, and failure; the integration of short-term future- and long-term future-oriented motives and behaviors; and, the integration of current motives and behaviors with previous plans and past behaviors. Each of these dimensions has certain psychological traits or personality characteristics that tend to affect them in particular. Thus, internal-external integration is affected by the traits of dominance and submissiveness, activity and passivity, independence and dependence. The pleasure-pain integration is affected by traits of high and low self-esteem, high and low vigilance, and high and low need achievement. The short- or long-term future integration is affected by traits of high and low future orientation, high and low planning ability, and high and low orientation to change. Finally, the present-past integration is affected by traits of high and low stability and high and low impulsiveness.

One manifestation of ego integration is intention. In common usage the term "intention" refers to a person's goal or objective while behaving in a certain way or pursuing a certain course of action. However, there may be multiple intentions for any single act. In addition, the actor may be more or less aware of particular intentions, even to the point where some are totally excluded from consciousness. It was the latter observation that led to the concept of "subintention," first developed in association with the study of suicide where ambivalent intent and partially or fully suppressed intent appeared to play an important role in many self-inflicted deaths and some "accidental" deaths (28). The concept of subintention refers to the assumed mental state of people who do not fully intend an action but pursue it inconsistently, who make a decision about it by default, who expose themselves knowingly to an increased chance of its happening, or who through some element of their behavior indicate that the action serves their purposes. The degrees of intention involved in death-producing behavior may be illustrated as follows: full intention involves carefully and purposefully choosing to die; somewhat less than full intention involves impulsively or ambivalently choosing to die; smaller degrees of intention (subintention) involve knowingly exposing oneself to increased chances of death; no intention involves death coming about as a result of factors that could not be anticipated or controlled.

The various degrees of intention result from the integrative action of the ego upon the various motivational, attitudinal, and belief systems. The pattern of integration is unique to each individual and depends upon different psychological traits, including his or her typical defense and coping style. Further illustration of the principles involved in the different levels of intention and the integrative action of the ego within the domain of reproduction comes from research which reported on the intendedness of conceptions (29, 30). In this research, each one of a large number of conceptions was carefully evaluated through discussions with the woman and was rated with regard to the degree to which it was intended. The intendedness scale was based on the assumption that it should incorporate both the intention to achieve conception and the intention to prevent it. Thus, at the high end of the scale were those conceptions occurring as the result of a full, conscious decision to have a baby, followed by specific behaviors designed to achieve that end. At the low end of the scale were those conceptions occurring in spite of the full, conscious decision not to have a baby, followed by effective contraceptive use and other behaviors designed to prevent conception. Between the two ends of the scale were those conceptions occurring as the result of different degrees of less than full intention. These intermediate points were defined in terms of the presence or absence of conceptive intent and in terms of the presence and adequacy of proceptive and contraceptive behavior reported by each subject. Conceptions that occurred as a result of proception guided by weak or ambivalent desire were placed on the scale just below the fully intended conceptions. Next were those conceptions that occurred without any deliberate conceptive intent but where no contraception was utilized. Next were those occurring without conceptive intent but with inconsistent contraceptive use. Finally, just above the low end of the scale, were located those conceptions that occurred without conceptive intent but with regular contraceptive use except on a single occasion. In one investigation,

45 percent of 379 conceptions were rated as fully intended, 11 percent as unintended (occurring as a result of a contraceptive method failure) and the remaining percentage were intermediate. In another investigation of 319 first conceptions leading to the birth of the first child within marriage, 59 percent were fully intended, 8 percent were unintended, and the remaining percentage were intermediate in intendedness.

Stages of Decision Making

Up to this point we have described the psychological processes fundamental to decision making. We are now in a position to define the specific process involved in decision making itself. It is useful to describe this process as taking place in a series of stages, although it is important to keep in mind that these are not clearly demarcated in the majority of instances, and that the duration, importance, and even the presence of a particular stage will vary with the type of decision. We identify five stages in the decision-making process, including a preawareness stage, an awareness stage, a consideration stage, an implementation stage, and an adaptation stage. This scheme is slightly modified from previous work (31), and it is depicted in Figure 3.5. In the preawareness stage, the individual is either unaware of the opportunity for a choice (such as when someone does not know that it is possible to be surgically sterilized), or unaware of the relevance of a choice to him or her (such as when a woman does not yet know that she is pregnant and must make a decision regarding whether or not to remain pregnant and have a baby). Movement into the awareness stage occurs when the individual is informed of, or discovers, the possibility or personal relevance of choice. During this stage, an individual thinks about him or herself as wanting or having to face the choice point and making a decision sometime in the future, but does not work on the decision as though the choice was currently and actively being confronted. As soon as active consideration is given to taking action in the present situation, then the consideration stage has been initiated.

The consideration stage itself takes different forms, depending on the particular decision, and it tends to have its own sequence of

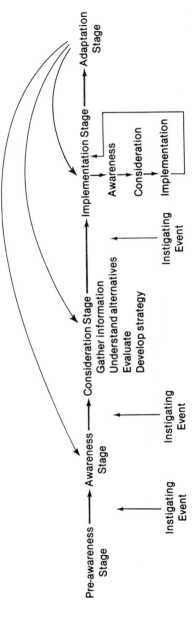

Figure 3.5. A schematic representation of the stages in the decision-making process, illustrating their relationships and components.

events, called the ''consideration process.'' The form consideration takes varies according to the degree to which it is intrapsychic or interpersonal. A decision maker may utilize one or the other of these forms of consideration primarily, or may proceed with both at once. Intrapsychic consideration consists of an intrapsychic dialog through which the decision maker explores subjective responses to the options. It involves a range of inner psychological phenomena varying from highly unstructured and only partially conscious fantasizing about a possible course of action and its consequences, to a rational and conscious deliberation about these matters. Fantasizing is an important part of the intrapsychic dialog because it allows the individual to tap feelings and latent wishes. On the other hand, rational thought is an important part of the dialog because it allows subjective states to be related to reality and to each other. Interpersonal consideration involves seeking out other people in order to discuss with them the choice point, the options, and the consequences. During this form of consideration, the decision maker gathers information, secures advice and opinions, clarifies his or her own thoughts and feelings, and reduces tension. Other important forms of the consideration process include the utilization of impersonal sources of information and opinion, such as books and the media, and the observation of other people who serve as potential models for the decision maker as they face and handle similar decisions. There are several common objectives of these different forms of the consideration process. These include the gathering of information, the development of an understanding of the possible courses of action and their consequences, the exploration of personal objectives and values, and the creation of a strategy for reaching goals. This last comprises the development of alternative actions and of contingency plans. To some extent these objectives are pursued in sequence. However, because of the sporadic nature of much consideration, they are just as often irregularly related to each other, occurring either out of sequence, simultaneously, or repeatedly.

Movement into the implementation stage begins with the actual pursuit of a course of action selected by the individual. Often this involves public behavior, but may not do so if the course of action does not occur in public or if what has been decided upon is the cessation of a segment of behavior. The implementation stage often confronts the decision maker with another decision. For example, if a woman decides to seek diagnosis for a lump in her breast, she must decide which medical resource to approach and when to do it. Here again is an illustration of the hierarchical and sequential organization of behavior. The subdecisions that may be confronted during and as a part of the implementation stage are indicated in Figure 3.5 by placing a subcycle of awareness, consideration, and implementation under the general stage of implementation.

Once the decision has been implemented, the stage of adaptation begins. In this stage, the individual adapts him or herself and adjusts the world in response to the changes affected by the decision. During this period, the decision is frequently reevaluated. This may result in efforts to undo or remake the decision. It is the feedback to the decision maker during this period of adaptation that is important in that person's learning about successful and unsuccessful decision making and further acquiring decision-making skills.

Movement from one of the decision-making stages to the next is often brought about by instigating factors. Commonly those are external events, but they may be internal, developmental processes. For example, an individual may not know about the possibility of prenatal diagnosis of genetic disorders through amniocentesis until reading about it in the newspaper. Another individual may not be aware of contraception until the developmental processes of adolescence have given a certain salience to sexuality and to the prevention of conception. Consideration of a tubal ligation or of geographic mobility may be precipitated by a pregnancy scare or by the loss of a job, respectively. Someone who has been considering going on a diet may be instigated into implementing that decision by an acute illness or by a health program seen on television. The important feature of instigating factors is that they serve to cue or release decision-making behavior at a time when the individual has already developed a strong tendency to act.

The Decision-Making Context

Our model would be incomplete if no discussion was directed to the situational aspects of decision making, namely, the context in which the decision is made. There are four especially important aspects of the decision-making context:

    (a) the dyadic or family context;

    (b) the community context;

    (c) the developmental-life cycle context;

    (d) and the random life event context.

The first two of these are indicated in Figure 3.1 by locating the individual decision maker first within the context of a couple or a family and next within the context of a community. The last two are extended in time and cannot readily be represented in Figure 3.1 which presents our decision-making model as though cross-sectioned in time.

Regarding the dyadic or family context, it is important to distinguish between two categories of decisions, or what, in reality, are the two ends of a decision-making spectrum. At one end lie decisions that are made by an individual about him or herself which may or may not take place in the context of a two-person relationship such as a marriage. At the other end lie dyadic decisions made by two people together about matters of common interest. For example, the decision to seek medical care for a painful symptom is commonly an individual one, whereas the decision to have a baby is commonly a dyadic one. In relationships that are not highly segmented or role segregated, most nontrivial decisions tend to have a large dyadic component. It is possible for a woman to make an individual decision to have a baby or for a man to make an individual decision to move geographically, but when this occurs in the context of a marriage it is likely that either the relationship is highly segmented or that one member of the couple is unusually dominant, at least in some areas of common interest. There is, of course, considerable couple variation on the degree to which nontrivial decisions are shared and there are some areas of common interest where it is very usual for one or the other member of a couple to assume dominance. For example, it is more usual for a woman to make an individual decision about contraceptive method selection, and for the man to make an individual decision about occupational change.

Dyadic decision making involves decision makers in a new level of complexity. First, there are two separate sets of motives, attitudes, and beliefs that must be combined. Then there is the superimposition of the processes of dyadic integration and decision making upon those processes taking place within each of the individual egos. Because of this complexity, there is some tendency for dyadic decision making to evolve toward the simplicity and efficiency of individual decision making. The increased efficiency of individual decision making is undoubtedly one of the reasons why each member of a married couple progressively assumes decision-making dominance for specific areas of life during the course of a marriage.

The community context of decision making can be usefully discussed with respect to four aspects of the community: its *opportunity structure,* its *normative structure,* its *rights structure,* and its *incentive structure.* These four specific structures, which are aspects of the overall social structure of the community, are composed of the patterns of social opportunity, of acceptable and expected behavior, of legal rights and obligations, and of incentives and disincentives existing in a community and its institutions. The first three tend to have an important influence on whether or not a decision can even be made. A person cannot decide to have an abortion unless there is an opportunity to obtain one in the community. Individuals are relatively limited in making childbearing decisions if the community norm is to have at least five children, or, as a more contemporary example, to have two and only two children. Someone cannot decide to move into a community, or a certain part of the community, if that person does not have the right to do so. Incentive structure may also influence whether or not a decision can be made. For example, the cost of pursuing a higher education may prohibit its serious consideration. However, in most cases, the pattern of incentives in a community interacts with the motivational, attitudinal, and belief systems of individuals to influence the direction each person's decision takes and to shape the statistical aggregate of all their decisions. For instance, the price structure of medical care in a community has a different impact upon individuals' decisions so that each seeks diagnosis and treatment at a different threshold of distress. A more complete examination of the interaction between individual decision making and community institutions will be developed in Chapter 5.

The life-cycle context of decision making consists of the stage of development within which the individual is located at the time of the decision. The concept of the life cycle has been applied to psychological development in infancy, childhood, and adolescence by Erikson (32) and more recently has been applied to the midlife period (33). It has also been used extensively for analyzing the family and family change (34). The basic notion of the life cycle is that individuals and families pass through a series of progressive stages, with the events that occur in one stage dependent at least in part on those that have occurred in a previous stage. Since the concept of a cycle suggests that there is a return to a starting point, it is more accurate to use the concept of "life course."

During the life cycle or life course of an individual there are various domains of behavior that appear to have their own developmental and progressive character. Such progression within any one of these domains is frequently referred to as a "career." Thus, an individual may be said to have a family career or an occupational career or an educational career. Stages within such careers tend to be demarcated by the appearance of certain psychological and behavioral characteristics and by the assumption of certain social roles. For example, the family career has been demarcated according to the occurrence of marriage, the birth of the first child, the birth of the last child, the departure of children from the home, the retirement of the parents from occupational activity, and the death of one of the parents. Each one of these family career stages has important implications for decision making, primarily through its associated psychology and social roles.

In order to illustrate how decision making varies during the individual and family life course, let us consider some of the factors influencing contraceptive decision making during the sexual, contraceptive, and reproductive careers of women. First, the selection of a contraceptive method will depend upon the location of the woman in her sexual career. During adolescence and before marriage, or in the post marital period as well, sexual patterns are variable and tend to be inconsistent. A woman is likely to have a number of sexual partners, each with a contraceptive preference or style, and she may well have long periods without sexual activity when the use of a contraceptive method such as the Pill would be inappropriate. Contraceptive method selection also depends upon the location of the woman in her reproductive career. Thus, a contraceptive method which is convenient but has a definite risk of failure may be more acceptable in the early period of marriage than it would be pre-maritally or when childbearing has been completed. The location of the woman in her stages of biological development also has a definite effect on her choice of a contraceptive method. For example, it is more difficult to insert an IUD prior to the birth of the first child. Similarly, oral contraception carries with its use an increase in the risk of undesirable medical side effects beginning midway in the fourth decade of life. Finally, psychological stages and development also affect contraceptive choice. The importance of spontaneity and general impulsivity in adolescent sexuality may dispose a young woman against selecting a coitus-dependent method of contraception such as the diaphragm—one that she may be perfectly happy with later in life.

The final important context of decision making is that of the random life event. The contexts discussed so far are a part of the social structure or they occur on a developmental, and therefore predictable, basis. There are, however, important changes introduced into individuals' lives through unpredictable events that have substantial effects on their decisions. In this category we include the effects of such events as the death of a spouse, an economic recession, an accident, and an inheritance. Major events like these tend to introduce severe perturbations in the ongoing stream of life. This affects decision making in at least three ways: it stresses the decision maker while he or she is making other decisions; it stimulates a reevaluation of personal goals, which may lead to a remaking of old decisions; and it confronts the decision maker with new decisions to be made.

EFFECTIVE DECISIONS

Effective decisions are those that achieve the desired results for the decision maker. There are two main factors which prevent effective decisions: ineffective decision making and decision outcome failures. The former occurs when there is a disruption or an inadequacy in the decision-making process. The latter occur when decisions are made effectively but still produce results contrary to the desires or best interests of the decision maker. In the former the emphasis is on decision-making ability and in the latter upon the outcomes that follow decisions. Ineffective decision making leads to decision outcome failures, but other factors contribute as well.

There are five major factors operating within individuals to produce ineffective decision making. These include *developmental factors, learning factors, conflict factors, stress factors,* and *risk taking.* Before certain kinds of decision making are possible, biological and psychological development must have proceeded to a point that allows the individual to understand adequately the choice situation and grasp the implications of the various options. The effect of development on decision making is most apparent in adolescence when individuals are called upon to make many major decisions with lifelong implications. Most adults find these same decisions difficult; yet adolescents also have to contend with them even though their decision-making capabilities are more limited than those of adults because of adolescents' greater concrete thinking, comparatively short-term future orientation, and greater emotional instability. Developmental factors affecting decision making are by no means limited to adolescents. Important biological developments continue throughout life; especially important are those associated with menopause and aging in general. Social-role developments and refinements also carry with them important psychological changes that tend to occur developmentally and that are important for decision making.

Learning is an important factor in ineffective decision making, both with respect to the content and process. It is through learning that people acquire both the information essential for adequate decision making and the necessary repertoire of decision-making skills. For example, in order to make decisions effectively with respect to having a child, it is necessary to have both the knowledge of what it is like to have a baby and the ability to work out within oneself and with one's spouse a gratifying and appropriate choice.

Conflict within an individual, manifested by strongly opposed or contradictory feelings, desires, or goals, also contributes to ineffective decision making. There are several important forms of such conflict. First, there is neurotic conflict developing out of the opposition of conscious desires and unconscious, symbolic meanings: a woman may feel conflicted about having a baby because of the unconscious meaning to her of having a helpless child dependent upon her. Second, there is the type of conflict that derives from the occupation of two different, contradictory roles: a woman may feel conflicted about having a baby because of the role conflict of being a mother and pursuing an occupation outside the home. Third, there is the conflict resulting from the opposition of what an individual wants and how he or she has been socialized and is expected to act: a woman may also feel conflicted about having a baby because it is expected of her in her community, even though she would prefer to devote herself to, say, painting.

Stress is another factor which creates ineffective decision making. It may result from crises at either the biological, psychological, or social-system level. Whatever its origin, stress tends to produce anxiety in an individual that, in turn, creates a general disruption of all aspects of decision making. Once the individual's level of coping has been exceeded, effectiveness in decision making may decrease rapidly.

There are several forms of risk taking relevant to decision making. First, there is the risk taking that occurs when an individual deals ineffectively with a risky situation. An example is someone who uses denial while exposing him or herself to the risks associated with frequent cigarette smoking or unprotected sexual intercourse. This type of risk taking commonly results from the utilization of certain defense or coping mechanisms. Second, there is the risk taking occurring when someone such as a sky-diver or mountain climber actually pursues a risky situation for the excitement, challenge, or inherent satisfaction that it brings. When this type of "risk-seeking" motivation dominates an individual's judgment, it interferes with effective decision making. Finally, there is the risk taking that occurs to everyone at some time when they take a "calculated risk." When decisions are made under conditions of risk or uncertainty, the decision maker can only choose to maximize the chances of reaching his or her goals. A certain percentage of the time the choice must lead to an undesired outcome. For example, many individuals select the contraceptive method that they utilize with a full awareness of the risks of pregnancy and the uncertainty of incurring a medical side effect. They are aware of the chances of their experiencing an undesired outcome but still select the method because it is the most desirable one, all possible outcomes having been taken into consideration. In this type of risk taking, the process of decision making is usually very effective. For this reason, it is primarily associated with a decision outcome failure.

All four aspects of the decision-making context previously discussed play a role in the production of ineffective decision making and decision failures. We will first consider the dyadic, family, and community contexts grouped together. These contexts can contribute to ineffective decision making by causing or promoting most of the factors we have just discussed. They do this, for example, by confronting decision makers with the need to make certain decisions before they are developmentally prepared. A good illustration involves adolescents who, because of the patterns of sexual behavior in their community, must make a decision about sexual intercourse before its personal implications and meaning have been fully worked out. Contexts can also contribute to ineffective decision

making by failing to provide an adequate learning environment for
the acquisition of decision-making skills. Many adolescents arrive
at adulthood in the United States without having mastered, or even
practiced, decision-making skills with respect to marriage or childbearing. Contexts can also create or maintain various types of conflict. Because of the normative structure of a community, a woman
may become conflicted while considering an abortion, even though
she would have pursued that option without hesitation before moving into that community. A particularly important type of conflict
generated by contexts has to do with coercion during decision making. One of the most frequently cited reasons for unhappiness following an abortion decision is the presence of coercion by the
woman's parents or spouse during decision making. Contexts can
also produce stress in the decision maker. Thus, families with high
levels of interpersonal conflict and tension are usually difficult contexts within which to make important life decisions. Finally, the
decision-making context of the dyad, family, and community
can promote ineffective decision making by failing to provide interpersonal and social support systems for help during developmental
crises, learning failures, conflicts, or stress.

The dyadic, family, and community contexts can also produce
decision outcome failures in ways independent from their impact on
effective decision making. They can do this by providing misinformation or limited information to the decision maker. In many communities, the amount of information women have about menopause
and fecundity is limited. As a result of frequently erroneous media
sources, they may also have considerable misinformation about the
risks of oral contraception. It is worth emphasizing that with such
misinformation an entirely adequate decision-making process may
result in a decision outcome failure. Contexts can also produce
decision outcome failures if there is rapid change or disorganization
in the social environment. For example, effective decision making
about job training can result in the acquisition of skills that prove to
be useless in a changing community. Finally, decision-making contexts may produce decision outcome failures by limiting the options
of decision makers. Until recently in many communities it was next

to impossible for a woman to obtain elective sterilization for contraceptive purposes, unless she had borne a certain number of children and was a certain age. The inevitable result was that many women who had decided to terminate their fertility but could not choose the most effective method of accomplishing this, subsequently became pregnant. A more contemporary example is the failure of many communities to provide adequate child-care facilities, thereby forcing many women who had decided to work into unsatisfactory child-care plans. In both of these examples, the restricted opportunity structure of a community promotes the undesirable outcomes that follow a decision.

Ineffective decision making and decision outcome failures occur in characteristic ways at characteristic times throughout the life course. The times when they occur often appear to be those at which two or more of the individual factors we have described are working simultaneously. A particular example of a life course patterning of ineffective decision making and outcome failures in the area of reproduction is the series of eight stages during the sexual careers of women in the United States when they are vulnerable to unwanted pregnancy (35, 36). The first stage occurs during early adolescence when, because of subfecundity, a young woman has not developed the contraceptive vigilance that would aid her in avoiding an undue risk of pregnancy. The second stage occurs at the beginning of a woman's sexual career, whenever that may be in terms of age. It has two parts. The first occurs at the time of the first few instances of sexual intercourse, for which there is typically no contraceptive preparation, and often very little anticipation. The second part occurs during the several months to a year following initial intercourse, during which time a young woman is characteristically coming to grips with the fact that she is sexually active and must learn to recognize her sexual anxiety, her pregnancy anxiety, and her contraceptive anxiety so that she may cope meaningfully with each. The third stage occurs in relation to a stable, nonmarital sexual partner. There are three particularly difficult parts within this stage. The first occurs during formation of the relationship, when stable patterns of communication and of sexual and contraceptive behavior are being established. The second occurs during conflict or separation, at which time patterns of communication and cooperation may be disrupted. At this time there may also be an acute sense of personal loss, with the intensification of desire for physical closeness and, in some cases, the development of a wish for a child to serve as a replacement. The third phase occurs after termination of a relationship with a particular partner when a woman is situationally reexposed to him after a hiatus. This may be a time when sexual activity is desirable and natural, but the woman may not be contraceptively prepared in the same way that she was when the relationship was well established.

The fourth vulnerable stage occurs following geographic mobility, at which time there are commonly major changes in a woman's social field altering the sexual and contraceptive norms and opportunities she confronts. Most commonly, this type of change occurs after a woman moves away from the nuclear family of orientation or to a new sociocultural area. The fifth vulnerable stage occurs in relation to marriage. Because of the stress and conflict associated with the transition to marriage and because of the natural decrease in contraceptive vigilance occurring when the negative consequences of unplanned pregnancy decrease, the period just before and just after marriage is a vulnerable one. In addition, the same problems that occur during conflict or threatened separation and after separation in relation to a nonmarital sexual partner occur as well with a marital partner. The sixth vulnerable stage occurs following pregnancy. There are two parts within this stage: the first during the postpartum period, when there is a natural subfecundity, when previous patterns of sexuality are altered and commonly decreased, and when an interim, unfamiliar contraceptive method is often employed. These changes can increase the degree of contraceptive risk taking which is tolerated. The second occurs when the new demands brought about by the presence of a young baby make the level of contraceptive vigilance and the amount of contraceptive risk taking which was in effect prior to the pregnancy no longer appropriate.

The seventh vulnerable stage occurs in relation to the end of childbearing when a woman considers not having any more children and often contends—in some cases very ambivalently—with all the options alternative to domestic work and child rearing. At this time the conflicted desire to have another child may interfere with effective contraceptive use. The eighth and final vulnerable stage occurs just before and during menopause, when a woman's fecundity is decreasing significantly and, as a result, her contraceptive vigilance may relax.

In this discussion of contexts, we consider finally and briefly the effects of random life events on the effectiveness of decision making. It has been shown that major life events have typically stressful effects at all ages (37, 38). By creating stress or conflict or by exposing individuals to conditions for which they have not been prepared, such events may promote ineffective decision making. Further, by fundamentally changing the conditions of an individual's life, they may promote decision outcome failures secondary to decisions that were previously well considered.

ADAPTATION

We turn now to a brief discussion of adaptation. As we indicated at the beginning of the chapter, there is a significant range of overlap between what we are calling decision-making behavior and what we are calling adaptive behavior. In addition, adaptive behavior is organized hierarchically and sequentially in the same way the decision-making behavior is. For these reasons, much of what we have said up to this point regarding decision making applies well in the analysis of adaptive behavior. In this analysis, it is useful to consider five aspects of adaptation: the broad goals of adaptation, the specific goals, the process by which adaptation is accomplished, the context of adaptation, and maladaptation or adaptive failure. For the sake of brevity, we will deal almost exclusively with the first and third of these aspects.

The broad goals of adaptation may be described in many ways, depending on the purposes and point of view of the author. We select five broad goals of adaptation which are generally inclusive and because they concern different systems on different levels of organization, in keeping with a general systems approach to analysis. These five goals are:

 (a) internal regulation;
 (b) defense against distress;
 (c) securing of gratification;
 (d) maintenance of self-image and self-esteem;
 (e) and regulation of interpersonal relationships.

The first of these is constituted by the adaptive regulation of the physical body by the central nervous system, especially the higher brain centers. The human body is composed of a complex, interlocking set of self-regulatory physiological systems that act to maintain a constant internal milieu. A significant portion of this regulation occurs as a result of voluntary behavior governed by the ego. Examples of this behavior include how people act to avoid pain, to satisfy appetites, to maintain temperature within a comfortable range, and to avoid or to seek stimulation. The second, third, and fourth of these broad goals—defense against distress, the securing of gratification, and the maintenance of a self-image and self-esteem—all represent the ego's adaptive regulation of its own positive and negative experience. The first two of this triad involve primarily the affective and emotional components of behavior, while the maintenance of self-image and self-esteem involves more the cognitive and holistic aspects of behavior and is pursued through the integrative efforts of the ego. The regulation of interpersonal relationships, the fifth and final goal, is constituted by the adaptive regulation of contact with members of one's social network by the ego. From infancy to death the individual is a member of social groups that regulate the behavior of their members. Through the regulation of interpersonal contact, the ego is able to maintain an external, social milieu and to influence the degree and type of its regulation by that milieu.

We shall discuss the specific goals of adaptation to population-related phenomena or stimuli in considerable detail in the next chapter. Now, we turn briefly to a consideration of the process by which adaptation is accomplished. A variety of models for conceptualizing adaptive behavior have been developed by behavioral scientists (39). A contemporary and particularly well-developed one is the model of Lazarus (40). He formulates the process of adaptation and coping in the following way. An individual is said to be presented with a situation that confronts him or her with the possibility of harm when he or she anticipates that some motives will be thwarted. The individual responds to this situation first with an appraisal of the threat, then with an affective response such as anxiety which serves as a signal of danger, and finally with a secondary appraisal. The latter is a cognitive process that evaluates the various available strategies for dealing with the threat and that precedes any actual coping response. The coping reactions themselves fall into various patterns, such as avoidance of the situation, strengthening of the individual's protective resources, attacking, and defensive reappraisal of the threat. In the general model, there are two classes of determinants of coping behavior (41). These include the different personality characteristics of the individual and the situational factors. There are three sources of the individual's interpretation of the situational factors: biological sources built into the human organism through evolution; cultural sources learned by the human organism during socialization; and individual sources acquired by the individual during idiosyncratic personal experience.

The model developed by Lazarus has a generally negative emphasis as indicated by the terms "threat," "coping," and "defense." However, it is perfectly possible to extend this model to include opportunity for gratification as well as threat, positive adaptation as well as coping, and mastery as well as defense. Another description of the process of coping and adaptation which has a more positive basis is one based upon a summary condensation of a number of distinct behavioral science models of coping and adaptation (42). It suggests a sequence of behaviors common to the process of adaptation in most situations. This common process involves the steps of appraisal, information seeking and utilization, contingency planning, rehearsal and trial action, and utilization of feedback. The steps in the process are shaped from within the individual by motivation (including hope), and from without by social forces. A comparison of this process with the stages in the process of decision making discussed earlier in this chapter makes their similarity immediately apparent.

The influences of the context on adaptation may be analyzed in much the same way as we have analyzed them for the context of decision making. There are dyadic, family, and community influences to which individuals must adapt and to which individuals shape their pattern of adaptation. In addition, the content and process of adaptation varies during the life course and is significantly influenced by major life events. Finally, the topic maladaptation and adaptive failure is similar in many respects to ineffective decision making and decision outcome failures. Maladaptation and adaptive failure have their sources both within the individual and within the adaptive context and, as with ineffective decision making and decision outcome failures, many of these sources are susceptible to social action programs of prevention and intervention.

SUMMARY

In this and the next chapter we discuss individual decision making and adaptation as they relate to the various domains of behavior relevant to population. This chapter focuses on the psychological *processes* commonly involved in decision making and adaptation. We begin with some initial definitions and illustrations, including a more extended discussion of five fundamental aspects of decision making. These five aspects include: its taking place over some variable time duration; its involving various degrees of probability; its taking place under variable types and amounts of rationality; its being entered into more or less actively or passively; and its taking place to a greater or lesser extent within some dyadic or interpersonal context.

We next examine some of the models of decision making proposed by behavioral scientists. Some of these models offer relatively little regarding the processes of decision making. We then introduce our own comprehensive decision-making model, attempting to incorporate the five aspects of decision making already discussed and to build on the strengths and avoid the weaknesses of the other behavioral science models. There are five important components in this comprehensive model: the motivational, attitudinal, and belief systems (M-A-B systems) of the individual decision maker; the organization of the decision maker's goal-directed behaviors in a hierarchical and sequential way; the integration of M-A-B systems and behavior by the decision maker's ego across levels of organization and across time; the progression of the decision maker through stages of pre-awareness, awareness, consideration, implementation, and adaptation while making a decision; and the influence on the decision maker of a variety of contextual or situational factors, such as those occurring within the family and community or at different points during the life course. Having elaborated our comprehensive model, we relate it to one of the basic themes of the book—the problems of making effective decisions. These problems are based upon two overlapping considerations: ineffective decision making, which occurs when there is a disruption or inadequacy in the decision making process; and decision outcome failures, which occur when decisions produce results contrary to the desires or best interests of the decision maker, either as a result of ineffective decision making or because of influences external to the decision maker. We then discuss five major factors that operate to produce ineffective decision making: developmental limitations, learning deficits, conflict, stress, and risk taking. Next we discuss the different ways that the decision-making context can interfere with effective decision making or produce decision outcome failures even in the face of effective decision making. The chapter concludes with a brief section on adaptation which again focuses on processes. It emphasizes the many similarities in these processes between decision making and adaptation and discusses the parallel, on the one hand, between ineffective decision making and maladaptation, and on the other hand, between decision outcome failures and adaptive failures.

PSYCHO-DEMOGRAPHY AND DEMOPSYCHOLOGY[*]

4

In the previous chapter we discussed the psychology of decision making and adaptation with emphasis on the different forms that such behavior takes. In other words, we focused on the process of decision making and adaptation and on how individuals make decisions and adapt to various conditions. In this chapter, we turn to the content or substance of decision making and adaptation that is relevant to the issues of population. In other words, we now focus our interest upon what population-related decisions and adaptations are made and what specific motivations, attitudes, and beliefs direct or influence them. Although we recognize that, in reality, form is not separate from substance, or content from process, it is useful to make such a distinction for analytic purposes. In addition, the distinction has practical implications because it is possible to formulate policies and design intervention programs that deal separately,

* Adapted from Chapter 44, "Psychological and Psychiatric Aspects of Population Problems," by Warren B. Miller, M.D. in the *American Handbook of Psychiatry,*†
volume VI, edited by David A. Hamburg and H. Keith H. Brodie, © 1975 by Basic Books, Inc., Publishers, New York.
† Second edition, Silvano Arieti, Editor-in-Chief.

for example, with the skills an individual brings to the decision-making process and the desires or goals an individual has in making a specific decision.

We are guided in our discussion of the substantive aspects of decision making and adaptation by the systems model introduced in Chapter 1. In order to capture conceptually the linkage between the individual psychological level and the aggregate demographic level embodied in that model, we introduce here the terms "psychodemography" and "demopsychology." The former means the study of the effect of individual decision making and other psychological processes upon aggregate population factors. The latter is the study of the effect of aggregate population characteristics upon individual behavior. By organizing our discussion of the substantive aspects of decision making and adaptation according to these two concepts, we hope not only to achieve a further explication of our model but also to promote both an understanding of aggregate-level problems in individual human terms and an appreciation of the importance of aggregate level phenomena for the full understanding of individual behavior.

In Chapter 1 we distinguished between two demographic factors useful for analyzing a discrete population. These were the structural and dynamic factors. Included in the former were *size, geographic distribution,* and *status distribution or composition.* Included in the latter were *fertility, mortality, geographic mobility,* and *status mobility.* It was suggested that these seven factors interact with each other and with additional factors at the institutional and individual levels and that taken together all of them constitute a population regulation system. In this chapter we carry this analysis further by discussing the psychodemographic and demopsychological material in three main sections, each representing a subsystem of structural and dynamic demographic factors. The subsystems represent two or three of the demographic factors which appear to be especially interactive with each other. The three subsystems include the triad of fertility, mortality, and size, the dyad of geographic distribution and geographic mobility, and the dyad of status distribution and status mobility. We emphasize that these subsystems are by no means independent. In fact, for some populations a different sub-system organization of component factors is more appropriate. For example, at the present time in the United States, it is the balance between the birthrates and deathrates that largely determines the net growth rate and thus the population size. However, in populations in other countries or in subpopulations within this country, geographic mobility in the form of in- or out-migration may play a major role in determining net growth rate and population size. This is especially likely in economically expanding or depressed areas, or in areas ravaged by war or natural disaster. Thus, the groupings of demographic structural and dynamic factors followed in this discussion should be seen as heuristic arrangements, important primarily because of the dynamic framework they provide for the discussion of psychodemography and demopsychology.

At the psychological level a different but complementary framework will be utilized in organizing the discussion. Individual behavior may be described according to certain broad domains corresponding roughly to the basic biological functions necessary for adaptation and survival. To some extent behavior within each of these domains is determined by the biological substrate that the human species has evolved and that each individual has uniquely inherited from his or her parents. To a large extent, however, behavior within each of these domains is determined by culture-specific patterns of learned behavior. The behavioral domains to which we refer include the following:

  (a) union and reproduction;
  (b) self-care and self-preservation;
  (c) maintenance of shelter, home, and community;
  (d) subsistence, production, and occupation;
  (e) and development, socialization, and education.

It will be immediately apparent that each of these domains corresponds in a general way to one or more of the demographic factors; the first to the dynamic factor of fertility, the second to mortality, the third to graphic distribution and mobility, and the fourth and fifth to population composition and status mobility.

Each of the three sections that follow in this chapter will consider

one of the three demographic factor subsystems and their components. In each section we will discuss the component demographic
factors in order. For each factor, we will first discuss some basic
demographic concepts. Next, we will discuss decision making and
adaptation within the corresponding behavior domains. Finally, we
will discuss current social issues of relevance to both the demographic and psychological levels of analysis. Many of these issues
will be of importance to the policy considerations which will be
treated in Chapter 7.

FERTILITY, MORTALITY, AND SIZE

The fertility-mortality-size triad forms an important population subsystem. In the United States the balance between annual birthrates
and deathrates plays the major role in the determination of population size. In part, this is because the immigration rate has been
highly regulated in recent decades. As a result, the net annual immigration rate has remained at or below 2 per 1,000 midyear population. Since the mortality rate has also held relatively constant at
about 10 per 1,000, the net annual growth rate in this country has
fluctuated between 0.8 and 1.8 percent almost as a direct function
of the fluctuations in birthrates.

Fertility:

Basic Concepts. Because of differences between demographers
and biologists in the use of terms, there is some general confusion
about the meaning of the concepts of fertility and fecundity. For the
demographer, fecundity is the biological capacity to have children,
and fertility is the number of children actually borne by an individual or a population. The biologist, on the other hand, commonly
uses these concepts in a directly opposite way. In this chapter and
in this book in general, we follow the demographic usage. We refer
to the decreased biological capacity to have children as subfecundity and to the biological inability to have children—the extreme
form of subfecundity—as sterility.

With respect to fertility, there are several important demographic concepts. One of these is the crude birthrate. This expression refers to the ratio of total births to the total population during a specific period of time, usually one year. Conventionally, it is stated in terms of births per 1000 members of the population, the latter being estimated at the midyear point. Thus, the crude birthrate for the United States in 1973 was 14.9/1000 midyear population (1). Because the denominator of the crude birthrate includes all ages and both sexes in the population, it may not reflect in an accurate way a population's reproductive activity during a one-year time interval. For this reason, more refined concepts have been developed. One of these is the general fertility rate, or the number of births each year per 1000 women in the fecund ages, generally assumed to be between 15 and 45. A further refinement of this concept leads to the age-specific fertility rate, calculated as the number of births per year to 1000 women of a specific age. In other words, it is the general fertility rate applied to a particular age group of women. Because different populations have different age compositions, a further refinement of this set of concepts leads to the total fertility rate. This is an estimate of the total number of children 1000 women would bear if they bore children during their reproductive years according to each of the age-specific fertility rates applying during a particular year. A final refinement of this set of concepts may be calculated by including only married women in the denominator. With this step it is possible to generate nuptial general fertility rates, nuptial age-specific fertility rates, and nuptial total fertility rates. Depending on the amount of out-of-wedlock childbearing in a population, this set of rates may give significant new information.

In general, marriage has an important bearing on fertility rates, and for this reason, demographic analysis commonly includes the calculation of rates of marriage. Included in these calculations are the crude marriage rate which is the number of marriages per year per 1000 persons in the population, and the general marriage rate which is the number of marriages per 1000 unmarried persons in the age range from 15 to 49—the primary nubile ages. Finally, there is the nuptiality rate, which is the number of marriages per year per 1000 persons of a specific age who are eligible to marry during that year.

Demographic analysis focuses not only upon rates but also on social norms. Reproductive norms are of special interest, in particular those concerning family formation, family size, and birth intervals. Measurement of these norms involves two general approaches. They may be measured by determining the actual timing of births with respect to marriage and previous births, and by determining actual family size. They may also be measured by asking people about their ideals, their desires, and their expectations with respect to the timing of births, the interval between births, and the size of their family. In connection with fertility, there is also an interest in marital norms, which again may be measured by actual behavior and by reported desires and expectations.

Union and Reproduction: Factors in Decision Making.   As an aid in the description of the substantive psychological factors operating in individual decision making and adaptation, figures have been drawn indicating the general relationship that exists among factors. Figure 4.1 illustrates the most important substantive factors that affect the individual decision maker at the point where he or she decides to marry. These factors are called proximate factors because they are dependent upon various additional factors, most of which are not included in the figure. For example, an individual's perception of the social structural factors affecting marriage depends on the community within which that individual is situated and its actual social structure. Similarly, the individual's perception of the potential mate depends upon the actual characteristics of the potential mate, as well as upon the history of their relationship. In addition, all of the proximate factors are influenced by the individual's motivations to marry, attitudes toward marriage, and beliefs about marriage, and by other motivational, attitudinal, and belief systems operating in different domains such as heterosexual relationships, gender-role orientation, procreation, education, and occupation. Some of the more important psychological dispositions affecting the marriage decision include the desire for com-

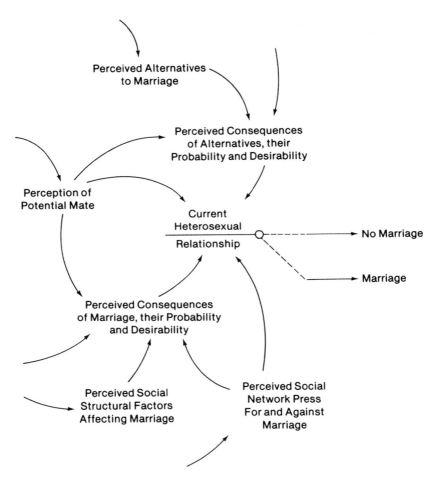

Figure 4.1. A schematic representation of the proximate substantive factors affecting a marriage decision, as perceived in the context of a particular heterosexual relationship. Arrows indicate the influence of factors upon the decision maker and each other or the influence of various unspecified motivations, attitudes, and beliefs upon the proximate factors.

panionship and intimacy, sexual drive, procreational desire, feelings of autonomy, and gender beliefs and identity. The reader is reminded that Figure 4.1 indicates very little about the decision-making process, a topic dealt with at length in Chapter 3, but rather deals primarily with the proximate substantive factors that shape the direction of the ultimate decision.

Discussion of each of the substantive factors depicted in Figure 4.1 will clarify their importance for the decision to marry. The perception of a potential mate refers to the qualities of that person in the eyes of the decision maker, especially the qualities that affect whether the potential mate is judged to be a good or bad companion, parent, provider, and sexual partner. Some of these qualities might be interpersonal sensitivity, nurturance, flexibility, assertiveness, and dominance. The perception of these qualities, and to some extent even their existence, will be influenced by the history of the relationship between the potential mate and the decision maker. In this regard, it is important to note that Figure 4.1 illustrates the factors at work at a single decision point and does not deal fully with the fact that there has been a heterosexual relationship which has progressed over a period of time and which is itself a process involving a sequence of decisions. This process has been called premarital dyad formation (2) and described as consisting of series of stages during which the couple moves from the perception of similarities in each other through the establishment of rapport, self-disclosure, and empathy to the achievement of interpersonal role fit and dyad crystallization. It is commonly at the end of this process that marriage becomes a significant option.

The perceived alternatives to marriage become important considerations at the point of decision making. One alternative might be to continue the relationship at its present level without increasing degrees of intimacy and mutual responsibility. Another alternative might be for the couple to live together, thereby further intensifying the relationship but without making the full commitment involved in a legal marriage. Of course, a third alternative might be to dissolve or deintensify the relationship. Whether marriage or one of the other alternatives is selected depends upon the decision maker's perception of the consequences of each course of action, the probability of their coming about, and their perceived positive or negative value. For example, marriage might be perceived as leading with certainty to highly desired levels of personal and sexual intimacy but with high probability to moderately undesirable levels of responsibility and loss of personal freedom. On the other hand, cohabitation might be perceived as very likely to achieve almost the same degree of desired intimacy, less likely to infringe upon freedom, but somewhat likely to lead to an undesirable premarital pregnancy.

A variety of social structural factors may be perceived as affecting marriage. Some of the more commonly mentioned include tax and welfare provisions that reduce the cost of marriage, laws restricting the choice of a spouse or affecting the availability of a divorce, social institutions that provide work roles compatible with marriage or social support for unmarried individuals, and customs and norms that affect personal or sexual availability of partners inside or outside of marriage (3). In addition, there are factors which affect how readily a marriage may be obtained, if and when the decision is made. These include laws which affect the ease of obtaining a marriage license and customs which affect the ease of communication between the decision maker and the potential parents-in-law. A distinct factor in the social field which affects marriage is the social network press for or against marriage. This factor is based upon the decision maker's perception of the important people in his or her life and the degree to which they promote or discourage marriage. For example, a decision maker's parents may encourage marriage in a variety of subtle and not so subtle ways because of their concern about the decision maker's increasing age and their own financial responsibility, or because of their desire for grandchildren.

The psychological factors involved in childbearing are more complex than those involved in the decision to marry because the birth of a child may come about either as the result of a direct decision to have a baby or as a result of a number of other decisions which only indirectly result in conception, and ultimately, the birth of a baby. Although many of the same motivational, attitudinal, and belief systems and many of the same individual behaviors are involved in the two different processes which may lead to child-bearing, they are sufficiently distinct that it is useful to illustrate and discuss them separately. The first of these processes was described in Chapter 3, in terms of stages of decision making. Figure 4.2 illustrates the psychological factors involved during this process, using a schema equivalent to the one used in the discussion of substantive factors and the marriage decision. The second of these processes was described in Chapter 3 in terms of the integrative activities of the ego. Figure 4.3 illustrates the substantive psychological factors relevant to that process.

Turning first to Figure 4.2, the decision is again represented as occurring at some point during the course of a heterosexual relationship. In the case of a childbearing decision, this usually involves a marital dyad. As we have described, the individual who makes the decision to marry has prior knowledge of what is being chosen, in this case the potential mate. In other decisions, such as occupational and geographic mobility decisions, as we shall discuss below, the same type of knowledge is possible. What is most unusual about the decision to have a baby is the decision maker's lack of knowledge of what he or she will be getting. Apart from the decision maker's own experiences with babies and children, the most meaningful knowledge about what the baby will be like derives from knowledge of the potential co-parent. This knowledge is based both upon the potential co-parent's genetic and biological contribution to the baby and on his or her potential influences on the new baby and child during the process of child rearing. For these reasons, the perception of the potential co-parent is an important factor in the decision to have a baby.

The perceived consequences of having a baby are numerous. For example, Hoffman has developed a scheme consisting of nine categories of reasons for which children are valued (4). Extending this work so that the categories fit better with cross-national empirical findings, Fawcett has identified five positive and five negative clusters of the value of children. These include emotional benefits, eco-

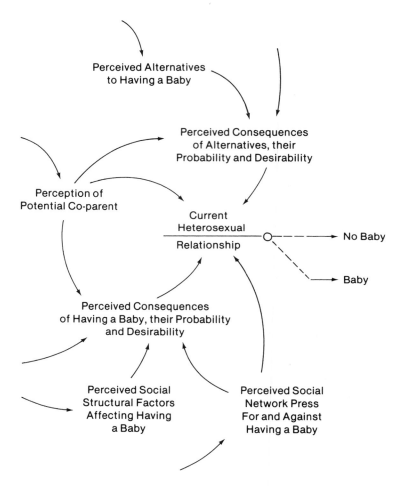

Figure 4.2. A schematic representation of the proximate substantive factors affecting a childbearing decision, as perceived in the context of a particular heterosexual relationship. Arrows indicate the influence of factors upon the decision maker and upon each other or the influence of various unspecified motivations, attitudes, and beliefs upon the proximate factors.

nomic benefits and security, self-enrichment and development, identification with children, family cohesiveness and continuity, emotional costs, economic costs, restrictions or opportunity costs, physical demands, and family costs (5). Within each of these categories are numerous subcategories which reflect a variety of specific perceived consequences of childbearing. Several other investigators (6, 7) have built into their theoretical model the fact that the perceived consequences of childbearing are modified in their influence on decision making by the perceived probability of the consequences taking place and by the desirability of the consequences in the mind of the decision maker.

The perceived alternatives to having a baby and their consequences may also affect the childbearing decision. A number of different alternatives are possible, depending upon the sex and the life-cycle stage of the decision maker. If the latter is a woman who has had no children, the chief alternative may be to remain at work. On the other hand, if she has had several children, the chief alternative may be to return to work. Although in both of these cases work is the alternative to childbearing, because of the different experiences with work and child rearing the woman has already undergone, her perceptions of the alternative will almost certainly be different. This observation has been imbedded in recent research that attempts to predict how women will make childbearing decisions (8). This research utilizes a model which assumes that employment is a competitive role activity to childbearing for women and that the most accurate prediction of childbearing decisions will be achieved by including the perceived rewards and costs of both childbearing and employment in the predictive formula.

As with the marriage decision, there are important perceived social structural factors that affect the childbearing decision, such as dependent tax deductions, free public schooling, the proximity of an extended family, normative and legal support for working women, job opportunities, and the availability of child care. There are also numerous sources of social network press for or against having a baby. For example, parents may want a grandchild, most other couples in the community may have young children, friends

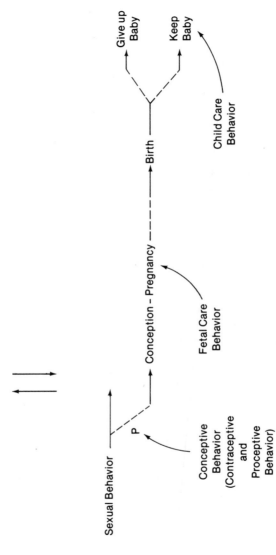

Figure 4.3. A schematic representation of the behaviors relevant to the occurrence of an unplanned conception, pregnancy, and birth and of the relationships between those behaviors.

from a consciousness-raising women's group may express antinatal sentiment, and children already present in the family may clamor for an additional brother or sister. All of these proximate factors entering into the decision to have a baby are affected by other considerations, including especially procreative motivations, attitudes, and beliefs as well as additional motivational, attitudinal, and belief systems from behavior domains relevant to childbearing. Some of the more important psychological dispositions on which these systems are based include the desire for generativity, feelings and attitudes about dependency, the desire for involvement and interaction, nurturant desires, and feelings of self-doubt and anxiety.

We turn now to a discussion of Figure 4.3 which illustrates the variety of behaviors bearing directly on the occurrence of an unplanned conception, pregnancy, and birth. The figure includes behavior from several different behavior domains. The way the ego integrates these behaviors, the decisions they involve, and the motivational, attitudinal, and belief systems that lie behind them determines whether or not a procreational outcome will take place, apart from a specific decision to have a baby. Both this figure and the previous Figure 4.2 are necessary to fully characterize the psychological factors antecedent to childbearing. Although the percentage of births that are fully planned will vary considerably in any population, depending on the age structure, the social-class structure, and other inherent factors, several recent investigations (9, 10) indicated that approximately one-half of the births occurring in a large contemporary population of women in the United States were fully planned. For such fully planned births, the procreational decision-making model depicted in Figure 4.2 is entirely appropriate. But for the large number of births that are unplanned, the model depicted in Figure 4.3 is necessary.

The central element in Figure 4.3 is sexual behavior. An individual may become involved in the latter as an end in itself, in order to achieve reproduction, or as behavior instrumental to other purposes. Examples of the instrumental use of sexual behavior vary from the more manipulative uses such as the seeking of power, dominance, or money, to more subtle and personal uses such as the communication of love, the achievement of closeness, or the reduction of tension. Whether the motive of sexual behavior be for sexual gratification, procreation, other instrumental purposes, or some combination of these, there is always associated with it a probability that a particular sexual act will result in conception and pregnancy. This probability is represented by the letter P in Figure 4.3. Behavior which is oriented toward affecting the probability of conception may be called conceptive behavior (11). There are two types of conceptive behavior: that which is oriented toward lowering the probabilities of conception and thus preventing its occurrence is called contraceptive behavior; that which is oriented toward increasing the probabilities of conception and thus achieving its occurrence is called proceptive behavior. Once conception and pregnancy have occurred, depending upon the influences exerted by various forms of fetal-care behavior, it may or may not progress to the birth of a child. One especially important type of fetal-care behavior is the seeking and securing of an abortion. Such behavior is at one end of a continuum of behavior that affects the probability of a conception progressing to the birth of a child. The other end of the continuum is characterized by behavior that results in good prenatal medical care. In between these two extremes lies a range of behaviors affecting the healthy growth and development of the fetus. After the birth of a baby, a variety of child-care behaviors occur. In many respects, they are a continuation of fetal-care behavior into the postnatal period, also varying along a continuum that affects the baby's health and development. One extreme of this continuum is characterized by infanticide, the other by health- and development-promoting child care. In the contemporary United States, when the parent is not motivated to provide the latter type of care, the child is usually given up to a member of the extended family or for adoption. None of the behaviors we have discussed as potentially important in the occurrence of unplanned births take place in social isolation. The behavior of others, especially that of the sexual and procreational partner, is frequently a strong influence.

All of the behaviors represented in Figure 4.3 are affected by procreational motivations, attitudes, and beliefs. For example, a woman who strongly desires a child but who is unable to have one because of some situational factor may be inclined by this desire to have sexual intercourse more frequently, to "forget" occasionally to use a contraceptive method while sexually active, or to reject an abortion should she become pregnant. Even more important is the fact that all of the behaviors represented in Figure 4.3 are affected by nonprocreational motivations, attitudes, and beliefs. The most important of these relate to sexuality, contraception, and abortion seeking. Space prevents us from describing in detail the substantive psychological factors influencing sexual, contraceptive, and abortion-seeking behavior. Other authors have described these at greater length (12, 13, 14, 15, 16). However, a brief review of these topics will be instructive. Some of the most important sexual dispositions are the desire for sexual pleasure, the wish to give pleasure to one's partner, the desire for intimacy and physical closeness, feelings of love, beliefs about the rightness or wrongness of sexual involvement, and feelings about one's own body and that of one's partner. The psychological dispositions affecting contraceptive behavior are oriented toward the particular contraceptive method used. For example, oral contraception is associated with the following: fear of harmful side effects, such as thrombophlebitis or cancer; feelings about physical side effects, such as changes in water retention, breast size, or menstrual distress; feelings about associated emotional changes, such as alterations in libido or flattening of mood; and feelings about the introduction of chemicals into the body, or "body pollution." Psychological dispositions affecting use of the IUD include feelings about alteration of menstrual bleeding and pain patterns, feelings about the introduction of foreign objects into the body, and feelings about giving up personal control (by using a method that has a known failure rate, which cannot be controlled by the contraceptor). Psychological dispositions associated with the diaphragm and other vaginal insertion methods include feelings about the introduction of an object into the vagina by the user and about the need to plan for or interrupt intercourse in order to do so. Use of the condom is associated with feelings about the decreased penile sensation that its use often produces in the man. Some of the more important psychological dispositions associated with abortion-seeking behavior include beliefs about the rightness or wrongness of abortion, feelings about destroying a "living thing," concern about the pain and discomfort associated with the operative procedure, and concern about the effects of the procedure on the body and on subsequent reproduction.

We have mentioned that for the large fraction of births in this country, which do not result from a conscious decision, the integrative activities of the ego are of central importance. This is because a series of decisions must be made by the individual regarding each of the behaviors represented in Figure 4.3 and these decisions, together with the motives and feelings that lie behind them, must be integrated by the ego across behavior domains and across time. Examples of some of the more important of these decisions include deciding to become sexually involved with a particular partner, deciding to discuss and plan contraception with that partner, deciding to use a contraceptive method, deciding to have sexual intercourse on a particular occasion, deciding what to do when it is suspected that a conception has occurred, deciding whether or not to interrupt a pregnancy, and deciding whether or not to keep and care for a child born following a pregnancy. Each of these decisions, and many that have not been mentioned but which also affect procreational outcomes, could be described with a model similar to the ones depicted in Figures 4.1 and 4.2. The direction of each of these decisions is strongly influenced by a variety of substantive psychological factors, including procreational motivations, attitudes, and beliefs, all of which must be taken into account if we are to fully understand and predict behavior resulting in childbearing.

Decisions to separate and divorce are important for childbearing because the termination of a union greatly reduces the likelihood of reproduction, at least until a new union occurs. There are three distinguishable ways that a separation and divorce decision can be made. First, it may be made by the partner and more or less imposed on the individual. Second, it may be made by the individual, either singly or jointly with the partner, in order to escape from or substantially alter a highly distressful situation. Third, it may be made by the individual, either with or without the partner's concurrence, in order to establish a new relationship under new, more satisfying conditions. In the first case, the individual makes no decision, except for those that must be made as part of adaptation to the state of being separated or divorced. In the second and third cases, the proximate substantive factors involved in the decision are generally similar to those represented in Figures 4.1 and 4.2 for marriage and childbearing, with two exceptions. First, the change or deviation from the ongoing state of affairs results in a loss rather than, as in the case of marriage and childbearing, an addition or a gain. Second, the type of separation and divorce decision in which the decision maker goes into another relationship includes a wholly new substantive factor, the decision maker's perception of that new person. Thus, in this type of separation and divorce decision the perceptions of both the current and the potential partner are important factors. The figure most closely approximating the formal relationship of the substantive factors in this type of decision is Figure 4.6, which represents the decision to move from one home to another. The latter decision is analogous because it includes the decision maker's perception of both the current home and the potential new home. One special set of perceived consequences in separation and divorce decisions includes the consequences for the spouse and any existing children. The latter, in particular, are likely to be passive participants. Both experience a loss and disruption. These features underscore the importance of the consequences for others of this particular decision.

Current Issues in Marriage and Childbearing.   There are a large number of important social and psychological issues in the area of marriage and childbearing. Many of these are currently undergoing fundamental changes. Some of these changes are undoubtedly a result of demographic and economic forces, but two additional considerations are important. On the biological level, technological advances have made conception control a reality within virtually everyone's grasp. On the social level, sweeping changes in ideology and values during the 1960s and 70s have changed the prevailing standards of acceptable and expected behavior in the areas of sexuality, reproduction, marriage, and family living (17, 18, 19). In other words, there has been a general increase in freedom of choice within the behavior domains that affect marriage and childbearing. This itself has introduced important new issues.

The United States has traditionally been a nation where marriage was almost universal. During the first three-quarters of the twentieth century, 90 to 95 percent of the individuals living in the United States have married at least once. The age at first marriage in the United States has decreased steadily from the late nineteenth century until the 1950s, and since that time it has steadily increased. Childbearing, too, has traditionally received wide normative support in this country. Depending on the decade, between 75 and 90 percent of all women have had at least one child and since the 1950s, when the higher percentage figure pertains, the majority of those going childless have done so for involuntary reasons associated with subfecundity, marital separation, and nonmarriage. In spite of high normative and institutional support for marriage, marital separation and divorce have steadily increased in this country until the present time, when approximately one out of four first marriages ends in divorce. However, this fact cannot be interpreted as a general disaffirmation of the institution of marriage because the great majority of divorced individuals promptly remarry. Many divorces occur after five or ten years of marriage and it is for this reason that 60 percent of all divorces involve couples who have children.

Since the mid-1960s women have postponed the age at first marriage by approximately one year (19). This postponement is partly explained by the marriage squeeze, an excess of young women over young men of marriageable age that resulted from the surge in numbers of young adults produced by the "baby boom" following World War II. Equally important in this postponement have been increases in women's college enrollment and employment, and decreases in fertility rates, all of which signal the assumption by women of new roles outside the home.

The above trends highlight a set of important contemporary decisions confronted by youth and young adults. These include whether to marry, when to marry, whether to have children, and when to have children. All four of these decisions are of crucial importance for individuals wishing to manage and plan their own life courses. They are, of course, to some extent mutually dependent. It is instructive to consider the approximate percentage of women who fall into the four different life courses made possible by the interaction of the two primary decisions, whether to marry and whether to have children: among women born since 1930, about 89 percent marry and have children; 5 percent marry and do not have children; 5 percent do not marry and do not have children; and 1 percent do not marry and do have children (20). At the present time (1977), only the first three of these courses fall within the bounds of normative behavior, and only the first course is fully accepted. In fact, it seems likely that only a very small minority of people in this country give active consideration to the possible advantages of singlehood or childlessness (21, 22). Nevertheless, given the number of normative and behavioral changes currently taking place in the area of marriage and reproduction and given the fact that each of these life courses has unique advantages that will appeal differentially to people with different life styles and goals, it seems very likely that there will be an increased exploration of each of these life courses by individuals and an increased demand for institutional support systems that will make them viable options within society.

In order to make effective decisions regarding the four life-course options we have been discussing, it is desirable to have some previous practical experience with their characteristic challenges and problems. Individuals who have had experience cohabiting with a heterosexual partner or taking care of an infant or child will have a better base of knowledge and understanding from which to make their decision about marriage and childbearing. Perhaps it is this need for an experience-based decision with regard to marriage that has led to the recent upswing in the number of young adults who are cohabiting (19). It can be anticipated that the search for an equivalent experience with infants and children by adolescents and young adults will become increasingly common and important, creating a demand for institutional and normative change to meet the need. If such change comes about it will help not only with deciding whether or not to have children but also, for those whose decision is affirmative, with the transition to parenthood, made so much more difficult in the United States by the general lack of preparation and guidelines (23).

The decisions whether or not to marry and/or have children are closely related to decisions about gender-role activities, especially for women. In spite of the fact that since World War II there has been a significant increase in the labor-force participation of American women with more women combining marriage, childbearing, and work than ever before (24), there remains a significant amount of role strain between the pursuit of a career and full-time parenthood for women. (The same applies to those men who invest an equivalent amount of time and energy in the home and parenting.) This role conflict is certainly one of the main reasons for the fact that women who work because they want to work have fewer children than those who work out of necessity, who in turn have fewer children than those who do not work at all (25).

When to marry and when to have the first child are also important contemporary social issues. Early marriage, especially teenage marriage, is associated with high rates of marital dissolution and the production of larger families (18). It is also more likely to interfere with educational achievement, the development of psychological autonomy, and the process of self-exploration and self-discovery. However, it does provide companionship and intimacy for a longer period during the early adult years and it does allow for an early initiation in family building. The early birth of the first child, provided it does not occur during the early teens, also has biological advantages since the risks of childbearing increase steadily from the late teens throughout the reproductive period. Early childbearing has psychological advantages and disadvantages. In general, a younger parent has more energy and gets more actively involved with the child more of the time. On the other hand, an older parent will tend to have a more tempered judgment and emotional response to a child. It is noteworthy that both energy and temperance are the advantages of youth and maturity respectively in most activities. For this reason, the decision regarding the timing of the first child depends to some extent on which activity the individual feels it is most important to pursue when youthful and energetic, and which when mature and wise. One person may elect to devote the younger years to childrearing, another to the pursuit of a career. Since it is perfectly feasible to follow one course and then the other, and in either order, there are no simple rules to guide decision making. In general, deciding when to marry and when to have the first child rests on a consideration of the best sequencing for an individual of the careers and subcareers of marriage, child rearing, education, and work during the life course. Although the current trend is in the direction of later marriage with childbearing postponed at least until after education is completed, there are enough advantages to early marriage and childbearing followed by periods of devotion to education and/or work, that institutional support for these options will almost certainly need to be increased.

Another important set of childbearing issues is associated with the decisions that must be made with regard to birth intervals. These decisions include determining the interval between marriage and the first birth, between the first and the second birth, and between all subsequent births. Recent research has examined the birth intervals desired by American women (26, 27, 28). It appears that the length of interval acceptable between marriage and the first birth can vary over a wide range, provided that the interval allows time for the married couple to become adjusted to marriage, to become financially ready for children, and to enjoy each other's company for a period of time before turning to parental responsibility. The acceptable range of interval between the first and second birth also appears to be wide, with general agreement that spacing children more than four years apart significantly reduces the likelihood of their becoming close companions. The most salient consideration in determining the length of interval between the second and third birth lies in providing the oldest child with time to develop sufficient independence so that the mother is not overburdened with demands from three children simultaneously. An important consideration determining the acceptable length of all birth intervals for a particular couple appears to be achievement of the total number of children desired within the span of time that they wish to devote to childbearing and the rearing of preschool children. For example, the woman who wants to have three children and also wants to limit the preprimary school years to twelve will find a birth interval of up to three years acceptable. With such an interval, she would be able to have three children during the first six years of her child-rearing career, with the youngest of these children starting primary school after about twelve years.

Another set of childbearing issues is associated with decisions about family size. During this century, family-size norms in the United States have fluctuated considerably, as have the birthrates. During the 1930s, the average woman was having 2.3 children. During the 1950s, at the height of the baby boom, this figure reached a peak of 3.8 children. It appears that women in the current decade will be having children at a rate equal to or even below that of the 1930s. The two-child family is currently considered ideal, in part because it represents a replacement level and, therefore, does not contribute to population growth. As a result of this popular sentiment, there is considerable normative pressure to have no more than two children. The effect of this pressure appears to be that it is reducing the family size options that are available to couples. However, if trends toward singlehood, marital childlessness, and one-child families develop and are sustained by institutional supports and government policy, then it is entirely possible for some couples to elect to have three, four and even more children without bringing about a net population growth. Not only would this increase individual freedom, but it would contribute to the heterogeneity of the population by allowing both parents and children to have different family-size experiences with the associated benefits and costs.

One of the considerations in decisions about family size is the possible consequences that any given size will have for the family, and especially for the children (29, 30). In particular, there appear to be a number of personal characteristics of children associated with the size of their sibship as well as with their sibling rank. In this regard, scientific investigation does not always confirm the popular impression. For example, the only child is commonly perceived as maladjusted, self-centered, self-willed, and temperamental in comparison with other children. However, if anything the reverse is true: they are more likely to be characterized by such positive traits as achievement orientation, independence, verbal intelligence, and trustworthiness. These latter characteristics appear to be equally attributable to first children. In comparison, second children are more likely to be described as active, aggressive, nonconforming, and peer-oriented. There is also some evidence that children from large families, regardless of sibling rank, tend to be less socially adjusted and to have more frustrated dependency needs. Probably the most consistent research finding is that intelligence decreases as family size increases and as the length of birth intervals decreases (31). With regard to all of these relationships between child characteristics and the ordinal position or sibship size of a child, it is important to remember that the research findings are generally weak and frequently inconsistent. In part this is due to the inadequacy of research in this area to date, but it must also be recognized that the characteristics of children are determined by so many factors such as genetic characteristics, parenting styles, and peer and community influences that sibship factors are only one part of a large overall set of determinants.

Another form of decision making affecting the characteristics of children is the predetermination and preselection of fetal characteristics through biological and genetic means. For example, recent technological developments make it possible to safely withdraw amniotic fluid during pregnancy and use this fluid to identify various characteristics of the fetus. In conjunction with selective induced abortion, this technology makes it possible to predetermine biological characteristics of the fetus and preselect which fetuses will proceed to a full-term. At present, these techniques are practical in only two situations: for predetermination of the presence of a small group of specific genetic abnormalities and for predetermination of the gender of the fetus. With regard to the former, it is increasingly recognized that the amount of hereditary disease in human populations is large—many estimates run as high as 5 to 10 percent of all births—and causes considerable burden on both the individuals involved and on society (32). It is now feasible to establish a network or large system of centers that would be capable of identifying important genetic diseases and counseling the involved individuals (33). Although current approaches to the prevention, treatment, and research of genetic disease raises important ethical issues (34), the potential benefits to future parents are very great, especially in view of the current emphasis on decision making and quality, as opposed to spontaneity and quantity, in procreation. All of these developments indicate the social importance of ongoing research that aims to develop a greater understanding of decision making under conditions of genetic uncertainty (35).

With regard to gender preselection, although the technology and other methods for accomplishing this are as yet unsuitable for large-scale use (36), there is considerable evidence that numbers of individuals and couples would exercise the option to predetermine the sex of their child if a suitable method were available (37). If such a choice became a social reality, the most important, lasting demographic consequence would be the increased probability of firstborn children being male and second-born children being female (38). If this were the case, whatever characteristics or traits are associated with being firstborn or second born would be concentrated differentially in the sexes. Beyond gender preselection, there appears to be a great potential for the practical application of recent genetic advances (39). If the ethical dilemmas can be adequately resolved, then the number of options available for the preselection of infant and child physical and psychological characteristics may become large, with presently unknown social and demographic consequences.

The childbearing issues discussed so far in this section apply only in a society where conception control and birth planning are technologically and normatively possible. However, as we have shown, research indicates that the incidence of unplanned and un-

wanted pregnancies within marriage in this country is substantial
(9, 10). Between 1960 and 1965 20 percent of all births within
marriage were "number failures." In other words, these births occurred after the couple had borne all the children they desired. Of
the remaining births, 43 percent were "timing failures." In other
words, they were unplanned but did not cause a couple to exceed
its desired family size. Although it is true that there has been a substantial reduction in unplanned births in the United States during
the 1960–1970 decade (40), the following facts make it apparent
that unplanned and unwanted conceptions and births continue to be
a major issue: the 1960–65 data regarding number and timing failures apply only to the married population; almost 10 percent of annual births in this country are out of wedlock (41); the rate of out-
of-wedlock births has been increasing in recent years (42); and
legal abortions in the United States have increased almost four
hundred fold from 1963 to 1974 (43, 44).

It is useful to make a distinction between planning a child and
wanting a child. Evidence indicates that virtually all conceptions
that are planned result in children who are wanted, whereas many
unplanned conceptions result in relatively or completely unwanted
children (10, 45). This association of being unwanted solely with
being unplanned does not mean that every couple either wants to
plan, or should plan, their children. In fact, many couples place a
particular value, either religious or otherwise, upon "letting nature
take its course" without any conscious intervention on their part to
affect conception. It seems that the most undesirable effects of
unplanned conceptions occur when premarital conceptions force a
marriage decision, commonly resulting in substantial economic and
educational disadvantage for the couple and often in marital dissolution (46, 47); or when marital or nonmarital conceptions significantly interfere with the execution and implementation of educational and occupational decisions.

As we have indicated in the previous section, sexual, contraceptive, fetal-care, and child-care behaviors are all important in the occurrence of unplanned conceptions. The relaxation of sexual norms that
began during the 1960s has had two consequences with opposite ef-

fects on unplanned conceptions. One consequence has been the removal of barriers against sexual activity among certain subpopulations. Most important for this discussion is the removal of barriers to teenage sexuality. The effect of this change has been to increase the likelihood of unplanned conceptions among teenagers because of their relative lack of preparation and social support for their sexual activity. The second consequence of normative relaxation has been to reduce some of the tensions and anxieties associated with sexuality in those groups where sexual activity is socially sanctioned. Since sexual anxiety can significantly interfere with effective partner communication (11, 12), the effect of normative relaxation for the group enjoying socially sanctioned sexual activity has been to decrease the likelihood of unplanned conceptions.

An important issue at the present time with respect to contraceptive behavior is that all current methods have significant problems or side effects associated with their use. The effective methods tend either to have important medical side effects for a number of users, to be irreversible, or to require behaviors affecting sexuality in ways that are undesirable to a number of users. The remaining methods carry too high a risk of failure to be satisfactory for conception control for most people in most situations. Because women commonly bear the heaviest burden associated with contraceptive use, another important current issue is the development of a male contraceptive method, preferably one which is not coitus dependent. Even if such a method can be developed, it is not clear how effectively men, who are of course once removed from the immediate consequences of ineffective contraceptive use, will utilize it. Within stable marriages enjoying good communication and where there is symmetrical gender-role activity, a male method may be used with great reliability. In other circumstances, however, male participation in contraceptive activity may be less than optimal.

A special set of issues regarding contraception occurs both at the beginning and at the end of the reproductive career. For teenagers, contraception presents special problems, and since sexual activity among teenagers has increased considerably, these problems are socially salient. At what age should teenagers begin prescription contraception? Should such contraception precede the initiation of the sexual career of a teenager? At what age or stage of development is a teenager ready to make a decision regarding contraception without his or her parents' knowledge? How can parents, and society in general, most effectively prepare teenagers for their sexuality and contraceptive use? These and a host of other questions illustrate the specific developmental issues teenagers face with respect to contraceptive use. The importance of these issues is underlined by the large number of out-of-wedlock births and pregnancy terminations and the large number of early-marriage births that are now occurring in the teenage population (48). A different set of social issues arises in connection with contraception at the terminal end of the reproductive career. These issues revolve around two basic considerations: whether to terminate fertility and have no more children, and whether to use an irreversible contraceptive method such as vasectomy or tubal ligation. Related to this latter consideration is the question of which member of the couple should undergo sterilization if such a method is selected. Since sterilization has become the most popular contraceptive method for married couples where the woman's age is thirty or above, (49), this set of issues has also assumed social salience.

One response to an unplanned or unwanted pregnancy is to seek an abortion. This option has become increasingly available in the United States during the last decade. Associated with these changes in behavior have been changes in public attitude toward abortion. Gallup Polls during the 1960s revealed an overwhelming majority of Americans as disapproving of abortion on request (50). Two polls in the early 1970s show a striking reversal of these figures, with a majority now favoring abortion on request (51). The increased use of abortion in the United States in recent years is not contraindicated by the behavioral science research evidence regarding the psychological consequences of abortion. Research conducted during the 1960s generally supported the relatively benign effects of induced abortion. In most instances, the operative procedure was followed with feelings of relief and hopefulness and with positive coping. More recent research has continued to support these observations and conclusions (52, 53).

The demographic and social consequences of the availability of induced abortion have also tended to be positive. One investigation estimated that induced abortion was responsible for a significant portion of the observed fertility decline during 1974 (54). Another investigation demonstrated that the availability of induced abortion allowed blacks to have fertility rates more comparable to whites and thus served as an important social equalizer (55). Since abortion is used most extensively by young unmarried women (44), its availability has the important demographic effect of postponing the birth of the first child for a large number of women. Since the parents' age at the birth of the first child is one of the most important determinants of family size, the significance of the availability of abortion for population regulation is readily apparent. One of the concerns regarding easy access to abortion has been that it would lead to the use of abortion rather than contraception for purposes of fertility regulation, and a to a high incidence of repeat abortions. To date, however, evidence indicates that the effective use of contraception increases following an abortion (56). In addition, the incidence of repeat abortion has not exceeded the rates to be expected when it is used primarily as a back-up method of fertility regulation following the failure of regularly used contraception (57). Perhaps the most persuasive argument in favor of maintaining the availability of legal induced abortion is the effect that its availability has on the occurrence of illegal abortion. Current evidence suggests that the utilization of legal abortion in the United States has resulted in a very dramatic reduction of morbidity and mortality from illegal abortion (54). A final important issue with respect to induced abortion is the effect that its availability has had, and will increasingly have, on child-care behavior. A great many unwanted births are prevented through this option, and there should be a far lower incidence of negative child-care behavior of all types, from subtle psychological rejection of the child to outright child abuse. One aspect of this change already observed is a reduction in the number of babies available for adoption. Unfortunately, this has the effect of reducing the options available for those individuals who, for various reasons, are unable to bear their own children.

Turning to consideration of proceptive behavior, it is noteworthy how little scientific information has been gathered on this subject. What is known suggests that proception is practiced far more casually and in far greater ignorance than contraception. A national survey found that most couples in 1960 were unable to speed up conception by orienting their sexual activity to the fertile period of the menstrual cycle. Only 20 percent of the sample ever reported trying to time their conceptions in this way, and of this group, only half had enough accurate information about the timing of ovulation during the menstrual cycle to have some chance of success (27). The complexity of American life and the importance for many couples of careful planning of conceptions in sequence with other planned events suggests that there is considerable need for an improvement in the practice and accuracy of proceptive behavior.

Of greater importance in its psychological implications than the ability to time conceptions is the relative inability of a woman to conceive at any time. This is the problem of subfecundity and sterility. On the basis of a national survey, it has been calculated that 31 percent of married couples between the ages of 18 and 39 are subfecund and that about one third of these (11 percent of all couples) are definitely sterile (25). The data for this study were collected more than fifteen years ago, so that the majority of sterile couples were involuntarily sterile, only about 2 percent out of the 11 having had contraceptive surgery. Thus, there appears to be a large proportion of the population who experience some difficulty in achieving conception and, thereby, run the risk of having fewer children than desired. There is also a small but significant proportion who will never be able to have children at all without practicing adoption. Medical diagnosis and treatment offers several important and hopeful steps for those individuals and couples who have been unable to conceive. One of the more interesting techniques is artificial insemination, though it is not yet systematically developed and made available to those who might select it (58). In general, the problems of the subfecund and sterile appear destined to continue for many people who wish to have the option of bearing children. Since the number of babies available for adoption will almost certainly continue to decrease, it appears that many potential parents will have to adjust to the frustrations and disappointments of not being able to achieve parenthood, even through a biologically unrelated child.

Mortality:

Basic Concepts. The most elementary mortality concept is that of the crude deathrate, that is, the number of deaths per year per 1,000 persons in the population. This measure is analogous to the fertility measure of the crude birthrate. As with fertility rates, there are more refined measures of mortality rates that are specific for age and sex. These measures are useful for demographers because they allow more accurate comparisons between populations with different age and sex compositions. Another important way of conceptualizing mortality is in terms of life expectancy. This is commonly expressed as the average expectation of life at birth, but the average expectation of life may be calculated for any age. In the United States in 1972, the life expectancy at birth for men was 67.4 years and for women was 75.2 years (59). These figures and the figures for life expectancy at any age are calculated from "life tables," (60) which themselves are calculated from age-specific mortality rates.

Self-Care and Self-Preservation: Factors in Decision Making. It is not uncommon for an individual to make a direct and conscious decision about whether or not to die. Two examples might be an elderly man who kills himself several months after his wife has died of natural causes leaving him alone and chronically ill, and a middle-aged woman who decides not to have her breast removed for cancer in order to avoid surgical mutilation. For such cases, a schematic representation of decision making very similar to the ones shown in Figures 4.1 and 4.2 could be developed. The two main options at the decision point would be between life and death. In making the decision the individual would consider the perceived consequences of choosing death and the perceived alternatives to death, with their perceived consequences. The decision would also be influenced by the individual's perception of the social network press for and against choosing death. All of these proximate factors would be influenced by the individual's motivations, attitudes, and beliefs regarding death.

The more common situation in mortality-related decision making is that death comes about in an unplanned fashion, as a result of decisions that are unrelated or, at best, indirectly related to the choice of death. Figure 4.4 presents a schematic representation of those behaviors indirectly affecting the occurrence of death. This schema is directly parallel to that shown in Figure 4.3 for unplanned fertility. Its central premise is that all behavior has a certain number of health-compromising results. There is nothing people do that does not have some probability of producing a somatic disease or death or both. It is true that there are certain common behaviors, such as overeating, smoking, and using drugs, that have higher levels of risk for people than have most other behaviors. But the fact is that even the most mundane behaviors, such as driving to work, exercising, and even sleeping in bed at night, have risks to health and life as a result of accident or disease associated with them. The risks of an auto accident as a result of human or mechanical failure are well recognized by all American drivers. A number of Americans drop dead of heart attacks each year while jogging. There is a small but definite risk of being overcome by gas, smoke, or fire or being attacked by an intruder while asleep at night. An interesting example of the importance of the health-compromising issue in ordinary behavior may be seen in the area of nutrition. For many years, experts have warned of the dangers of high-fat diets. Recently, not only have many other diets been identified as containing some risk to health, but so too has virtually every type of nutritional pattern. Some of the ultimate reasons for this have been discussed at length by Dubois in *The Mirage of Health* (61). Simply stated, the reasons are that individual human beings are highly complex organisms with a unique set of genetic and acquired char-

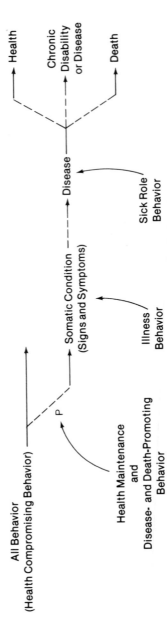

Figure 4.4. A schematic representation of the behaviors relevant to the occurrence of an unplanned death and of the relationships between those behaviors.

acteristics. Each human is adapted to living under a variety of environmental conditions. Because of this, no one set of conditions is likely to be fully adaptive and therefore comparatively risk free for any single individual. Nor is one set of conditions going to be of equivalent risk for different individuals in a population.

In Figure 4.4, the various risks to health and life of all behavior are indicated by the letter P. This symbol indicates that there is a certain probability, P, that any behavior will lead to a somatic condition, identified by objective signs and subjective symptoms, which condition may progress to a specific, diagnosed disease, and perhaps ultimately to death. Behavior oriented toward reducing the probability of the development of the disease or death is called health-maintenance behavior. Such behavior includes seeking preventive health care, maintaining physical fitness through appropriate amounts of exercise and rest, avoiding exposure to hazardous conditions or contagious diseases, and so forth. Behavior which is oriented toward increasing the probability of the occurrence of disease or death is called disease- or death-promoting behavior. Although such behavior may be less common, and certainly less socially acceptable, than health-maintenance behavior, there are definite benefits that may be derived from illness, the sick role, and dying (62, 63). Because of these benefits, certain behaviors are specifically intended to increase the chances of disease or death occurring. Disease- or death-promoting behavior includes deliberately seeking exposure to hazardous conditions or contagious diseases, allowing deterioration of one's physical condition, and failing to take adequate precautions against disease states. When distressful or dysfunctional signs or symptoms develop, individuals manifest what may be called "illness behavior." This behavior begins when the individual responds to signs and symptoms with attention, affective response, and interpretation of their meaning and continues to the point where he or she takes some action in order to deal with or seek help for these signs or symptoms. This behavior is modified by such factors as the individual's perception of the deviant physical signs and subjective symptoms, his or her knowledge or assumptions about their meaning, the extent to which these signs or symptoms pose a threat or disrupt ongoing functions, the individual's typical style of coping with physical threat, and the relative benefits and costs of seeking help (64). Once the somatic condition has been diagnosed, or in some way labeled as a disease, the individual responds with what may be called sick-role behavior. This behavior includes limiting effort and activity in accordance with the disease condition, being exempted from certain role obligations and expectations, and conforming to the treatment plan given by the physician or other agent of treatment. It also includes readjustment behaviors of the individual during recovery and return to health or during chronic disability or disease (62).

The behaviors represented in Figure 4.4 are influenced by a variety of motivations, attitudes, and beliefs. Perhaps the most obvious are those that have to do with self-preservation, self-care, self-injury, and self-destruction. However, since any behavior can be health compromising, virtually all motivations, attitudes, and beliefs are relevant to an individual's health status. It is the relative salience for an individual of self-preservation and self-care goals in comparison with all competing goals that determine the frequency and extent to which the individual will compromise his or her health.

There are three forms of mortality-relevant behavior which have not been mentioned so far but which do fit generally into the schema we have developed. The first of these is accident behavior, sometimes discussed in terms of "accident proneness." This is a complex topic and considerable attention has already been given to its analysis (65). In general, the accident-prone individual appears to be one who consistently displays a specific type of health-compromising behavior and is repeatedly victimized by "accidents." In some cases this accident proneness appears to be influenced by self-injurious and self-destructive motivations, attitudes, and beliefs, but in other cases nonmotivational psychological factors are influential (62).

The second and third forms of behavior as yet unmentioned are suicidal and homicidal behavior. In the first case the individual seeks death either directly as a result of conscious decision making or indirectly by different forms of risk taking. The latter is a special form of death-promoting behavior. There are, of course, gradations between the direct and indirect forms of suicide. The same distinction may be made in the case of homicidal behavior. Some homicides are the result of direct conscious decisions, others of spontaneous unplanned acts where another person's life is risked. In the latter case in particular, the behavior of both the victim and the perpetrator are important, since in the majority of murders both know each other and both seem to participate in the homicide process (66). To the extent that attack and death can be anticipated and to the extent that they are precipitated by psychological factors in the victim, his or her behavior is a form of health-compromising behavior. Since in many cases the victim's behavior is a type of suicide equivalent, it may more properly be seen as a type of death-promoting behavior. The fact that homicide involves two people indicates the importance of dyadic psychology for understanding the substantive influences that work in this type of behavior. This suggests that Figure 4.4 could be expanded to include the behavior of the partner in the homicidal process, much as Figure 4.3 included the sexual partner. Dyadic psychology has importance in other categories of mortality as well, most notably in suicidal deaths where family members, physicians, and significant others often participate and contribute in major ways to the result (67).

Current Issues in Health and Death. Each of the mortality-related types of behavior discussed is associated with one or more current social issues. For example, health-compromising behavior has emerged as a major contributor to loss of health and life through disease. Changes in the behavior of the American people which would result in the alteration of their dietary, smoking, exercise, and alcohol-consumption patterns and reduce the physical and psychological stress to which they subject themselves would have a far greater effect on American health and mortality than any currently anticipated technological developments or applications. As a specific example, alteration of existing patterns of behavior seems to be the best way of reducing the risk of heart disease (68). The importance of behavioral and decision-making factors in the health and life expectancy of the Canadian population—one closely similar to the American—is well supported in a report prepared by Lalonde, minister of health in Canada (69). He examined the causes of ''early death'' (those occurring before age seventy but not including those occurring before age five) in the Canadian population and calculated the total number of years of life lost within all of the disease categories during a one-year period. The five most important contributors to loss of man-years were, in descending order of importance, motor-vehicle accidents, ischemic heart disease, all other accidents, respiratory disease and lung cancer, and suicide. All the forms of behavior we have discussed, especially health-compromising behavior, play an important part in one or more of these five disease categories.

It has been demonstrated that obtaining adequate immunization for infants depends upon the parents' perception of the disease's seriousness and risk, their knowledge of the efficacy and length of the protection of the vaccine, and their degree of media exposure (70). This is just one example of the importance of psychological and behavioral factors in health maintenance. The American public seems to be increasingly aware of this importance because a major impetus to the many currently popular physical-fitness programs are their health-maintenance effects. These developments are coming at a time when there is increasing public and political pressure to provide quality health care to all people. More comprehensive health-care programs are being developed with increased emphasis on preventive and early detection techniques. As an element in these trends, health maintenance and illness behavior are assuming more importance in the minds of health professionals. At the same time, with the greater need to follow complicated treatment and rehabilitative regimes following medical diagnosis and surgery, sick-role behavior is receiving increased attention and investigation by health professionals and behavioral scientists, in the belief that designing service programs around basic psychological principles will greatly increase medical compliance (71, 72, 73).

All these developments have moved in the direction of preserv-

ing life; however, there has also been an important social development toward allowing life to end under appropriate circumstances.
Euthanasia has become an important popular and scientific issue
(74, 75). In the late 1940s, a Gallup Poll showed that a little more
than one third of the American respondents were willing to grant a
doctor the power to end the life of a patient suffering from an incur-
able disease (76, 77). By 1973, the percent had increased to over
one half of the respondents (78). Current sentiment seems to be
similar with respect to suicide. In 1975 a majority of the respondents to a Gallup Poll who were under thirty indicated that incur-
able disease or continuous pain confer upon persons the moral right
to end their own life (79). In 1976 the California state legislature
passed a law that made it legal for individuals to grant permission
to their physicians to withdraw their life-support systems. These
scattered pieces of evidence suggest that there is substantial and
growing public sentiment and institutional support for giving individuals the freedom to decide to die under certain circumstances.

Population Size

In considering the effects of population size upon individual psychology and, especially, human adaptation, it is possible to distinguish between direct effects where the individual is aware of population size and is affected by his perception and indirect effects
where the individual is affected by aspects of the social environment that are themselves the result of population size. Relevant to
the indirect effects is Barker's review of the literature on the effects
of institutional size on individual psychology (80). He concluded
that there was a negative relationship between group and organizational size, on the one hand, and the amount of participation, involvement, and satisfaction the individual developed during activities within that group or organization, on the other hand. If this is
true, and if larger populations generate larger and more complex
social institutions, then as populations grow, individuals will tend
to experience less participation, involvement, and satisfaction.
These experiences are consistent with observations of urban living.
Milgram has discussed three aspects of a city's population that af-

fect the psychology of interpersonal experience: number of people, density of people, and the heterogeneity of the people (81). He suggests that when all three of these variables affect the city dweller to a significant degree, they tend to produce noninvolvement, impersonality, competitiveness, and a functional approach to interpersonal relationships.

One way to conceptualize the direct effect of population size upon individual psychology is through the concept of personal identification. During the nineteenth century in the United States, it was not unusual for individuals to identify themselves primarily with relatively small demographic units such as the family, clan, or township. The nation itself was an upper limit of reference for most and often a relatively weak one. In contemporary United States, identification at the level of the smaller units continues to be important. However, many individuals also identify themselves readily with regional, national, and international units. For some, there is even an urgently felt identification with the whole human race, vividly suggested by the concept of "Spaceship Earth." It appears that both the size of the unit with which the individual personally identifies and the number of units from different levels has a significant effect on individual adaptation.

GEOGRAPHIC DISTRIBUTION AND
GEOGRAPHIC MOBILITY

The dyad of geographic distribution and geographic mobility constitutes a second important population subsystem. Together, these two factors reflect the structural and dynamic aspects of a population's location in space. Two sets of time-series data for the United States illustrate the important relationships between these factors. The first represents the impact of western migration on settlement patterns and area density as this country was developed over a two-century period. In 1776, the density of the United States was approximately eight persons per square mile and most were concentrated on the eastern seaboard. In 1876, the overall density of the United States had increased to approximately seventeen persons per square mile, with most of the population located in the eastern third of the nation where there was a density of over twenty-five persons per square mile. In 1976, the overall density of the United States has increased to almost sixty persons per square mile, the eastern third of the nation having a density of greater than one hundred persons per square mile, and the eastern half of the nation together with the western seaboard having a density of greater than twenty-five persons per square mile (82). The following time series illustrates the recent shifts of population between areas in the United States with different community types and life styles. In 1940, there were approximately thirty million inhabitants in the rural areas of this nation. The number has decreased each decade since then to the low level of approximately ten million persons in 1970. In contrast, the urban areas, which contained approximately forty-five million inhabitants in 1940, have gradually increased to approximately sixty-five million inhabitants in 1970. A more rapid increase may be found in the suburban areas. In 1940, these areas contained somewhat less than thirty million inhabitants (less than were located in the rural areas). Marked increases over the last three decades have brought the population of the suburban areas up to seventy-five million in 1970 (83). Much of the changing pattern represented in this last time series has been accomplished through geographic mobility. This has been made up of three primary components—rural to urban movement, urban to suburban movement, and suburban to suburban movement (84, 85). Since the rural, urban, and suburban areas have distinct and characteristic densities, this time series also illustrates some of the important changes in population density that took place within the United States during the decades between 1940 and 1970. At the present time the range of population density in the nation is very great. On the one hand, there remain large wilderness areas with essentially zero population per square mile; on the other, areas in residential Manhattan have a population density approaching 400,000 persons per square mile (86).

Much of the change in population distribution and density during the course of this country's history has been possible only because of the American people's willingness, and at times eagerness, to undergo geographic mobility. At the present time, geographic mobility is one of the most characteristic features of the American way of life. It has been estimated that one out of five Americans changes residence every year, and one out of sixteen migrates to another county or region of the country each year (60). A longitudinal perspective on the American patterns of geographic mobility indicates that the average American changes his residence as much as thirteen times and migrates to another county or region three or four times in a lifetime (87).

Geographic Distribution:

Basic Concepts.   There are many different demographic measures or expressions of density. These include the following: persons per unit space (e.g., people per square mile); persons per functional unit (e.g., people per room or per household); functional units per unit space (e.g., housing units per acre); and functional units per functional unit (e.g., housing units per building structure). The fact that each of these ratios measures a different aspect of population density with different demopsychological meanings is substantiated by a recent investigation which demonstrated that juvenile delinquency and public assistance rates were most strongly correlated with the measure of persons per room, and secondarily with the measure of housing units per structure, while mental hospitalization rates were most strongly correlated with the measure of rooms per housing unit (88).

A distinct population density measure is that of population potential (89). This is a summed, person-to-distance ratio that takes into account not only the number of people in a given area but also those in all the contiguous areas. Other factors that may interact in important ways with spatial density include temporal density (the number of persons per unit time to whom an individual is exposed), privacy (the total available private space, or the private-space–public-space ratio per individual), social isolation (the number of close relationships, or the ratio of the close to superficial relationships per individual), and use intensity (the amount of interpersonal contact per area of space per individual (90)).

Shelter, Home, and Community: Adaptation to Density.   The adaptation of individuals to density conditions in their home and community is mediated by a large number of psychological variables. Some of the more significant of these and the linkages between them and adaptive behavior are schematically represented in Figure 4.5. The surrounding circle in this figure indicates that the schema represents adaptive psychology and behavior within a specific density condition. The more important linkages between variables are represented by arrows. Although the arrows are generally drawn in one direction only, this is primarily for the sake of simplicity and emphasis. For most of the linkages, the direction of effect must be thought of as occurring in both directions over time. Three of the five general goals of adaptation listed in Chapter 3 are included in the figure, with bidirectional arrows drawn between them and adaptive behavior in order to emphasize their special interactive and superordinate relationship with the latter. The two general goals of adaptive behavior not included in the figure—regulation of the internal milieu and regulation of interpersonal relationships—could be included if a more detailed and complicated schema was desired.

An individual's previous experience with different density conditions will affect adaptation. For example, stress is generated when a person moves into a low- or a high-density condition without opportunity to develop appropriate adaptive mechanisms by previous exposure to such a condition. Cassel has indicated that the health effects of density are most apparent during the period of adjustment following an individual's or a population's change in living conditions and density exposure (91). An individual's sense of personal space and territory is also an important mediating factor in density-adaptive behavior. Horowitz has developed a concept of the body buffer zone, a small area extending from the surface of an individual's body into the surrounding space, that is perceived as an extension of the body and that affects how the individual manages the

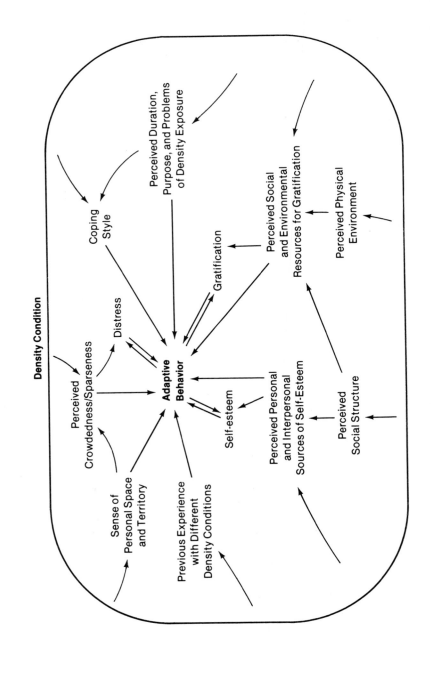

Density Condition

space between him or her and other people or objects (92). The anthropologist Hall has discussed personal space in terms of four types of distance that people maintain between themselves and others, depending upon the social situation (93). He has called these the intimate, personal, social, and public distances. They vary in the degree of their closeness between people, the first involving body contact and the last involving twenty-five feet or more of separation. Another aspect of personal space is reflected in the concept of "territory" (93). This concept was originally developed from observation of animals, but it also has useful application to humans. Many people develop a sense of special territory within the home or the work location, as well as more symbolic feelings of territory relating to fields of competence and reputation.

Perceived crowdedness and sparseness have a direct effect upon adaptation as well as an indirect one by affecting levels of distress. Which particular conditions are perceived as crowded or sparse depends greatly upon cultural values and conventions regarding interpersonal transactions (94). The perceived duration and purpose of the density exposure also affects adaptive behavior, both directly and indirectly. Very high density conditions, such as occur in a rush-hour subway train or in a packed football stadium can be well tolerated for short durations if the purpose of the exposure is highly valued by the individual. As with all adaptive behavior, the individual's unique coping style, which has been constructed out of both constitutional and experiential factors, influences the response to density conditions. To some extent, this style may be modified by the individual as the purposes of the density exposure vary, and the problems are anticipated and encountered.

A number of social-ecological aspects of the community moderate the effect of population density upon individual psychology and behavior. These moderating aspects include the perceived physical environment and the perceived social structure. The former in-

Figure 4.5. A schematic representation of the proximate substantive factors affecting adaptation to a particular density condition. Arrows indicate the influence of factors upon the adapting individual and each other or the influence of various unspecified motivations, attitudes, and beliefs upon the proximate factors.

cludes such factors as noise, light, temperature, and arrangement of architectural space. Other factors such as institutional and role complexity, the homogeneity of values and norms, and the availability of specific community resources also play a part.

Two special features of the schema represented in Figure 4.5 deserve final mention. First, all of the proximate factors we have discussed as affecting adaptive behavior are themselves influenced by the individual's motivational, attitudinal, and belief systems, including some which are specific to density, such as the desire for either interpersonal closeness or for privacy, and many which are totally unrelated to density. Second, the specific forms of adaptive behavior have not been mentioned. This is because there is such a large number of ways of adapting to different density conditions and so many different density conditions which might be considered that an adequate discussion would be too long for this context. Suffice it to say that one important form of adaptation is geographic mobility.

Current Issues Related to Population Distribution. A major issue current in the area of population distribution involves the way that population density affects the quality of life. Many lines of research, including animal studies, sociological studies of human communities, and experimental studies of individuals under relatively controlled conditions, provide some helpful evidence (95). On the basis of work to date, certain general conclusions may tentatively be drawn (15):

   (a) For any individual there is an optimal range of population density beyond which, in either direction, he or she begins to experience distress, decreased gratification, and decreased self-esteem.

   (b) The population density range within which an individual can function well and be content is influenced by many different factors (those discussed in the previous section).

   (c) The effects of the extremes of density act to disrupt different types of behavior—for example, interpersonal behavior or task performance—beginning at different points along the density range.

(d) The range of densities to which a large population of different individuals can adapt is far wider than the range to which any single individual can adapt.

(e) Moving individuals or subpopulations along the density dimension to a point outside their usual density experience creates stress and strain that is relieved over time with adaptation to the new conditions.

Readers may tend to construe the above comments as applying solely or primarily to high-density conditions, since it is these conditions most commonly associated in people's minds with the issues of population. However, high density is only one facet of the problem. During the 1960s over one-half of the counties in the United States actually lost population (85, 96). Thus, there appears to be an important potential for adaptational problems developing at the sparsity or low density end of the range of density conditions. Of course, apart from specific, density-dependent effects, depopulation has its own set of problems associated with changes in population structure and economic and business activity (96).

Geographic Mobility:

Basic Concepts. There are numerous types of geographic mobility such as the wandering and ranging of primitive people, the impelled movement of groups of slaves, refugees, or disaster victims, and the pioneer migration of individuals and small groups to frontier areas (97). In the United States, there are currently three important types of geographic mobility: local moving, intranational migration, and international migration. The first refers to a local change of residence, while the second two refer to the crossing of some geographic or cultural boundary. Intranational migration consists of movement to either another county, state, or region within the United States; international migration involves movement into or out of the United States itself.

As with the other dynamic factors geographic mobility is expressed in terms of rates for a given population. Frequently, the rates are per 100 persons in that population, or alternatively, as a percentage. Most commonly rates are for a one-year period, but they may be for a five- or ten-year period. Geographic mobility varies considerably by age and sex. Hence, age- and sex-specific rates are frequently calculated in order to improve accuracy. Also, it is possible to calculate general and age-specific migration expectancy, using the same principles as in calculating life expectancy. There are two aspects of geographic mobility that make it somewhat different from the other dynamic demographic factors. First, it is common to have multiple moves within a one-year interval. Second, two moves—an out-move and an in-move—may bring an individual back to the point of origin. As a result, it is possible and important to consider both out-migration and in-migration rates, as well as net-migration (the difference between out- and in-migration) and gross-migration (the sum of out- and in-migration) rates.

Shelter Home, and Community: Factors in the Decision to Move. Relatively little research has been conducted by behavioral scientists on the psychology of geographic mobility, but that which has was recently reviewed and synthesized (98). In keeping with our previous discussion of decision making, it may be noted that the decision to move contains a number of subdecisions. The most important of these are whether or not to move, when to move, and where to move. Figure 4.6 presents a schematic representation of the psychological factors influencing these decisions, most specifically the decision whether or not to move. It is similar to the marriage and the childbearing schemata presented earlier in this chapter. The individual's perception of the current home and community as well as the potential home and community are both included in the geographic mobility schema. Also included are the perceived consequences of moving and the alternatives to moving which are considered. The schema also includes the perceived social network press and for and against geographic mobility, such as the pressure from family or friends to remain in an area or join them in another area. Finally, the schema includes perceived social-struc-

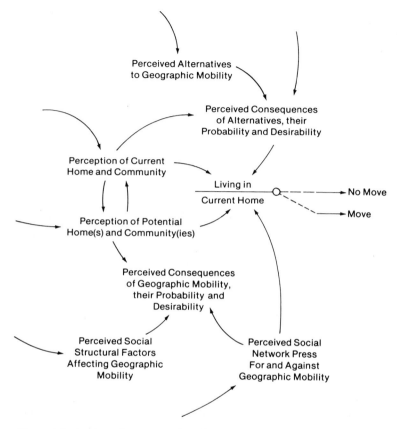

Figure 4.6. A schematic representation of the proximate substantive factors affecting a geographic mobility decision, as perceived in the context of a particular home and community. Arrows indicate the influence of factors upon the decision maker and upon each other or the influence of various unspecified motivations, attitudes, and beliefs upon the proximate factors.

tural factors affecting geographic mobility. Among these factors are those acting on the process of moving itself, such as the reliability and effectiveness of the moving industry; and those acting either in the individual's home community, or in the potential destination community, such as the local occupational, educational, or recreational resources.

The factors in the schema of Figure 4.6 are all affected by motivational, attitudinal, and belief systems. What are the major motivational factors behind the movement of people? It appears that migration is most commonly motivated by economic and vocational considerations (searching for work, changing jobs, accepting a job promotion), and next, most commonly by family life cycle considerations (getting married, expanding the family, getting divorced). Migratory streams into Florida and the southwestern United States in recent years have shown that health and retirement motivations have also become important in migration (85, 99, 100, 101). The motivation for local moves most commonly seem to be related to family, house, and neighborhood considerations (100, 102).

Current Issues in Local Moving and Migration. An important issue regarding geographic mobility is the effect that it has on the quality of life. There are at least four easily identified stress points during the process of moving. The first of these is the configuration of family, community, and occupational events, which leads to the decision to move. The second is the separation from one's family, social network, and home, which is necessary with any move. The third is the move itself, including the process of travel, lodging, transport of family possessions, and contact with unfamiliar social groups. The fourth is the experience of getting established in a new area, which includes locating a new home and achieving economic and social assimilation into the new social system.

Relatively little research has been conducted with respect to the first and the third of these stress points. With regard to the second, it has recently been demonstrated that forced relocation can cause considerable stress and grief for the lost home (103). When relocation is not forced, however, there may be relatively few psychosocial consequences (104), provided the mover is not prevented from replacing his or her lost social organization. When the individual's family remains behind, some migrant groups rely appreciably on the "stem family" as a source of support (105). With regard to the fourth stress point, the psychological and behavioral problems associated with establishment in a new area are affected by many factors. Among the most important of these are the degree of cultural difference between the new community and the community of origin, the distance of the community from the community of origin (thus affecting the ease of remigration and/or maintenance of the old interpersonal network), the extent to which the migrant has family or friends in the new community, the amount of family burden in the form of responsibilities or demands the migrant brings with him or her, the degree to which the move is associated with status mobility, the ability of the new community to respond supportively to new members, the availability of work, and the migrant's psychological and health resources.

STATUS DISTRIBUTION AND STATUS MOBILITY

The dyad of status distribution and status mobility constitute the third and final important subsystem to be considered in this chapter. As we have previously indicated, these two factors measure the structural and dynamic aspects of a population's composition. The status distribution of a population is determined by the distribution within it of a variety of demographic or social statuses. The statuses of greatest interest to demographers are: *age, sex, marital status, religion, education, occupation, race,* and *social class.* Status mobility refers to the movement of individuals in a population through social and psychological space from one status to another. Status mobility, like fertility, mortality, and geographic mobility, is a descriptive rather than a capacity concept. It refers to actual movement across statuses that can be described with rates per interval of time and not to the latent ability an individual may have to move across statuses. Thus defined, status mobility denotes what some social scientists have meant by the term "social mobility" (106).

Status Distribution

One of the most important status categories for demographers is that of *age*. It is biologically based and affects everyone. In addition, virtually all of the demographic dynamic factors such as fertility, mortality, and geographic mobility, are affected by it. The age structure of the United States has undergone some dramatic changes during the last five decades and these changes have had important effects on both social institutions and individuals. During the depression years of the 1930s, fertility rates dropped to about replacement level. After the end of World War II, during the late 1940s and 1950s, there was a marriage and baby "boom" which saw a marked reversal of the downward fertility trend of the previous half century. This "boom" was itself reversed in the late 1960s to the point where, in the early 1970s, fertility was back to replacement level. The result of this zigzag course of fertility rates has been a marked variation in the size of consecutive five-year age cohorts, with those of 1945 to 1965 substantially larger than the previous and subsequent cohorts. These changes in age-status distribution have meant that schools, colleges, and universities first had to expand and are now having to contract and consolidate or face empty classrooms and bugetary deficits. At the individual level, this pattern of age-status distribution has increased the competition in the marriage market through the marriage squeeze (107). When one age cohort is significantly smaller than the next younger age cohort and both are in the primary years of marriage, since women tend to marry men several years older than themselves, there is a relative abundance of eligible women in the marriage market. This relative unavailability of potential mates may present many women with major adaptational challenges. Of course, men will have to adapt to the same situation when the "boom" moves through to older age groups and the older cohort within the primary years of marriage becomes larger than the next younger one. This should take place beginning about 1985.

The effect of a population's age distribution on society and on individual adaptation may be further illustrated by the changes that would be brought about if the United States achieved zero population growth by maintaining a stationary population size. One result would be a very different age structure from what currently exists. The mean age would change from the current one of about twenty-eight to one of about forty. The proportion of those under fifteen years of age would change from 30 percent to about 20 percent. There probably would be a shift of aggregate values, beliefs, and behavioral traits away from those associated with youth and toward those associated with middle and late life. It seems likely that other alterations in society secondary to zero population growth would include changes in the rate of social change, the processes of job advancement, the importance of job security, and the types of educational and recreational resources available.

In a no-growth society, one subpopulation that would face special adaptation problems is the group sixty-five years of age and over (108). There would be over one-third more women than men in that age group compared with today. Fewer of both of the sexes would have living children, and of those who did, more would have only one surviving child. Also, fewer of them would have living grandchildren and, because of the overall decrease in fertility, fewer would have living siblings. In general, the older living Americans of the no-growth society would be more likely to be without families in the sense of having no living relatives. As a result, more of them would be living alone, more would be living in age-segregated communities, and more would be living in institutions.

The distribution of other statuses in the population of the United States has equally important adaptational effects. For example, *racial status* confers obvious and well-recognized problems upon those who are members of a minority race. In the United States, blacks in particular have been concerned with the genocidal issues, which are potentially present in any family planning or population regulation program (109). Concern has reached high levels, especially among black men, in spite of the fact that current evidence indicates that any changes in the black subpopulation over the next seventy-five years will, if they occur at all, be small and most probably in the direction of a proportional increase. There are other status categories where being a "minority" presents a special adaptational challenge. Examples include being an unmarried adult, being a childless adult, and being a career woman. These three statuses are all different from the status of race, sex, and age in that they are likely, at least to some degree, to occur as a result of selection by the individual. This can change the adaptational process, both in the sense that individuals have a different psychological investment in something they have selected and in the sense that it is usually possible for individuals to select themselves out of such statuses.

Status Mobility

Of the demographically important status categories subject to individual decision making, apart from those we have already discussed in the earlier sections of this chapter, the two of greatest importance in the United States are education and occupation. These represent, respectively, the broad behavior domains of education and self-development in the first case, and subsistence, production, and occupation in the second. As with the other broad behavior domains we have discussed, it is possible with each of these status categories to develop a more or less detailed schema of the substantive factors entering into decision making. However, because of space limitations and the fact that such schemata would be very similar in form to those represented in Figures 4.1, 4.2, and 4.6, we will not present additional figures or detailed discussion here. Suffice it to say that the motivations, attitudes, and beliefs of individuals, their perceptions of the available options and the consequences of selecting those options, and their perceptions of the social setting all influence their decisions with regard to education and occupation.

Education is becoming an increasingly prevalent and important option for everyone in the United States. In October 1974, at least one in every four persons in this country was enrolled in school, not including students in technical or vocational school, or those in adult education classes (110). Changes that have taken place in school enrollment patterns between 1950 and 1974 demonstrate that school attendance has shown the greatest increase during those periods in life when attendance is voluntary and therefore more completely subject to decision making. There was almost no increase during this interval in the percentage of children between the ages of six and fifteen who were enrolled in regular school. However, for children under six years of age, the enrollment rate increased by about 50 percent, and for adolescents and young adults sixteen to twenty-nine years of age, enrollment increased by 80 percent. The latter increase was most marked among women. Other current patterns of education have important implications. Over 80 percent of contemporary youth are completing high school. Of those who do complete high school, less than 20 percent plan not to attend any additional college or school (111). Although one-half of college students are eighteen to twenty-one years of age, those twenty-five years old and over make up approximately one-third of all college students (110). There is increased enrollment in two-year and community colleges, where being a part-time student and attending college while married are becoming more prevalent. In addition, high schools and universities have widely accepted the legitimacy of students interrupting their education in order to pursue an alternative activity for a planned interval. Finally, graduate and professional training programs are becoming far more accepting of women and minority applicants. All of these patterns of change suggest that education is becoming an option for more people, that it is not being pursued in a lockstep fashion at one point in the life course, but rather distributed over an increasingly large portion thereof, and that it is being admixed with other family, occupational, and recreational pursuits. In short, its timing and nature have become subject to greatly increased voluntary decision making.

Occupational status mobility has traditionally been measured in two ways, intergenerationally and intragenerationally. The former has commonly been measured by the change of occupation from father to son, the latter by the change from an individual's first job to the current one. As might be expected, research in the United States has indicated that there is considerable occupational mobility both across and within generations and that the degree of mobility varies according to the occupation initially held by the father or by the individual (112). The occurrence and type of occupational mobility are based upon decisions about whether to enter the labor force, whether to work full time or part time, what job to take, whether to change jobs, and whether to leave the labor force. In recent decades all of these decisions have been faced with increasing frequency by women. For example, between 1950 and 1973, overall labor-force participation by women rose by over 30 percent. It rose by over 80 percent for married women who were living with their husbands, and by almost 300 percent for married women with preschool children (113). The reasons for these changes are numerous. They include greater educational achievement by women in the past several decades; greater fertility control, which has allowed the postponement of marriage and the postponement of childbearing for many women; greater child-care support services, which have allowed women with young children to work; greater ideological support for women who seek and maintain independence and autonomy through occupational activities; and an increase in the United States economy of service-related jobs, traditionally occupied by women.

Other current social trends in the occupational area are affecting both men and women. Many employers now recognize the increase in individual well-being and in job efficiency that occurs when working hours are flexible and the job structured so that it may be easily integrated with family, educational, and leisure activities. In addition, new ways to work are being developed. An example is job sharing, where two individuals share one full-time job and prorate staff benefits according to the percentage of the time worked by each. There is also greater recognition that an individual may appropriately pursue two or more careers consecutively. Thus, someone who has mastered one area and performed well in it for a decade or more may decide to completely alter his or her career path. Finally, there is increased recognition of the legitimacy of ordering educational, occupational, and family activities and commitments in different ways, either concurrently or consecutively. This means that some women may finish high school, then bear and raise their children, and then go back to school or work, while others may complete their education first, then initiate their work or pursue their careers, and later begin their families. Of course, a third alternative is for some to simultaneously raise their families and begin their work after completing their education. Although all three of these patterns have occurred in the past, they have been less a matter of free choice than is now beginning to be the case. Now, when women look at occupational options, they are more likely to select the one that best fits in with their overall life-course planning. Thus, although it is true that free choice has been limited in significant ways by unemployment and related constraints during the 1970s, it appears that the general effect of most current trends in both job design and occupational selection has been in the direction of increased voluntary decision making by individuals, with less constraint by social structure and social norm.

SUMMARY

In this chapter we continue the discussion of individual decision making and adaptation as they are relevant to population with an emphasis upon their *substantive* aspects. We examine what decisions and adaptations are made and what the underlying motivations, attitudes, and beliefs are within those broad domains of behavior which have an important bearing on the population regulation system. These domains include: union and reproduction; self-care and self-preservation; maintenance of shelter, home, and community; subsistence, production, and occupation; and development, socialization, and education.

The analysis within the chapter proceeds in three primary sections, each one dealing with a subgroup of the seven major dynamic and structural demographic factors. Each subgroup appears to comprise a natural demographic subsystem. We begin with a section dealing with individual decision making and adaptation as it relates to the triad of fertility, mortality, and size. Next we move to a consideration of the same individual behaviors as they relate to the dyad of geographic distribution and geographic mobility. Finally, we consider individual decision making and adaptation as they relate to the dyad of status distribution and status mobility. Within each of these main sections of the chapter there are three important steps in our analysis. First, we introduce and discuss the basic demographic concepts that are relevant to each of the particular sections. Second, we examine the important substantive psychological factors that appear to influence decisions and adaptations within the respective behavior domains. In a number of cases, these factors and their relationships are represented in a schematic illustration. Third, we discuss the important current social issues relevant to the respective sections. Throughout the chapter the organizing principle is our effort to describe and analyze the linkages between the substance of individual decisions and the dynamic demographic factors of fertility, mortality, geographic and status mobility, and between the structural demographic factors of size, geographic and status distribution, and the substance of individual adaptation. It is the analysis of these sets of linkages that constitute the meaning of the terms psychodemography and demopsychology.

CULTURE, INSTITUTIONS, AND POPULATION PSYCHOLOGY

5

The culture of a society reflects the accumulation through generations of the artifacts, knowledge, beliefs, and values through which individuals in that society have dealt with the world (1). Culture influences individual decisions in two ways. First, it determines, in part, the options that individuals have and the constraints upon those options; and second, culture also helps to shape the form of individual thinking about these options (2). Because culture influences both the substantive issues about which decisions are made and the way they are made, explanation and prediction of individual behavior cannot be removed from the culture in which it occurs. Olsen defines culture as a relatively unified set of shared ideas associated with patterns of social order within the process of social organization (3). These patterns of social order—the informal and formal rules that govern human interaction—are the institutions of society. The family, schools, corporations, governments, and peer groups provide examples of social institutions. Each has its own norms or working rules that in part reflect the culture of the society and in part distinguish it from other institutions.

When studying a culture and its institutions, the units of analysis are the interactions among individuals rather than the individual as such. In the study of human behavior we often encounter the individualistic fallacy, that is the attempt to explain individual behavior without reference to the situation, the institution, or the culture in which the individual is imbedded. Because different cultures and institutions, like different species, evolve and adapt through time, cultural or institutional phenomena are more than the sum of all individual actions at one point in time; they cannot be explained by simply summing all individual actions. The whole is more than the sum of its parts. Institutions provide roles for their membership (for example, those of mother, daughter, citizen, student, employee, patient, counselor). These roles have two closely related consequences for individuals. First, roles provide guidelines for action. Each time individuals enter an institutionalized situation, if they are familiar with the working rules, they know what actions are appropriate. For example, when someone changes doctors, he or she knows that upon entering the doctor's office he or she should go to the receptionist, fill out a brief medical history, take a seat, and expect to wait. Institutionalized roles eliminate much of the trial-and-error searching for appropriate actions.

Just as roles provide guidelines for our actions, they give regularity and predictability to our social interactions. Social roles in this way aid all of us in anticipating, predicting, and interpreting the actions of other persons with whom we interact. For example, when the nurse ushers the patient into a small room where the doctor's examination will take place and requests the patient to remove all clothing, the patient is able to "understand" these requests and their meaning. If this same person went to a minister for counseling and the same requests were made, the individual's reaction to and interpretation of the requests would likely be quite different!

Because institutions provide the working rules that guide the interpretation of action and interaction, they exert considerable control over individuals. Some rules, because they occur again and again, become accepted as "right" and are internalized—that is, these rules are accepted by individuals as their own personal standards of action. These norms and role expectations are not just learned, but are incorporated by individuals into their motivational, attitudinal, and belief systems. They abide by these rules not because of immediate external forces or rational decisions, but because they want to (3).

Institutions provide a second type of control over individual actions through the process of identification of the individual with an organization. An individual will accept the working rules or standards of an organization from a desire to establish a relationship with that organization. These working rules may not become internalized, but no overt, external controls such as the threat of sanction are necessary. Examples of this type of acceptance of institutional rules are ubiquitous. Students adopt the dress code of the group of which they are members or wish to become members. Persons moving into a suburb that is strongly Republican or those working in a conservatively oriented corporation may choose to support the Republican Party, while persons moving into a Democratic neighborhood or those joining a liberally oriented sociology department may choose to adopt the Democratic Party. The rules of etiquette are examples of working rules that have been institutionalized to provide persons with guidelines for their social actions and to give regularity and predictability to social interaction. For some persons these rules may be internalized and used as a means of judging themselves and others; for others these rules may be complied with on the basis of expediency.

When individuals internalize the norms and rules of an institution, their freedom (range of options) is narrowed because alternative courses of action are not considered. Institutions also limit freedom by making certain options so costly as to be, for all intents and purposes, irrelevant. The current emphasis on individualism has increased the options available to individuals through the "deinstitutionalization" of society. This process, coupled with the increases in technology, has acted to enlarge social and technological freedom in many areas. However, the increase in options may, or may not, actually increase freedom because each new option makes greater demands on the ego for integration. As the discussion of the eight "vulnerable stages" in the sexual careers of women indicates, dramatic changes occur in life roles that often reduce the ability of persons to decide effectively. If there are too many options for the ego to integrate successfully, not only is ineffective decision making probable, but also the level of anxiety may rise to the point where individuals wish to "escape from freedom" (4).

Although culture, institutions, and roles influence human behavior and thereby constrain it, this control does not necessarily reduce the quality of life. Human beings are born into the process of collective action and it is only through social interaction that Homo sapiens become "human." As John R. Commons so succinctly pointed out in *The Economics of Collective Action,*

> Collective action means more than mere "control" of individual action. It means liberation and expansion of individual action; thus, collective action is literally the means to liberty. The only way in which "liberty" can be obtained is by imposing duties on others who might interfere with the activity of the "liberated" individual. The American people obtained liberty for the slaves by imposing duties on the slave-owners.(5)

If blacks are free to live, eat, and lodge wherever they choose, then whites are not free to exclude. If a woman and her doctor are subject to fines or imprisonment if the doctor performs an abortion, the freedom of both is limited. Conversely, the "liberalization of abortion" limits the freedom of the fetus.

Institutions can also encourage freedom and expand the options available to individuals. If society values the questioning of social norms and the critical examination of institutions, and if it sets up institutions to encourage such questioning, then it is more probable that persons will extend their freedoms and options. The constitutional protections of free speech, free press, and free assembly are examples of working rules designed to expand liberty. The norm of academic freedom is valued because educational institutions are supposedly established not only to socialize students to the existing norms of society, but also to help them critically examine those norms through the advancement of knowledge. The continuing tension between these two duties of education is symptomatic of the conflict between maintaining sufficient order for liberty and ensuring that such order does not destroy liberty and the adaptive ability of a particular social order (6).

INSTITUTIONAL EFFECTS ON POPULATION DECISIONS

In Chapter 3 we described a general decision model that we believe is appropriate to individual decision making, and in Chapter 4 this model was used to examine and explain population decisions related to marriage, childbearing, mortality, and geographic and status mobility. In each case important variables included the motivational, attitudinal, and belief systems of the individual, the perceived social structural factors related to the decision, the perceived social network pressures related to the decision, the perceived alternatives to any given option, and the perceived consequences of each option and its alternatives. As the introductory section of this chapter indicates, the individual's motivational, attitudinal, and belief systems are strongly influenced by the culture and its institutions. In addition, the perceived social structural and network factors, the perceived alternatives, and the perceived consequences of all options are influenced by the cultural and institutional setting.

Davis and Blake in their article, "Social Structure and Fertility: An Analytic Model," outline a model that describes the institutional factors determining fertility rates (7). According to this model, fertility rates are a function of the eleven variables associated with exposure to sexual intercourse, conception, and gestation shown in Table 5.1. It is clear that variables 1, 2, 3a, 4, 6, 8, 9, and 11 are strongly affected by the institutional norms and incentives of a particular culture. The individual's motivations, attitudes, and beliefs about the appropriate age of entry into a sexual union are highly conditioned by the institutions and their norms related to premarital sex, kinship, property, and the available alternatives to marriage. The perceived consequences of a sexual union are also influenced by these same institutions. For example, in Ireland immediately following the potato famine, it became socially unacceptable for a male to marry until he had sufficient land or other prop-

TABLE 5.1

I.   *Factors Affecting Exposure to Intercourse ("Intercourse Variables")*.
A.   Those governing the formation and dissolution of unions in the reproductive period:
   (1) age of entry into sexual unions;
   (2) permanent celibacy: proportion of women never entering sexual unions;
   (3) amount of reproductive period spent after or between unions
      (a) when unions are broken by divorce, separation, or desertion
      (b) when unions are broken by death of husband.

B.   Those governing the exposure to intercourse within unions:
   (4) voluntary abstinence;
   (5) involuntary abstinence (from impotence, illness, unavoidable or temporary separations);
   (6) coital frequency (excluding periods of abstinence).

II. *Factors Affecting Exposure to Conception ("Conception Variables")*:
   (7) fecundity or infecundity, as affected by involuntary causes;
   (8) use or nonuse of contraception
      (a) by mechanical and chemical means
      (b) by other means;
   (9) fecundity or infecundity, as affected by voluntary causes (sterilization, subincision, medical treatment, etc.).

III. *Factors Affecting Gestation and Successful Parturition ("Gestation Variable")*:
   (10) fetal mortality from involuntary causes;
   (11) fetal mortality from voluntary causes.

erty to support a wife and family, and the laws did not allow either the subdivision of lands or joint ownership of land between a father and an adult son. This meant that marriage would be postponed for the eldest son until the father either died or was willing to relinquish all legal rights to the land. The younger sons were given strong incentives to migrate under these rules because they had little hope of obtaining sufficient property to marry. Thus, the institutions surrounding kinship and property discouraged early sexual unions and thereby exerted a strong negative influence on fertility (7).

In contrast to the Irish kinship and property institutions, many traditional socioeconomic systems encourage early sexual unions through an extended family system in which the parents of a child maintain their authority even after the child is married and has children. This means that if the culture is patrilineal, when a male marries, his wife and children extend the property and authority of the son's father (8). In addition, in societies where infant mortality is high and economic security in old age depends on the support of the parents by the child, persons cannot afford the loss of fertility which would accompany late entry into sexual unions.

Work institutions may also influence the age of entry into sexual unions. Where wage-earning opportunities are limited to males by cultural norms, the incentive for women to delay the age of entrance may be decreased. A possible example recently of a reduction in this influence is the increasing age of American women when they marry. As they have more educational and employment opportunities, the necessity of marrying to obtain acceptable status and roles has been reduced. These same opportunities may also affect the individual's motivational, attitudinal, and belief systems and the perceived consequences related to the frequency of intercourse, the use of contraception and sterilization, and the frequency of abortion.

As we have indicated above, mortality rates and institutions are also related through a series of intermediate variables that govern an individual's exposure to death and his or her accessibility to methods of preventing or delaying death. Although these intermediate variables are more numerous and therefore not as readily categorized as the eleven intermediate fertility variables of Davis and Blake, their relationships to institutional factors are well documented in the actuarial tables of insurance companies. When we consider geographic and status mobility and their relationship to institutional factors, the intermediate variables are even less readily categorized. In part, this is because there is no simple biological funnel, relatively narrow in the case of fertility and relatively wide in the case of mortality, through which these variables converge. When dealing with fertility the decision process and institutional influences are largely funneled through their effect upon the probability of the single physiological event—the combination of the two gametes. After conception only two intermediate variables, voluntary and involuntary fetal mortality, remain. With mortality there are many more physiological events that can cause death and therefore a correspondingly higher number of variables and combination of variables that can influence health-compromising behavior that lead to death. Geographic and social mobility are not physiologically determined. They may be related to physiological characteristics (for example, a higher proportion of men than women fill the occupational positions of higher status), but this association is directly related to cultural and institutional norms rather than to physiological imperatives. This lack of a biological funnel for geographic and status mobility does not, however, mean that decision processes and the influence of institutions upon them are dissimilar.

THE FAMILY AND POPULATION PSYCHOLOGY

The family undoubtedly constitutes the single most influential institution in the determination of individual population decisions and the demographic patterns found throughout society. Many sociologists and anthropologists argue not only that the family is the most important institution related to population factors, but also that without the institution of the family "society" would not be possible (9). Social scientists using the structural-functionalist paradigm stress the importance of the family in fulfilling the functions of social placement of the members of society, regulating social alliances, and socializing the young for future roles—particularly sexual, marital, and parental roles (10). In Chapter 2 we saw how the institution of the family has evolved and adapted from a set of relationships functional in gathering-hunting society to different sets of relationships that were suited to agricultural and industrial societies. The institution of the family continues to adapt and is currently responding to and influencing changes in the roles of men and women in marriage, child rearing, and employment. These changes represent fundamental alterations in the patterns of dominance within the family and the norms governing interactions among family members. Finally, individual attitudes and behaviors with regard to achievement, political participation, and tolerance toward diverse ideas are largely products of early socialization by the family (11).

Both the determination of desired family size and the ability to achieve the desired number of children are heavily influenced by the structure of family relationships. As indicated above, property and kinship norms influence intermediate fertility variables such as age of entry into sexual unions, the dissolution of these unions, and exposure to intercourse. However, these broad social norms and legal requirements that constrain and orient the institution of the family are not the only family factors influencing fertility patterns. Communication processes and role differentiation among family members are also important influences on the intermediate variables that determine fertility. Rainwater found that among working-class families, those husbands and wives with more effective communication and greater equality in family decision making were more effective contraceptors (11). Beshers discovered similar patterns in his analysis of fertility and family planning in Puerto Rico (12).

As noted above, the family plays an important part in socializing children to various marital role expectations. Although these expectations are also influenced by the larger culture, the media, and various peer-group subcultures, the first concepts of appropriate husband and wife roles are derived from the individual's parents. For the female, the mother's influence especially appears to be one of the most important sources of the norms about marriage (10). These childhood acquired role expectations then became part of the working rules governing the expected patterns of behavior within the family. These rules influence the level of equality between marriage partners, the amount and type of communication that is likely to occur, whether or not and under what conditions the wife will enter the labor force, and the many other social interactions, both within the family and outside it, that affect fertility by influencing exposure to intercourse, to conception, and to gestation.

Household Decision Making and the New Home Economics

The emergence of household economics from the "Chicago School" of microeconomic theory has led to some of the more extensive and exciting debates both within and among the disciplines of demography, sociology, and economics. Briefly stated (and much oversimplified) household economics, as it has been developed by Gary Becker, Theodore Schultz, and many of their students and colleagues, treats fertility decisions as economic decisions. In other words, they assume that a couple or family will calculate the expected benefits and costs of a child, as they do with other "goods," before deciding whether or not to make a "purchase" (13). In addition, household economics treats the family as a single decision unit in much the same way that the economic theory of the firm treats a firm as the single decision unit even though it is made up of many individuals. Other critical elements of household economics are its consideration of time as a valuable good and its examination of quality versus quantity in decisions related to family size (14, 15).

Undoubtedly, the most criticized element of household economics is its treatment of the decision to have a child in economic terms. For many sociologists such an approach appears ridiculous and not to be taken seriously. Udry is typical of this view:

> For the individuals deciding on parenthood, the fact cannot be avoided that *every decision to have a child means a decision to accept a lower standard of living in return for the satisfactions of parenthood.* If parenthood were strictly a rational economic matter, few of us would ever have been born. (10, p. 391)

Such a view, however, misunderstands the theory. The economic theory of fertility does not suggest that the income produced by the child must be greater than the cost of raising it. Rather the theory suggests that the total expected benefits the child will provide, which include both tangible economic goods such as economic security in old age and less tangible "goods" such as the production of reciprocal caring, the achievement of immortality via the offspring, and the meeting of parental and peer expectations, must outweigh the total costs, such as income forgone, time spent, and possible grief. The decision to have a child means that other possibilities must be forgone; but the decision to purchase flowers for one's spouse, not to work on Sunday, or any other similar "purchase" means a decision to accept a lower standard of living—that is, to forgo other options in exchange for the expected benefits of a pleased spouse or a day of leisure.

Although there are excellent reasons to view children as different types of purchases than consumer durables (16), the assumption that persons weigh the economic costs of an additional family member seems to be justified. A far greater difficulty with this assumption is the definition of "family." The economic models of fertility treat the "family" in a static rather than a dynamic fashion. For example, a couple is often assumed to decide upon the total number of children, and their timing, at or before their marriage and without ever reconsidering these decisions, except perhaps in the case of the death of a child (17). Having made this assumption, the family can then be considered to include all potential members and their utilities for various goods. Although the assumption may be useful for the purposes of model specification, it is certainly unrealistic, and current researchers working with these models are attempting to relax this assumption while maintaining models that can be used in empirical studies of fertility.

The assumption that the family acts as a single unit leads us to examine the importance of reciprocal caring. In most families, one spouse derives pleasure from the pleasure of the other, parents derive pleasure from their children's happiness, and vice versa. Given this common type of combined utility in the family, decisions are made differently than would be the case in the absence of reciprocal caring. A parent may give up certain goods in order that the child may have others. The single-unit assumption also makes it unnecessary to separate family utilities into individual-member utilities. In the family, there may be a division of labor in the production of goods and services, but there is joint consumption. For this reason the single-unit assumption is, in many respects, a far more realistic view than the attempt to treat each family member as an individual producer and consumer—especially since there is joint ownership of many goods.

A particularly useful contribution toward understanding population decisions has been the inclusion of the value of time in the calculations that both the individual and the family unit must make. Although many people, particularly ecologists, would not agree with Theodore Schultz that "the ultimate economic limit of affluence (economic growth) is not the scarcity of material goods but the scarcity of human time for consumption" (14), persons certainly do value their time. This prizing of time becomes particularly important in considering the effects of both husbands and wives working, and the issues of quantity versus quality in childbearing.

In the United States, as in many other countries, there is a strong negative relationship between participation in the labor force by a woman and her completed family size. When a woman has a child this usually means an extended period of nonparticipation in employment outside the home. As a result, the cost of a child is not only its consumption of goods and services, which must be purchased outside the family, but also the income that would have been produced had the mother remained in the labor force (18). These costs, the forgone opportunities that must be sacrificed in choosing one thing rather than another, are known as "opportunity costs" (19). For example, if a woman is earning $10,000 per year and each child requires her to leave the labor force for three years, then the cost of the child must include the $30,000 of income that would have been earned if the child had not been born. Thus, we may expect that should salary inequities between males and females decrease and employers be effectively prohibited from sex discrimination in employment, the costs of children would rise and, *ceteris paribus*, fertility rates would fall.

Beyond linking female employment and fertility, the microeconomic theory of fertility helps explain several other relationships between demographic behavior and family characteristics. Researchers from several disciplines have found that the number of siblings a child has and its place in the birth order are related to its lifetime earnings, educational level, ability (as measured by I.Q.

tests) and health, even after the effects of socioeconomic status have been accounted for (20, 21, 22). These investigations tend to indicate that firstborn children and children with fewer siblings have an advantage over children born in the middle of the birth order and children with more siblings. A partial explanation of these differences is the greater level of investment that the parents can make in each child. Given the limitations of available resources for investment, for any given family the larger the number of children, the fewer the resources available to each child. These investments include parental instruction, formal education outside the family, nutrition, and inherited wealth. Similarly, it is easier for parents to invest greater time and energy in the firstborn child because during the period between its birth and the birth of later children all the time and other resources available for investment in children can be devoted to that child alone.

Leibowitz has demonstrated that parental investment of time in a child is positively related not only to the early educational achievement of the child, but also to the earnings of the child over its entire lifetime (22). Figure 5.1 schematizes the different types of investments in children and how these may be expected to relate to the child's education and earning capacity. As Figure 5.1 implies, the quantity and the quality of investments by the family in a child are both important. If these are mutually reinforcing, and are patterned along class lines, they become the instruments through which the family structure contributes to the determination of social stratification and social mobility in a society. A recent study comparing the social mobility of Japanese Americans and Mexican Americans has indicated how this may occur (23). The authors, using completed family size as a surrogate measure for the ability to make investments in children, demonstrate not only how larger family sizes may create a comparative disadvantage for children within a generation, but also how this comparative disadvantage is compounded across generations. This occurs because in the first generation the children from smaller families receive more education since their parents can better afford to send them to college. These same children are likely to inherit more money since there

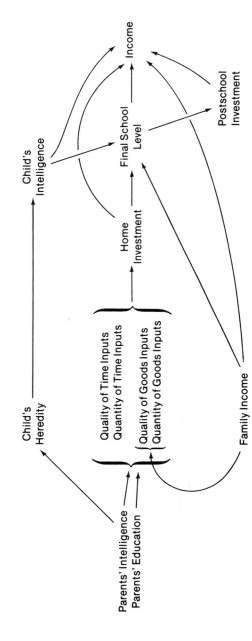

Figure 5.1. A schematic representation of some of the factors affecting a child's educational and earning achievements. The arrows indicate the direction of influence between factors. (Adapted from Leibowitz, 22.)

are fewer children to share the inheritance. These children, following the schema in Figure 5.1, can, in turn, afford to make higher investments in their own children if they maintain the small family size. Thus, over successive generations, if one ethnic group has a small family norm and the other a large one, the two groups will find themselves at different levels in the social class structure within a few generations, even though they began in similar class positions, with similar social disadvantages.

Using the framework of household economics may also help explain family interactions in migration decisions. In the United States, men's careers have tended to be given a higher priority in the family than the wife's career. This is, of course, partially explained by the role expectations that persons have internalized when they enter the marriage—the father as "breadwinner," the mother as "child raiser" and/or "facilitator" to the husband's profession. The wife tends to be categorized by the position of her husband. As a result, it is commonly a consideration of the man's career that determines job-related geographic mobility.

In the family decision process, how difficult is it to obtain equality of career roles if the husband and wife desire it? That is, if the husband and wife are aware of these role expectations and decide that they are inequitable or for other reasons decide not to accept the norm, what are the social, psychological, and economic costs for breaking the norm? Komorovsky in her examination of male and female views toward equality of career objectives shows that when their wives are perceived as intellectually superior or as earning greater amounts the men are perceived by others as less masculine and may perceive themselves as less masculine (24, 25). However, even if the couple can overcome these stereotypes, there are likely to be true economic costs if both members share equally the tasks of "breadwinner" and "homemaker." First, women do receive lower pay for the same level and quality of work. As a result, if the male must reduce his time in the labor force by the same amount that the woman increases her participation, there is likely to be a net loss. This loss can be further compounded by the double taxation that the Social Security system places on families where both spouses work and their combined income is greater than $15,300, the maximum income for each individual that is subject to social security withholding. In addition, social stereotyping of sex roles has led to a system where the wife's education can be used to substantially benefit her husband's occupation and earnings through her supportive role ("behind every successful man . . ."). In contrast, the husband has a more difficult time in finding socially acceptable ways of supporting his wife's career (26). Further, if the wife's employment has been interrupted for childbearing, then her skills depreciate and her wages are even lower because of the interruptions in work (18). Finally, if the family has moved to allow the husband to change jobs, or if he was transferred by his company and the wife accompanied him, it is likely that while his move was a vertical move and meant an increase in earnings, the wife, even if she entered the labor force immediately after the move, misses steps on the employment ladder if she is forced to begin with a new company and lose many of the benefits accumulated from her previous employment (18).

All of the above forces act to give preferential treatment to the husband's occupation and career advancement. Thus, if husband and wife decide to allocate time spent in career activities and home activities on the basis of economic costs or probable social costs, and both have competing demands on their time, on the basis of comparative advantage the husband will pursue career objectives more frequently than the wife. Constrained by this system, in the United States which gives priority in many different ways to the husband, definition of what is fair and equitable within the family will be difficult for the husband and wife to resolve, while what is monetarily profitable and socially acceptable will not.

Although the existing social and occupational norms and rewards encourage patterns of spatial and occupational mobility centered around the husband's labor-force participation, there is evidence that when the wife's income is nearly equal to or greater than the husband's, the family's decisions concerning migration are affected substantially. When the wife's income provides 50 percent or more of the combined income, the propensity of the family to migrate is considerably reduced (27). This reduction probably reflects the difficulty of finding two new jobs in a new location and the increased "power" of the wife to prevent a disrupting move. The combined utility of the entire family is also reflected in the reduced geographic mobility of families with children, especially children in secondary school (28, 29). Presumably this decrease in mobility is caused by the desire of the family not to disrupt the social life and schooling of their children. Seidenberg has indicated how disrupting geographic mobility can be to family members other than the one for whom the move meant career advancement (30). Almost all the data concerning geographic mobility suggests that reciprocal caring among family members leads to quite different decisions than decisions occurring in the absence of such motivation.

Although the above discussion of the family has stressed an economic perspective, it is important to emphasize that an "economic" explanation does not compete with anthropological, sociological, or psychological explanations. We have used an economic paradigm primarily in order to point out that the constraints which culture and institutions place on either family or individual decisions make an economic explanation possible. Freedoms are never unlimited, whether they are sociological, technological, biological, or psychological. Because norms have been internalized, many options are never considered; other options are closed by social pressures. The impact of the family institution on individual decisions cannot be adequately understood unless consideration is given to the cultural, economic, and social constraints it imposes, and unless we develop a framework of the decision process allowing for altruism within the family and the fact that, through the process of love (reciprocal caring), one family member's satisfactions are also another's. Without this explicit recognition, policy recommendations designed to effect population-related decisions are likely to be highly misleading.

EDUCATIONAL INSTITUTIONS AND POPULATION PSYCHOLOGY

After the family, educational institutions may be the most influential in the entire range of population-related decisions. Because

most individuals in the United States are exposed to formal education from ages six to sixteen, with the majority enrolled for even
longer periods, educational institutions have great potential for establishing norms, developing ways of thinking about the world,
structuring perceptions of reality, and accomplishing general socialization for participation in society. In addition, because educational
institutions are subject to more direct governmental control than is
the family, the potential for introducing society-wide change is
greater.

The use of school busing to achieve integration provides only
one of numerous examples of government attempts to use educational institutions to promote social change. Because of the preemi-
nent position of education, many of the most heated political controversies revolve around its appropriate role. The long and
continuing conflict over the presence of prayers and sex education
in school systems gives evidence of the public's perception, if not
the reality, of the influence that educational institutions can have on
the attitudes, values, and behaviors of individuals. Controversies
over sexism in textbooks and past and present debates over whether
communists, atheists, or homosexuals should be expelled from the
teaching profession give further evidence of the fears and expectations of society concerning the potential influence of education.

General Orientations and Specific Attitudes

In discussing the role of education in the process of population regulation, it is important to differentiate the specific role of educational institutions in developing attitudes and behaviors toward
quite specific objects such as contraception, sex roles, and the desirability of mobility, from the general role education has in developing the ability to seek, process, and utilize information. Education is not a "thing"; it is a category within which are included a
variety of activities. These activities include learning (or not learning) specific skills, such as reading, writing, and mathematics; obtaining general information about subjects such as history, religion,
and government; and interacting with peer groups and figures of authority outside the family. All of these activities and their interac-

tions with the rest of life's experience affect the development of a general set of expectations and orientations to life.

In the literature on the determinants of fertility, perhaps the most fully investigated relationship is that between education and fertility (31). Although the strength of the relationship varies from country to country, the evidence is quite consistent that greater education of potential parents increases their contraceptive usage and the spacing of their children, and decreases their completed family size (26, 27, 28, 32). These family-planning behaviors appear to be associated with the common effects which education has, regardless of country or culture, on attitudes and behavioral dispositions. Among these effects are openness to new experience, readiness to experience social change, the dispositions to hold opinions, an awareness of the diversity of attitudes and opinions that exist in society, the orientation toward planning, and an awareness of and respect for the dignity of others (33).

Most people positively value the general orientations described above and regard them as what may be expected from a liberating education that expands psychological freedom. Presumably these general orientations to life are the result of experiences that students have in school and the information to which they are exposed. It is difficult, however, to attribute these orientations to the norms and rules that pattern interactions among students, faculty, and administration. For example, sexism in text books has been quite pronounced (34, 35). Also, most schools are not characterized by either flexibility of rules or equality of authority. In fact, the educational systems in the United States and other countries have been severely attacked for the regularity of their authority patterns, their inequality, and their stress on conventional values and norms (36). How then does the educational process lead to openness, acceptance of diversity, and respect for others in spite of these limitations of the school system? A partial answer is that education provides the necessary skills, such as reading, mathematics, and verbal ability, that allow individuals to broaden their own experiences. Certainly the differential rates of migration of the more and less educated members of society is partially based upon their differential ability to occupy positions requiring skills obtained from educational institutions. Similarly, to use contraception effectively, people must be aware that it is available and know how to obtain information concerning its use. Previous research concerning contraceptive use indicates that effective users have more and better information, while nonusers often have mistaken beliefs about their harmful effects (37, 38, 39).

Beyond the provision of information and skills, educational institutions seem to provide individuals with a sense of efficacy and willingness to plan. Rather than leaving things to "fate" or "the will of God," the educated individual acquires a more active orientation (33). It seems likely that as individuals learn more about the processes of nature, technology, and society there is a spillover to everyday aspects of life, with the result that fewer things seem beyond his or her ability to control. Other effects that schooling may have are learning to live by schedules, and the meaning of "time." These behaviors further facilitate the ability to plan and to make effective population-related decisions.

Education and Freedom

In the introductory chapter we discussed three different types of freedom: (1) biological and technological, (2) psychological, and (3) social. Educational institutions, because they both produce and disseminate knowledge, play a crucial role with respect to these freedoms. The types of research encouraged or even allowed are determined, at least in part, by social, economic and political forces. Researchers are not socially free to choose what research will be done or how it will be done; nor are educators free to teach whatever they choose. What is taught must be taught within limits established both inside and outside the educational institutions.

Research requires time and money. In the United States, and other countries as well, the availability of these resources is determined by society and often by the political system. Contemporary issues surrounding the subject of nuclear energy are in most respects typical of how educational institutions affect and are affected by the level of social and psychological freedom in society. Because of the early start and strong government funding nuclear research received during the Second World War and the nuclear arms race, many new technological options relating to nuclear energy have been developed. As a result, many physicists and other energy "experts" can currently argue that only nuclear energy can be increased to the level required to meet anticipated energy needs. Because of the large number of research grants, traineeships, and graduate fellowships provided to support the education of nuclear physicists, the United States has an abundance of persons trained to do further nuclear research and who have a strong vested interest in the continuation of nuclear research programs. It is very probable, however, that if similar funding for research and education had been devoted to solar energy, it would currently be the only "feasible" way to meet anticipated energy needs. Because of the differential availability of funds, the technological options of society have been significantly limited. Furthermore, funding of the production and dissemination of knowledge in the field of nuclear energy has greatly constrained the ability of educational institutions to evaluate alternative options with respect to their effects on social norms and freedom.

The relationship between education's role in the production and dissemination of knowledge and its role in the evaluation of social norms and the level of free decision making in society is clearly evident in the field of population. The collection of basic data by demographers provided a major impetus to the social evaluation of population levels and growth rates (40). Demographic research helped to force attention upon the consequences of abortion for both fertility and mortality. Technological advances in contraception, abortion, and sterilization created entire new sets of opportunities for both individual freedom and social control. New information on the incidence of illegitimacy, premarital sex, and venereal disease spurred the reevaluation of existing policies concerning sex education, the provision of contraception to minors, and abortion laws. Research on female employment was encouraged by the force of the women's movement and provided further substantiation of sex discrimination.

Educational institutions are not limited, however, to the production of new knowledge. They are involved with its dissemination as well. In addition, the same persons who do the research and teaching are often called upon to evaluate and even formulate legislation. Many members of the academic community move back and forth between academic and governmental positions, and many more are dependent on governmental funding (41). In such a web of information production, dissemination, and evaluation, it becomes particularly important, although all the more difficult, to ensure that the norms and procedural rules of educational institutions foster a true critique of societal issues.

THE MEDIA AND POPULATION PSYCHOLOGY

After the family and education, the institution many perceive as influencing population decisions most strongly involves the mass media. Early in population regulation research, attention was focused on the media as a means for achieving the diffusion of contraceptive information and attitude changes. As with educational institutions, the media have received close attention from all sectors of society because of their pervasiveness and the belief that they could change attitudes, beliefs, and values. Commercials using ethnic or sex-role stereotypes receive complaints from the aggrieved parties; equal time is required in political races; cigarette commercials are banned from television; and, programs during the "family hour" are highly censored. These are just a few examples indicating that society believes the media to be important determinants of attitudes and behavior.

Although the various media are believed by many to be highly influential, it has been far more difficult to actually document this influence. Study after study has shown that television and radio have not been particularly successful in affecting contraceptive behavior (42). As a means for the diffusion of innovation, the mass media have generally proven far less successful than more personal forms of communication (12). In influencing social norms or in changing attitudes, the media tend to be better suited to the reinforcement of preexisting norms and attitudes than as agents of change (43). O'Keefe, in his summary of mass communication research, lists the following conclusions consistently found in studies of the influence of mass media (43):

- (a) the media may help form attitudes toward new subjects where little prior opinion exists;
- (b) they may influence attitudes weakly held;
- (c) they may strengthen one attitude at the expense of others if all the relevant attitudes are not equally held;
- (d) they may change strongly held attitudes if new information about the environment is revealed;
- (e) they may suggest new courses of action in the pursuit of a goal already desired;
- (f) and they may frequently reinforce and strengthen previous dispositions.

One of the difficulties in understanding the role of the media in individual decision making is that they most often reflect existing norms and values rather than advocate values that are contrary to the traditional social norms. On television one rarely sees police stories that show the police as villains and the criminal as the protagonist, stories in which communism is good and capitalism bad, or stories in which extramarital sex is enjoyable while sex within marriage is dull. Newspaper editorials rarely argue for positions that are not already held by a large number of persons. For these reasons, the identification of any independent effect of the media becomes difficult. Television, radio, newspapers, and magazines do not generally introduce and advocate new ideas and values; rather they deal with the more familiar and accepted norms. *Maude* did not reach T.V. until long after the women's movement had gained substantial support outside the media; blacks did not become heroes and heroines until long after *Brown* v. *Board of Education*. The following rather than leading role of the media does not mean, however, that they are unimportant either in facilitating or inhibiting social change. The extent to which they expose persons to different ideas and customs and the way that they portray (and implicitly evaluate) these ideas and customs certainly plays an important part in expanding or restricting social and psychological freedom. Particularly in the provision of previously unperceived alternatives, the media have the opportunity to broadly expand individual freedom in decision making.

If the only women's roles that a girl sees on television or reads about in newspapers and magazines are those of wife and mother, as an adult she probably will not search for alternatives as much as if many other roles were presented to her by the media. Similarly, if individuals are exposed by the media only to information about their immediate community, they are less likely to examine the alternatives that migration might offer. Even if the media were to concentrate solely on the reinforcement of conventional norms and behavioral patterns, their influence could have significant behavioral consequences—possibly even more significant than if they devoted more time and space to the portrayal of the unusual. In her study of the effects of pornography on adolescent females, Patricia Schiller found that these females were far more likely to be ''turned on'' by the romantic content of movies, pop music, and television than by more clearly erotic pornographic materials (44). The explanation Schiller gave to these findings was that the materials that actually aroused these females were those that fitted into their role and norm expectations and fit situations in which they were likely to find themselves. The media awakened previous fantasies and feelings of ''love'' as these young women had been socialized to expect love and sexual interaction. Clearly the mass media have important consequences for individual decision making and behavior. Their most significant effect, however, appears to be the reinforcement of existing social norms rather than changing these norms. This suggests that the media may provide to the consumer cues as to what are acceptable norms during periods of rapid social change.

The Media and Attitude Change

As we have mentioned, family planning advocates have been keenly interested in the potential of the media as tools for encouraging population planning and fertility reduction. Although research results concerning the impact of media information and propaganda have not been uniform, the dominant conclusions have been that the media are neither helpful in changing attitudes toward family planning nor effective in reducing desired family size. Although some studies in the field of family planning and reproduction have shown some behavior change (42, 45), perhaps the most extensive literature on the effects of the mass media and attitude change is found in the evaluation of antismoking campaigns and other medically oriented efforts to encourage individuals to take health-maintenance steps in order to increase their life span. This research has largely supported the six general findings reported above. Particularly pronounced have been the findings that strongly held attitudes are not likely to be changed and that the media campaigns are more successful in achieving behavioral change if they are supplemented by personal communications (43, 46). These findings are quite similar to those of Freedman and Takeshita in which the best results were obtained when field workers were utilized to encourage contraceptive use (47).

Although the studies of media influence on attitude and behavior have not demonstrated dramatic changes, the general literature on attitude change would indicate that expectations to that effect would be unrealistic. The mass media are only one of many institutions that shape and constrain individuals' motivations, attitudes, and beliefs. Among these institutions the media are, perhaps, the most diffuse and the least personal. In spite of this, they are in an ideal position to provide new information to society. Although new information does not necessarily change attitudes, attitudes are rarely changed without new information. By presenting new information, the media allow potential decision makers at least to enter the stage of awareness. Subsequent experience, perhaps unrelated to media influence, may contribute to a realignment of attitudes. In this way, all three levels of freedom may be increased. On the other hand, if the media act to reinforce existing social norms, all levels of freedom, especially social freedom, may be decreased. This occurs in particular where censorship, either formal or informal, is practiced.

THE INSTITUTION OF COUNSELING AND
POPULATION PSYCHOLOGY

In addition to the family, education, and the media, another institution influencing population-related decisions and adaptions is that of counseling. However, unlike those we have discussed, the institution of counseling does not exist in a specific type of social organization; rather, it exits within a wide variety of different organizations. Counseling exists within educational organizations, social service agencies, industry, prisons, hospitals and medical clinics, and in the general community. Within specific organizational settings, counselors and counselees deal with the special problems of life associated with those settings. They may also deal with more general problems and issues in the general community setting. In all of these cases, the activities of the counselor and counselee fulfill the definition of an institution in that there is a patterned social interaction that serves certain functions, is governed by certain norms and rules, and is characterized by certain roles. The purpose of counseling is for the counselor to help the counselee with a problem, most commonly in the area of decision making or adaptation. The role of the counselor is to help and the most important tool the counselor has for reaching this goal, whether working with a situational problem or in intensive psychotherapy, is the ability to listen (48). The role of the counselee is to resolve the problem or difficulty that brought him or her to counseling. The most important way that this may be accomplished is through talking and self-discovery.

In this last respect, the institution of counseling is significantly different from others, at least in degree. In order to provide a framework for personal satisfactions, most institutions regulate and control behavior and to some extent feelings and thoughts. In the institution of counseling, however, the rules that are established and the regulation that takes place are solely for the purpose of creating a type of psychological set in the participants and a type of interpersonal relationship between or among them that will make possible the exploration and understanding of self on the part of the counselee. The major goal, therefore, is an increase in psychological freedom. Among all other institutions, education approaches this goal most closely. However, in the institution of counseling, there is the least interference through the introduction of performance expectations or imposed personal values.

There are different forms of both counseling and psychotherapy (49). In general the former is educational, situational, and problem solving in its orientation, while the latter is more exploratory, analytic, and reconstructive. To some extent, and paralleling the just cited differences, counseling focuses more on decision making, while psychotherapy focuses on adaptation. However, these differences are tenuous at best. It is the similarities between counseling and psychotherapy that are most apparent and that justify their being placed together within the same institutional category. Nothing makes this more apparent than the wide diversity of professional backgrounds leading to counseling or psychotherapeutic activities. The following helping professions spend a major portion of their time pursuing the art of counseling or psychotherapy: clinical psychologists, counseling psychologists, school psychologists, social workers, psychiatrists, pastoral counselors, and marriage and family counselors. In addition there are many other professionals and paraprofessionals who, on the basis of work experience, supplementary training, and native ability, move naturally into roles and positions that involve counseling.

All of the population-related decisions and the adaptations we discussed in Chapter 4 are the subject of special counseling efforts in the United States. Perhaps the most obvious are marriage and family counselors, educational counselors, and vocational counselors. However, many additional types of counselors actively influence population-related decision making and adaptation. For example, both psychiatrists and social workers, whether institutionally based or in private practice in the community, commonly counsel and conduct psychotherapy with individuals in crisis over the decision to marry, the decision to have a baby, the decision to divorce, what to do about an unwanted pregnancy, the inability to conceive, the decision to adopt, and many other fertility-related problems. Hospitals and clinics both commonly counsel and conduct psychotherapy with patients reacting to acute physical illness and with others adjusting to chronic disability. Both are also called on to consult and work with individuals whose character traits predispose them to unusually high levels of health-compromising behavior. There is one area where psychological clinicians are relatively inactive, although there is great need—this is the area of geographic mobility (50). Both in the community of origin and in the community of destination, psychological clinicians can provide important direct counseling services, channeled through various community organizations immediately involved with migrants.

In order to illustrate the degree to which extant counseling already deals with the wide variety of population-related personal problems, we mention here some of the major types of counseling that bear on reproduction and fertility. First, there is sex counseling, important because of the fundamental role of sexual behavior in all reproductive decision making and adaptations. Next, there is contraceptive counseling, important for the influence it may give the individual over reproductive outcomes. Since most reproduction occurs within marriage, marriage counseling is also important. It includes premarital counseling, which is aimed at helping the individual with the decision to marry, marital counseling, which is aimed at dealing with the problems and conflicts that may occur within marriage, and divorce counseling, which focuses on the decision to divorce and its associated problems. Next, there is family planning or procreational counseling, which deals with decisions and problems related to planning for children. There are several types of closely related counseling: (a) pregnancy counseling deals with the processes and problems associated with pregnancy; (b) genetic counseling deals with the decisions and problems associated with preventing the occurrence of genetically determined, undesirable characteristics in a child and with selecting genetically determined, desirable characteristics; (c) infertility counseling deals with the decisions and problems leading to and resulting from infertility; (d) adoption counseling deals with the decisions and problems associated with the problems of adoption; and (e) sterilization counseling deals with the problems associated with termination of the procreational period through sterilization; (f) problem-pregnancy counseling deals with the problems that arise as the result of an unwanted or ambivalently regarded pregnancy, which depending on the situation may take one of two special forms: abortion counseling or child-placement counseling. The length of this list itself suggests the potential impact that the institution of counseling may have on population-related decision making.

GOVERNMENTAL INSTITUTIONS AND POPULATION PSYCHOLOGY

One of the major purposes of the institutions of government is to allocate rights and duties in society and to serve as the final arbiter in disputes among individuals and institutions. In democratic societies, governmental institutions must sort out the countless, diverse, and often incompatible demands of its citizens and allocate rights and resources that reflect the desires of the majority. Although we are accustomed in most of our transactions with others to think of most of these transactions as "private," governmental institutions exert a strong influence upon the ways in which these interactions take place. For example, if your neighbor has a habit of playing his stereo while you would like to sleep, the property rights that have been determined by governmental institutions will either allow your neighbor to continue or allow you to require that he discontinue his stereo playing. The manner in which a store advertises its goods and the duties of a store to customers are also determined by the governmental distribution of rights.

One of the most important and most difficult tasks of government is the determination of rights and duties on issues of morality. Even in the absence of government it is possible for you and your neighbor to arrive at some price that you will pay him to turn down his stereo or that he will pay you to allow him to continue playing. (Who pays whom is, however, determined by the initial distribution of rights, or, in the absence of these, by might.) However, when it comes to an issue such as abortion, it is unlikely that those who consider abortion to be murder will set a price they must be paid to allow abortion to occur in the community. The woman who considers the option of abortion to be a "natural right" to determine how her body will be treated will be equally unwilling to set a price on this right. Even if each individual could set a price on the "murder" or the "natural right," because so many individuals with different prices are involved, it becomes necessary for some institution or set of institutions to decide the issue. This same set of institutions determines the procedures by which the issue will be decided.

Because the issues related to population are often moral ones, money loses much of its usefulness as a medium of exchange. As exchange mechanisms other than money become available, governmental institutions are likely to play an increasingly important role. Whether individuals have the *right* to "die with dignity," whether United States foreign aid will support abortions, whether minors have the *right* to contraceptive information and to contraception without parental consent, whether the fetus has the *right* to protection by the state, whether parents have the *right* to prevent or to require sex education in the public schools, whether individuals have the *right* to welfare benefits in their new location after migration, whether employers have the *right* to use sex or ethnic origin as criteria in employment decisions are all population-related issues that have been decided by government in the last decade.

The ways in which governmental institutions decide these and similar issues will have great significance to individuals in their population-related decisions. For instance, biological and technological freedoms are influenced by government through its funding of research and education as well as through public financing (or the lack of it) in the area of medical care. Individuals' access to counseling and psychological services is partially determined by the amount of public resources devoted to these activities. This amount influences the level of psychological freedom in society. Moreover, governmental institutions influence the levels of social and psychological freedom in society through their allocation of rights to other social institutions such as the family, education, and the media. If governmental institutions are considered legitimate by the citizenry, they act as the final arbiters of disputes in society. However, governmental institutions reflect, as well as shape, the constraints and freedoms in society. Just as the economic system reflects social inequalities when persons have unequal purchasing and bargaining power, the political system and its associated institutions reflect inequities in political power. In general, governmental regulation will be effective only in those instances where the regulations reflect existing distributions of values and power in society or in those situations where attitudes and values are not strongly held. The ability of governmental institutions to lead society through radical change, is, therefore, severely limited in a pluralistic political system such as the United States where values are so heterogeneous and power is so widely distributed.

Governments rarely regulate change when the required changes limit the privileges of the more advantaged sectors of society. More typically, those who are the original targets of regulation become the regulators (51). For example, State Medical Boards, which regulate physicians, are made up of physicians not patients; the membership of the Interstate Commerce Commission is derived from past and future members of railroad, airline, and trucking companies; and the Federal Reserve Board is composed entirely of bankers. Since zoning boards, which determine land use and settlement patterns in communities, are dominated by realtors, builders, and bankers, it comes as no surprise that the settlement patterns of unzoned communities do not differ from communities with strict zoning regulations (52). We suggest, therefore, that although governmental institutions will be involved in most population issues, it would be naive to expect government to solve most population problems. Most social and political problems are problems because someone benefits from the existing pattern of activities. If we wish to reduce population growth, we must recognize that this will impose costs on persons and organizations. Even a relatively simple operation such as the distribution of contraceptive information by the public sector costs the taxpayers and offends some groups in society. When issues arise such as those associated with unrestricted access to abortion, the enforcement of equal opportunity for women and minorities in the labor force, or equal access to quality medical care, the resolution of these issues will be a long and difficult process and will require the cooperation of the other major institutions that influence attitudes and values in society.

ORGANIZATIONAL SIZE AND COMPOSITION

As we mentioned in Chapter 1, an important aspect of resolving commons-type issues is the development of a sense of community and belongingness among the users of the commons. This sense of community creates a situation in which if you and I are members of that community, I will not wish to increase my benefits at your expense, nor you at mine, since our utilities are partially combined through reciprocal caring. Earlier in this chapter we discussed this situation in its most frequent form, the family. However, the development of a "sense of community" becomes difficult to imagine with respect to a region, the nation, or the world when one considers the limited ability of individuals to identify their interests with persons whom they do not know and who are very different from themselves in many respects. In addition, it is difficult for the individual in such large contexts to see any impact of his contribution to the collective good. As was noted in Chapter 4, increases in the size, density, and heterogeneity of a city tends to reduce the sense of belongingness and produces noninvolvement, impersonality, and competitiveness rather than cooperation. Given that our society is not likely to grow smaller or less urban, can organizations be structured within urban areas in a way that will facilitate a sense of belongingness?

Barker, Wicker, Williams, and other social psychologists investigating the impact of organization size on schools and churches have consistently found that smaller-sized units not only encourage participation, but also feelings of effectiveness and competency among members of these smaller organizations (53, 54, 55, 56). Verba and Nie in their study of political participation found that persons living in smaller-sized communities participate more and believe more strongly that they can influence the governmental decisions in their community and that governmental decision makers do, in fact, behave in ways that are more consistent with the preferences of the citizens (57). Porter and Lawler have found that it is not necessarily the total size of the organization that encourages participation and responsibility. A large work organization can obtain many of the positive effects of smaller size if it is structured into subunits with sufficient autonomy to determine many of the work rules and task definitions of members, while continuing to meet the production demands of the larger unit (58). Most of the literature concerning the benefits of smaller-sized units relies on the psychological benefits of small groups and face-to-face interaction (59). Olson has shown that even if individuals act only on the basis of their economic self-interest, smaller-sized units will be far more likely to solve commons-type problems (60).

If smaller organizational units provide these benefits, why do Americans continue to develop ever larger organizations, whether these organizations relate to work, church, education, or government? One reason has been the belief that larger organizations are more efficient because of economics of scale. During the period from 1940 to 1970 local governments in all parts of the nation consolidated jurisdictions for purposes of efficiency (59, 61). A second reason, particularly in the private sector, is that executives did not wish to give workers authority over parts of the production process (62). More recent studies of governmental services have indicated that only a few services, such as water and sewage, benefit from economies of scale beyond a size of 25,000 citizens, and many services, such as police and fire protection, become less rather than more efficient as the size of the organization increases (63, 64).

Certainly for the purposes of resolving commons-type issues as well as providing individuals with opportunities to take responsibility for their own actions, decentralization may offer exceptional opportunities to structure institutions in a way that aids the accomplishment of both objectives. However, it is also possible that decentralization may pit one community, neighborhood, or ethnic group against another. Of the many issues currently being studied by the social sciences, this one is particularly appropriate to psychologists, anthropologists, biologists, and political scientists and provides important opportunities for comparative research.

In our discussion of social institutions, individual psychology, and population, we have emphasized that freedoms are both constrained and made possible by the social order and control that institutions provide. All the institutions we discussed in this chapter—the family, education, media, counseling, and government—are interdependent and mutually affect each other. This interdependency is inevitable in a society with complex social, economic, and political systems. The complexity of these systems and the interdependency of the relevant institutions means that attempts to change population patterns and population decision making will be frustrated by our fragmented and partial knowledge. Nevertheless, we believe that useful and appropriate population policies can be identified that will encourage organizational and community participation by individuals and promote environments that facilitate individual responsibility and effective decision making. In Chapters 6 and 7 we will discuss how this might be accomplished.

SUMMARY

In our discussion of social institutions, individual psychology, and population, we have suggested that the individual's behavior cannot be understood apart from the cultural institutions in which it is embedded. By establishing the norms, values, and roles in society, these institutions create the social order that both constrains and makes possible individual freedom. Of the institutions examined in this chapter, the family typically exerts the greatest influence on individual population decisions. Through it, the norms and values concerning the appropriate patterns for parenting, husband and wife relationships, and other basic roles are first introduced to the individual. Although the family may be the institution of greatest importance, it both affects and is affected by other institutions including education, the mass media, counseling, and government, each of which we discuss in turn. The interdependencies and complexities of these institutional systems mean that attempts to change population patterns and population decision making will often be frustrated both by the exertion of counteractive, self-regulatory forces within the overall population regulation system and by our fragmented and partial knowledge of these forces. Nevertheless, we believe that useful and appropriate population policies can be identified that will encourage individuals to develop the capacity for effective decision making and well-adaptive behavior and that will promote environments that facilitate these qualities. In Chapters 6 and 7 we will discuss how this might be accomplished.

TYPES OF GOVERNMENTAL POLICIES

6

We move in this chapter to an examination of those actions that might be taken by governments to improve the quality of life in society through the resolution of demographic issues. First, however, we must remind the reader that governmental institutions are only one of many influences and that, in most aspects of life, they are relatively less important than other institutions. Nevertheless, because governmental institutions can change the future ability of social institutions to affect demographic factors by expanding or restricting their rights and authority, and because all persons living within a country are at least potentially influenced by the rules of the state, governmental rules become the natural tools that society relies upon to change its demographic characteristics.

Before analyzing potential population policies, we must have a preliminary definition of "policy." For our purposes we will simply define a policy as "something a government chooses to do or not to do" (1). By defining policy in this manner we "force" all governments to have policies on all issues. For example, using this definition every governmental body will have population policies concerning fertility. These policies may be pronatal, antinatal, or neutral; and they may be stated explicitly in a public document or left unstated. To those unfamiliar with the policy-analysis literature, this definition may appear too broad to be useful. Is it not misleading and unnecessary, for example, to suggest that every government, whether it is a water district, city, county, state, or nation, will have population policies? We suggest that an understanding of both the power and limits of government requires this broad definition. The saying that "not to make a decision is to decide" has an analogue for governments: not to take an action with regard to an issue is to allow other influences to determine the outcome.

The importance of "nondecisions" in understanding public policies can be seen by comparing the city government of Petaluma, California, with other city governments. After observing the effects of population increases on other communities in its area, Petaluma decided to restrict the building of new residences each year to an amount not greater than 6 percent of the existing housing stock. In this way, the town hoped to avoid the disruptions attendant on rapid growth, and to maintain the present character of the town. This action certainly constitutes a population policy and will significantly affect the population size, as well as the age, income distribution, and mobility of current and potential residents of Petaluma. Cities that have not taken actions to restrict growth have decided, actively or passively, to have a policy allowing the existing social and economic forces influencing their growth to remain unchanged by the city government. Similarly, many states prior to the Supreme Court decision liberalizing abortion, changed their abortion laws by eliminating previous legal obstacles to abortion. Those states not taking these actions also had an abortion policy—the maintenance of antiabortion laws.

POLICIES AND RIGHTS

All policies are coercive to someone when they determine rights and duties in society.* Using the examples of Petaluma and of

---

* "Coercion," "coercive," and "to coerce" in their ordinary language usage tend to connotate extreme or excessive influence. As used in this book, however, coer-

abortion liberalization we can examine how policies change rights and thereby coerce someone not previously coerced. When the government of Petaluma decided not to allow more than a specified number of housing units to be built, it coerced both residents and nonresidents of the community. Presumably, at least some citizens of Petaluma such as the builders and real-estate agents did not wish growth restricted, because the action would negatively affect their incomes. Prior to the government's decision, these individuals had the right to build and sell as many dwelling units as were needed to meet the demand for housing in Petaluma and that could be built in accordance with existing zoning regulations. The city's decision attenuated this right. Similarly, persons who wished to move to Petaluma suffered a reduction in rights. Prior to the policy, individuals outside Petaluma could move there if they could purchase an existing unit or if they could find land to build on. After the decision only a few individuals could move to Petaluma. Presumably, the number desiring such a move is greater than the number allowed, otherwise Petaluma's government would not have taken this action. Thus, some individuals lost their previously held right to move. Even those who do enter Petaluma will probably have to pay a much higher price for the privilege since the supply of housing has been reduced while the demand has not. The Petaluma government, therefore, increased the rights of current home owners and reduced the rights or income of future or potential owners.

In the liberalization of abortion laws, who experienced coercion? At a first glance it would appear that the change in laws reduced society's coercive power over women by giving them rights they did not previously have, and certainly this increase of rights for women did occur. However, in most of the state policies, and definitely in the case of the Supreme Court decision (2), several identifiable parties experienced a reduction in rights. Husbands, whose permission was previously required if their wives terminated a pregnancy, lost this right. Persons who believed that abortion constituted murder,

---

cion includes the entire range of incentives, disincentives, constraints, and persuasions that are employed to produce behaviors considered desirable by the coercing party when those behaviors would not otherwise have occurred.

and who formerly had the right to stop this murder through the use of the state's enforcement power, lost that right. Finally, the right of the fetus to protection by the state was abridged.

From the above illustrations it should be clear that when governmental policies change rights, one person's gain must be another's loss. A function of government is the allocation of rights in society. Since a "right" equals the ability to impose costs on others, changes in rights either give or take away the ability of one individual or group to impose a cost on another (3). As the quotation in the previous chapter from John R. Commons suggested, some coercion by collective action is necessary for liberty. The slaves obtained their right to liberty when the right to own persons was revoked. Without some allocation of rights, duties, and privileges it would be impossible to have ordered transactions among persons.

EVALUATING POLICY ALTERNATIVES

Numerous criteria have been set up for the evaluation of population policies. Bernard Berelson in his well-known article, "Beyond Family Planning," lists six criteria for evaluating population policies (4).

(a) scientific, medical, and technological readiness;
(b) political feasibility;
(c) administrative feasibility;
(d) economic feasibility;
(e) moral and ethical acceptability;
(f) and expected effectiveness.

Berelson suggests that among all potential policies for reducing fertility, "family planning" programs best serve the combination of these six criteria. The major justification for this choice was the "voluntary" nature of the programs. They do not appear coercive. Additional criteria that have been suggested include:

(a) policies should expand options rather than reduce them (5);
(b) policies should internalize externalities; that is, they should return costs and benefits of behavior as directly as possible to those who create them (5);
(c) policies should increase the level of equality in society (6);

(d) and policies should fit within the cultural tradition of the so-
     ciety (7, 8).

While all of the above criteria have certain merits, they presup-
pose that a fundamental consensus on what constitutes "social justice" exists in the society. However a closer examination of them
would suggest that this fundamental consensus does not exist. For
example, a policy that will internalize externalities is often suggested to resolve problems such as that described in Garrett Hardin's, *The Tragedy of Commons,* where persons acting on the basis
of individual self-interest brought about the collective destruction of
the commons (8). If costs and benefits are to be completely borne
by those who create them, all property must be held privately with
the owner having the rights to the profit, the use, or the sale of that
property (5, 9). There exists, however, a prior question: "What is
the optimal distribution of property (rights) in society?" As an
illustration, take the rights of society, parents, and children to determine whether or not a child will enter the labor force at an early
age or attend college. Let us assume that a given family (a father,
mother, and two children) owns a medium-size family farm that
earns a profit. If three people in the family work the farm, there is
sufficient profit to allow the fourth person to go through the educational system and attain a college degree. Let us further assume that
the demand for college-educated labor is such that the society can
utilize efficiently one, and only one, child who has attained a college education from each family, and that beyond this number the
economy of that society cannot efficiently utilize the human capital
investment in education. Because only one child can attend school
someone, presumably the parents, must decide which child will
pursue a college education and which child will be taken out of
school to work with them on the farm in order to invest in the other
child's education. This allocation of resources will maximize the
productivity of the household and will not create any external costs
to the society. In fact, such an allocation would come close to max-
imizing the net social productivity for that society. Such a distribution of rights, however, would violate the criterion of individual
equality since both children might desire to go to college if the ex-

pected utility of occupations requiring a college degree is higher than occupations not requiring a college degree.

The above example is only one of an infinite number that could be chosen to indicate how conflicts arise among different evaluative criteria. The function of the political system is to allocate rights. These allocations typically are justified on the basis that they will improve the quality of life for individuals living within the government's jurisdiction or are affected by its actions. Not everyone places the same value on different rights, such as the right to abortion, the right to migrate, and the right to use one's land as one pleases. In addition, the values of many rights that are important to the quality of life cannot be expressed in monetary terms. For these reasons the political system must deal with noncomparable utilities when it allocates rights, duties, and privileges. As we indicated in Chapter 5, it is appropriate that government determine the distribution of rights so that peaceful transactions can take place and social order can be maintained. But how can we evaluate governmental policies if the criteria used inevitably conflict?

Equity Criteria

"Is it fair?" "Is it effective?" "Is it efficient?" While policy evaluation requires that each of these three questions be addressed, the first is by far the most complex. To determine whether a policy is "fair," "just," or "equitable" philosophical analyses such as those of Plato, Bentham, or, most recently, Rawls might be used (10). These works identify and distinguish among the various underlying dimensions of equity. For example, we typically distinguish between ends and means and require not only that the governmental action be equitable with respect to end results, but also, that the means employed to achieve these results be fair as well.

Procedural or Allocative Equity.   In the study of politics, means and ends are equivalent to procedural and allocative equity, respectively. Procedural equity tends to focus on the impartiality of the decision process. Emphasis on "due process" and "equality of opportunity" provide examples of the concern with procedural equity.

When the focus of the evaluation relates to the consequences or ends of the action, the allocative dimension of equity is emphasized (11).

There is, of course, an association between decision procedures and the allocations that they can be expected to produce, and this association quite often is negative. Procedures that treat unequals equally will tend to perpetuate the original inequality. For example, when an outbreak of the swine flu was expected in the winter of 1976–77, persons who were most likely to experience the greatest harm if they caught the flu were given first priority in receiving the inoculations. Equal opportunity would have led to unequal mortality risks as well as a higher mortality rate overall.

Individual or Categorical Equity. A second equity dimension concerns the issue of equity between individuals and equity between categories of people. Philosophical analyses are typically more useful in identifying inequities in the treatment of individuals. Was person A treated fairly when compared with the treatment of person B? In the governmental sector the courts and other judicial institutions are familiar with handling these issues and do so on a case-by-case basis. The equity or inequity of an action is usually determined after the fact. Public policy, however, to the extent that it tries to promote equity, must often deal with categories of people that are imperfectly defined and measured. Examples of such categories include blacks and whites, men and women, and rich and poor. These categories are difficult to define precisely, and the category itself is often a surrogate measure for some other category (for example, in "affirmative action" policies the categories of blacks, women, and Chicanos are used as surrogate indicators for "individuals who experience discrimination"). Because of the rough and imperfect nature of the categories, in order to evaluate the equity or impact on social justice of any policy, it becomes necessary to relax many of the assumptions of philosophical analyses oriented to the individual level and look not only at individual effects but at the effects upon categories of persons as well (12).

To illustrate the difficulties of using policies to achieve social justice and of evaluating their impact, we will take the Department of Health, Education and Welfare's attempts to reduce discrimination on the basis of race or ethnic background. Presumably these policies were designed to facilitate equality by compensating for the previous disadvantaged position of individuals. Because *on the average* blacks and Chicanos experience greater social and educational disadvantages than whites, organizations may be encouraged to use hiring quotas. However, these quotas may result in the child of a black physician being given preference over the child of a white migrant worker. Thus, a policy designed to promote equity across categories of people may produce an injustice in individual cases.

Freedom or Equality. Theories of equity or social justice must eventually face the conflict between freedom and equality. This conflict has been particularly acute in the United States. Following John Locke and classical liberal theory, the state has been regarded as the primary source of coercion, while coercion by other institutions such as the "market" and "private" contractual relationships have been perceived as "natural" and noncoercive (13). The major difficulty with the traditional image of freedom and liberty arises from its failure to consider adequately the coercions that arise from nongovernmental sources. The concept of liberty as "doing what one wants so long as it does not interfere with another's right to do the same" is a status quo concept because it does not take into account the unequal distribution of wealth and opportunities with which individuals begin life. For persons living in poverty in an urban ghetto or a rural depressed area who have little opportunity to improve their life, doing what one wants is often a hollow freedom. The inadequacies that stem from defining liberty as the absence of governmental constraints are almost infinite. For example, the Supreme Court once found child labor laws unconstitutional on the grounds that they interfered with "freedom of contract." Similarly, the white dominated culture has been "free" to socialize minorities into accepting their inferior status. Until Brown v. Board of Education and subsequent civil-rights legislation, whites were "free" to exclude blacks from their schools, hotels, and restaurants. Until more recent environmental protection legislation, factories were "free" to pollute and persons "free" to breathe any clean air they could find.

A more complete definition of freedom would need to take into consideration an individual's ability to exercise choices and all the coercions present in the social structure. The classical liberal definition of freedom as the absence of governmental coercion must be extended to include the concept of a balance of coercive forces: psychological, economic, social, and environmental, as well as governmental. From both a sociological and psychological point of view, nongovernmental sources of coercion may be more damaging than governmental coercion. As John Stuart Mill pointed out, the tyrannies of custom and prejudice can do extensive damage to individuals in society whether or not these tyrannies are de jure as well as de facto. One means of reducing legal, social, and psychological coercion is to reduce the inequality among persons. If one person is not more powerful than another, it is more difficult for extensive coercion to occur. Thus, a concept of freedom expanded beyond the classical liberal definition should also take into consideration equality of opportunity and power.

An Evaluative Framework for Public Policy.   Inequalities in social, political, and economic resources are unavoidable in any absolute sense. In fact, some have argued that they may be necessary to stimulate productivity (10, 14) and that if each individual were required to have the same exact amount of political power, political decision making in a complex society would be intolerably debilitated (15). An alternative to an absolute equality criterion for social justice would be one requiring the random distribution of inequalities among a selected set of attributes. In such an arrangement, the probabilities that a given individual had above-average or below-average political influence or income would be independent of (not statistically associated with) attributes such as sex or race. Such a concept of social justice is illustrated in Table 6.1, where the fullest possible justice would require that the associations between any two attributes denoted by X not be significantly different from zero.

TABLE 6.1
A Measurement of the Level of Social Justice in Society

	Individuals			
Individuals	Access to Health Services	Political Power	Economic Wealth	Education
Economic Wealth	X	X		
Education	X	X		
Economic Wealth of Parents	X	X	X	X
Education of Parents	X	X	X	X
Race	X	X	X	X
Sex	X	X	X	X

A society's level of social justice becomes higher as the level of association between row and column attributes denoted by an X approaches zero.

The set of variables that should be included in the matrix is crucial. Culture certainly plays a part in defining the set of variables, but this definition is a dynamic process. In the United States there is a general consensus that the attributes of race, sex, and income should not be associated with health care, education, and occupational opportunities. Substantial disagreement undoubtedly exists over the level of association judged to be politically insignificant and the rate at which the level of association should be reduced. Nevertheless, this concept of social justice is amenable to policy evaluation, while other, more individually oriented definitions of social justice require levels of information that are beyond the resources of governmental institutions. If this method of measuring the aggregate level of social justice in society proved acceptable, then it would be possible to evaluate the justness or fairness of different policies, the effects of which involved noncomparable utilities for different members of the population.

When the impact of a policy cannot be adjusted with reference to comparable utility units, fairness requires that some other means be used. For example, prior to the 1964 Civil Rights legislation, whites were free to exclude blacks (and vice versa) from their restaurants, hotels, employment, and neighborhoods. In this case the rights to serve and to sell property to whomever one pleases competes with the right to equal opportunity to service and housing. Each group may believe its claim to the right in question is a just one. How can society determine the appropriate allocation of rights? In this case, we suggest that the right to equality of opportunity takes precedence since this raises the level of social justice in society. This is in accord with the often-used criterion that the rights to food, shelter, and security are more basic than the right to discriminate in selling food and shelter (16). It is certainly also in accord with the concept represented in Table 6.1.

Effectiveness and Efficiency Criteria

Criteria for policy evaluation such as technological, economic, and administrative feasibility reflect the policymakers' desire to use as few resources as possible to reach the policy objective. Although estimates of feasibility can be expected to change (often quite rapidly), they are obviously important in the determination of policy choices since it is usually unproductive to suggest policies that are beyond the resources of a society. In addition, when comparing two or more policies with equal or nearly equal social-justice implications, the economic, administrative, and technological costs can become the critical considerations. Given the almost infinite number of policies that affect fertility, mortality, geographic mobility, and status mobility, a systematic analysis and application of these criteria is beyond the scope of this book. In Chapter 7 where specific policy suggestions will be made, these criteria will be utilized in selecting those policies which are chosen for discussion.

CATEGORIES OF POLICIES

Throughout the first five chapters we have referred to population issues as being related to fertility, mortality, geographic mobility, or status mobility. Although such a classification by substantive area aids in the discussion of these demographic concerns, it does not provide a means for understanding, comparing, and evaluating policy options within each substantive area. In this book, our interest lies in making distinctions among policies that will provide guides for evaluating the ability of different policies to solve the problems in the field of population. In Chapter 1, we suggested that there were three basic categories of population problems related to individual free choice: (a) problems associated with ineffective decisions, that is, decisions that do not effect results desired by the decision maker; (b) problems associated with conflicts of interest between individuals and/or groups; and (c) problems associated with conflicts between individual interests and the interests of society as a whole. For the purpose of evaluating whether a particular policy is appropriate for the resolution of these problems we have chosen a fourfold typology developed by Lowi and elaborated by Salisbury and Heinz (17, 18, 19). These authors divide policies into distributive, redistributive, regulatory, and self-regulatory categories.

Distributive Policies

These policies take resources from the general fund and distribute them to particular individuals or groups. Family planning programs are a typical distributive policy. A government allocates certain dollars to purchase and distribute contraceptive information and methods, either free or at a low cost, to those who desire them. In the area of mortality, government funds given to pay for kidney machines distribute benefits to persons with these illnesses and to persons in the future who may have these illnesses. Similarly, in connection with geographic mobility, an example of a distributive policy would be the distribution of government funds to persons in depressed areas so that they could move to locations where there were jobs. With each of these policies the persons who benefit from them are generally aware that the policies exist and that they are the beneficiaries. The persons paying for the programs, the taxpayers, do not necessarily perceive themselves as being coerced by the policy, and are often even unaware of the programs.

Political decision makers like distributive policies for many reasons. First, the winners (beneficiaries) are aware of their benefits, while those paying for the program are not aware that they are doing so. Second, the beneficiaries of distributive measures usually provide all the information that the political decision makers need to justify the policy. This reduces the information and decision costs of the policy makers. Third, the policies appear voluntaristic—no one seems forced by the government to utilize the contraceptive services, use the kidney machines, or take the migration subsidy. For the politician these policies represent the best of all possible worlds. The beneficiaries know that they have gained, the public does not know that they are paying, and the decision costs are low (18, 19, 20).

Redistributive Policies

This type of governmental action takes resources from specific individuals or groups and gives them to other individuals and groups. For example, a statute to disallow income tax deductions for children and to replace such deductions with a tax on each child would be a redistributive policy. In this case, the persons who are coerced, those who have children, know that they have lost previous rights or privileges. The government's decision to subsidize medical care to the aged is clearly a redistribution from the young to the old. A potential redistributive geographic-mobility policy would be levying a special tax on residents of suburbs in order to enable owners of houses in the center city to refurbish their property rather than move to the suburbs.

At first glance, the difference between distributive and redistributive programs may appear nonexistent or small. In both cases, money is being taken from one set of individuals and given to a second set. To the politician, however, the differences between the two policy types are large. In distributive policies, those who are paying for the program are generally unaware of both the specifics of the program and that they are paying for it. At the same time, the individuals receiving the direct benefits of the program are very much aware that they are receiving these gains. By contrast, the persons who pay for a redistributive policy are quite aware that they—as individuals or members of some group or class—are being forced to give up some previous benefits or income so that another group can receive these benefits. Thus, the costs to the decision makers are much higher in redistributive than with distributive policies. Only when the demand for redistributive policies is particularly strong and well-organized will decision makers use these measures (18, 19).

Self-Regulatory Policies

Self-regulatory policies distribute rights and authority as opposed to monetary resources. They take the rights from the general fund (that is, the state or the general public previously holding the rights) and give them to a particular group. When the courts determined that states did not have the right to deny individuals access to contraception this was an example of a self-regulatory policy. These policies are permissive or enabling but do not compel action.

A self-regulatory policy in the area of mortality would be to give patients the right to decide not to continue a treatment necessary to keep them alive or to give individuals the right to purchase drugs such as heroin free of legal restraints. Sex-education programs could be classified as self-regulatory because they permit individuals access to instruction concerning reproduction, contraception, and related topics. No one is required to make use of this information, but by gaining access to it, his or her options are increased.

For the most part, self-regulatory policies are politically popular because the persons requesting a right provide the necessary information to policy makers to justify their appropriation of the authority, and the individuals losing the right are generally not aware that it is lost. In some cases, however, such as in gaining the rights to abortion and sex education, self-regulatory policies involve strongly held values, and some individuals may wish to limit the options available to others. When this occurs the policies are no longer perceived as self-regulatory but as regulatory.

Regulatory Policies

Regulatory policies redistribute power, authority, and rights. A governmental institution may take rights previously held by individuals, groups, or other governmental bodies and vest these in dif-

ferent units. Regulatory statutes generally include clear induce-
ments or sanctions and are immediately and clearly coercive.
Examples of regulatory policies would include a law requiring a
license in order to bear a child, a limitation on the number of
children a woman may bear, a law prohibiting murder, and a limitation on the right to change jobs or to travel. In short, regulatory
policies determine that "thou shall" or "thou shall not" behave in
specified ways.

Regulatory policies do not appear voluntaristic and the individuals gaining *and losing* rights and privileges are almost always
aware of their gain or loss. In particular, those who have lost a
right are normally very aware of the attenuation of previously held
powers. Because of the clarity of this loss to the losers, regulatory
statutes are quite difficult to pass. As we will discuss below, even
when they are enacted, they often change through time into distributive policies (18).

THE POLITICS OF POPULATION POLICIES

An important aspect of the above policy typology is that the distinction between a distributive and a redistributive or between a self-
regulatory and a regulatory policy rests mainly in the perceptions of
the policy makers and the public. For example, governmental action that gives an income-tax credit or deduction such as an investment tax credit, an oil depletion allowance, or a deduction of interest paid on home mortgages would normally be classified as a
distributive policy. This categorization is based on the fact that
most citizens are unaware of these "loopholes" unless they themselves are taking advantage of them, and the fact that citizens who
do not receive these distributions do not perceive themselves as directly paying for them. Of the many hundreds of special exemp-
tions or deductions in the tax laws, the average citizen is aware of
only a few. Compare these governmental actions with the graduated
income tax where persons with higher taxable incomes pay a higher
percentage of taxes on this income than persons with lower taxable
incomes. In this case, because the individuals in the higher tax

bracket are aware that they are paying more so that those in the lower income categories can pay less, the policy is perceived, and therefore classified, as redistributive.

In reality, all of the above policies (the tax loopholes as well as the graduated income tax), redistribute income among different groups of persons, and the basis for distinction between distributive and redistributive lies solely in the perceptions and the awareness of the citizenry. This difference in perception has tremendous implications for the politics surrounding the policies and the probability that a proposed policy action will be adopted. Legislative committees typically dominate distributive policies. As a result, the actions of these committees, and of the legislature as a whole, may be characterized as having a "low profile." Once distributive policies are enacted they become highly resistant to change, since those who benefit tend to show their appreciation through campaign support or other mechanisms that a legislator appreciates, and those who pay for the distributive policies are rarely aware that they exist and therefore rarely complain. The politics of redistributive policies differ substantially. Rather than being initiated by the legislature and characterized by consensus and a voluntaristic appearance, redistributive policies tend to be: (a) initiated by the executive branch of government; (b) class-oriented; (c) visible to the public; and (d) highly partisan. When redistributive policies are proposed the losers are typically quite vocal. Conflict rather than consensus characterizes the decision process. This combination of characteristics means that the costs to the decision makers are high because they can expect the losers to support other candidates in future elections. For all these reasons redistributive policies tend to be proposed far less frequently than distributive policies; and among those proposed few are adopted (17, 18, 19).

The difference between self-regulatory and regulatory policies, like that between distributive and redistributive policies, is based on the differences in the perception, not necessarily the reality, of what the policy does. In our discussion of self-regulatory and regulatory policies, we classified the decision that states could not deny access to contraceptive services as a self-regulatory policy, and a decision to limit the number of children a woman could have was classified as regulatory. This classification was based on the public's perception that the government was changing rights in a way that, in the first case, increased individual freedom with respect to contraception and, in the second case, decreased individual freedom with respect to having children. In the first case it appears that the government is taking rights from the state and giving them to the individuals most directly concerned, whereas in the second case it appears that the state is taking rights from individuals and vesting them in the government. Thus, the first action appears to expand voluntary activity whereas the second seems to reduce it.

While these differences are "real" in the sense that they exist in the minds of the citizenry, a closer examination of the two actions shows that each is taking rights from one set of individuals and vesting them in another. In the contraceptive-services decision, the courts took rights from the general public. As a consequence of this action, individuals (acting through their representatives) could no longer proscribe certain behaviors. If someone believed that the use of contraception was immoral, the previously held right to prevent its use (if the legislative majority necessary to pass the law could be achieved), was lost. On the other hand, a decision to limit the number of children would take away individuals' rights to have the number of children they desired, while giving them the right to join with others interested in reducing population growth and limiting the number of children born.

As a general rule self-regulatory policies take rights from "the public" and give them to the individual, while regulatory policies take rights from the individual and give them to "the public" or to another specified set of individuals. With many policy actions, however, it is not clear beforehand whether rights will be perceived as being given or being taken. Civil-rights legislation disallowed the state to segregate by race. Was this self-regulatory or regulatory? To blacks the decision might appear self-regulatory, while to whites the legislation might appear regulatory. The Supreme Court decisions to allow unwed minors to have access to contraceptive services and to abortion without parental consent reduced the right of the state to prevent an action by giving minors more opportunity to self-regulate the reproductive aspects of their lives. Thus, the minors may see the policies as self-regulatory. The parents, on the other hand, have lost certain rights to regulate the reproductive aspects of their minor children's lives and may see the action as regulatory.

As with distributive and redistributive policies, whether a policy that changes rights is perceived as self-regulatory or as regulatory significantly affects the politics surrounding the policy, the probability that the policy will be adopted, and how the policy decision is implemented. Quite often self-regulatory policies require the development of bureaucracies to implement their propagandistic or educational components. For example, a Department of Population Planning might be set up to implement programs that alert persons to the "need" to limit family size, or to inform them concerning the availability and utility of counseling services, contraception or abortion services, or to describe the severity of the problems. Such bureaucracies have been set up in many developing countries. The courts in the United States have also played a large role in establishing self-regulatory programs by overturning statutes limiting the availability of contraception and abortion, and rights to travel.

Organized interest groups constitute one of the dominant features of regulatory politics. A typical regulatory law will follow a pattern where one interest group or coalition of interest groups will approach the legislature requesting certain rights. These groups will be countered by other interest groups seeking to deny any restriction on their existing rights. For example, state land-use control represents one of the most important tools state governments have available to direct and to control their population size and distribution (20). In several states including Oregon, Florida, Hawaii, Vermont, and Delaware, environmental interest groups have attempted to pressure the state government to control development so that wilderness and scenic areas, as well as ecologically fragile and historically significant sites, will be protected (21). Other interest groups representing neighborhood organizations have also advocated state control so that multiple-family units and low-income housing can be excluded from their neighborhoods. Countering both sets of demands have been interest groups representing home builders, the Chambers of Commerce, and banks, all of which rely heavily on development for their economic profit. Because each group is politically powerful and can punish policy makers, and because each group has sufficient resources to gather and present information to justify its side, many attempts to pass regulatory policies end in a stalemate among competing groups (17, 21). This stalemate encourages the legislatures to delegate decisions to bureaucracies. When this occurs the bureaucracy distributes to each interest group much of what that group desires by taking resources from the unorganized general public and distributing them to the organized groups. In order to administer and oversee regulatory policies and laws, bureaucracies commonly appoint regulatory bodies. However, because members of the very interest group that is being regulated are the people most informed and competent regarding the interest area, the regulatory bodies tend to be staffed and directed by persons affiliated with the regulated groups. In the above example of land-use regulation the leadership of the bureaucracies was made up of environmentalists, realtors, bankers, and lawyers whose business was property protection. Similarly, the Interstate Commerce Commission is headed by representatives of trucking, rail, and airline executives; the Federal Reserve Board is headed by bankers; and the State Medical Boards are composed entirely of physicians. Thus, the regulated become the regulators (17).

Political Feasibility and Political Effectiveness

As might be expected, the political feasibility of each policy type varies inversely with its probability of effecting major social change. Distributive policies, because of their voluntaristic appearance, their low information costs to policy makers, the ability of beneficiaries to realize that they are beneficiaries, and the lack of awareness of those who must pay the costs, combine high political benefits with low political costs. However, because the behavior change intended by the policy is not required by it, distributive policies do not usually facilitate major social change. In addition, because the requests for these policies normally come from those individuals and groups in society that could be characterized as "more advantaged," and the benefits go to those who are requesting the actions, these policies rarely raise the level of social justice in society.

Self-regulatory policies, because they do not appear to require compliance and their information cost to decision makers is low, are generally politically feasible. Their feasibility is slightly lower than distributive policies because of their greater visibility and their potential for infringing upon the deeply held values of certain groups. These policies can be quite low in effectiveness however, because they do not take effect where they are most needed. For example, persons who strongly value large families will not have smaller families just because contraception becomes available to them. Similarly, persons whose ties to a particular geographical area are quite strong will not be especially responsive to policies that allow them to be geographically mobile. Self-regulatory policies are effective only where those who already wish to behave in a given way but do not currently have the legal right to do so are granted the required rights.

Redistributive and regulatory policies tend to be much more effective in creating social change because they clearly and definitely change the incentive structure for all parties involved in the situation. However, because the "losers" can readily identify themselves as losers, and because the redistribution of either substantive resources or rights means that the losers will have the incentive to punish the politician, redistributive and regulatory measures tend to be less politically feasible than distributive and self-regulatory measures. For these policies to be passed, some kind of crisis may be necessary.

THE APPLICATION OF POLICY CATEGORIES
TO DIFFERENT POPULATION PROBLEMS

We have suggested that population problems related to free choice can be divided into three types and governmental actions into four categories. In this section we will suggest how one can determine which category of policies is likely to be well suited to resolving a given problem. We will be using this framework in a prescriptive manner, that is, a manner for determining which type of policy ought to be used to achieve desired goals. Thus, the framework will allow us to evaluate governmental actions and will serve as a guide for our suggestions for new policies.

Ineffective Decisions

Chapters 3 and 4 described models of individual decision making and reviewed many of the problems created when individuals make ineffective decisions and therefore behave in ways detrimental to themselves and to society. We have suggested, for example, that ineffective decision making causes a large percentage of unintended and unwanted pregnancies which in turn result in large numbers of abortions, out-of-wedlock births, mistreated children, and related emotional problems for the women and their families. Ineffective decision making may increase health-compromising and risk-taking behavior and, in this way, increase mortality. Decision outcome failures in geographic and status mobility may also be related to ineffective decision making.

Presumably both society and the individual would be better off if the latter made more effective decisions. In the case of unwanted pregnancies, for instance, the individual would be spared them and their associated negative effects. The society presumably prefers not to expend its scarce medical resources on "unnecessary" abortions or births, and prefers not to experience the other negative effects that may be expected when individuals do not make effective population decisions. For this reason society may wish to distribute resources to aid individuals in making effective decisions.

When a population problem is created by ineffective decisions the appropriate policy should generally be distributive or self-regulatory in nature. For instance, in the above example of unwanted pregnancies if the individual cannot make an effective decision concerning contraception because contraceptive methods are not available or are not available at a price that he or she can afford, then society should be willing to pay the costs of providing the necessary contraceptive methods so long as these costs are less than the costs to society of an unwanted pregnancy and its attendant negative effects. Similarly, if the individual cannot make an effective decision regarding contraception because legal restrictions deny him or her the right to make that decision, then society should grant the individual the right so long as the value to society of its control of contraceptive decisions is less than the value to society of reducing the negative effects of unwanted pregnancies. The granting of this right to the individual would be a self-regulatory policy. Two useful examples of situations where self-regulatory policies have been deemed appropriate include the previous abandonment by the states of their regulations that denied contraception to individuals and the current media campaigns to inform individuals about the dangers of not using seat belts while riding in cars. In the first case, individuals did not have access to the necessary facilities to carry out effective contraception. The state, by removing its own previous restrictions, transferred rights from the general public to the individual. Such an action should be followed when the costs to the society of withholding the rights from the individual exceed the gains to the society. In the case of seat belts, the purposes of the campaign may be twofold. First, there is the informational aspect of the message where the benefits to the individual are explained so that he or she can make a better estimation of the ''true costs'' of not using the belts. The second aspect of the campaign may be propagandistic in the sense that society wishes the individual to change his or her evaluation of the costs even if no additional information is received. For example, the society may perceive that because the social costs of accidents are so high, it is necessary to change the individual's valuation of the use of the seat belt. By suggesting to the individual that a good ''citizen,'' ''father,'' or ''mother'' would use seat belts the campaign may change the social norms to the degree necessary to make most persons use seat belts.

Evaluation of the propagandistic aspects of campaigns to stop smoking, to have fewer (or more) children, to move to other locations, or other similar messages can be made by examining the expected impact of these campaigns on the level of social justice in society. If the attitude change raises the level of social justice (decreases the associations in the matrix in Figure 6.1), then a self-regulatory policy providing propaganda as well as information would be considered justified. On the other hand, if the propaganda decreases social justice (increases these associations), the propagandistic aspects of a self-regulatory policy would not be normatively justified.

The issues surrounding the propaganda aspects of self-regulatory policies can be related not only to the criterion of social justice but also to the concept of perceived freedom discussed in Chapter 5. All institutions limit freedom in that they impose unperceived external constraints on the individual, particularly through the internalization of social norms. As we have indicated earlier, however, some internalizations are necessary and useful to the individual so that he or she can have a minimal amount of order and predictability in life and will not have to "rationally" think out each and every behavior. When, however, such internalization serves the interests of others at the expense of the individual, it must be characterized as generally undesirable. As will be explained in the four examples below, even when such internalization raises the level of social justice in society, we suggest that redistributive or regulatory policies may be preferred to distributive and self-regulatory policies.

Conflicts Between Individuals or Groups

Examples of conflicting interests in fertility, mortality, and geographic and status mobility include:

(a) the conflict between the presumed father, who wishes to have the right to approve or disapprove of an abortion and the pregnant woman, who believes she has the greater interest and therefore the right to approve or disapprove of an abortion;

(b) the conflict between persons who believe health care should be provided on a private basis and purchased in a manner similar to other private goods and services and persons who believe that health care, like education, should be available to all on an equal basis;

(c) the conflict between those who believe in the right to geographic mobility and those who believe a community should be able to determine its size and/or demographic composition;

(d) and the conflict between persons who wish to eliminate intergenerational inheritance because it interferes with their concept of equal opportunity and those who wish to maintain the right to pass on some of their assets to their children or to others whom they choose.

These issues differ from those produced by ineffective decisions in that the reduction of ineffective decisions presumably is in the best interest of all. In conflicts between interests, if some person or group wins, another person or group must lose.

For this type of conflict we suggest that redistributive or regulatory policies would be more appropriate. In the case of abortion the two conflicting individuals, the mother and her husband, both claim to have an interest in the fate of the fetus. Because of the importance of time, it is not possible to have the courts decide each conflict on an individual basis. Therefore, one of the conflicting parties must be given the right by the state to impose a cost on the other party. Presumably after the right has been allocated, then, in individual cases, the party not having the right could purchase that right. For example, if the woman has the right to decide, she could require that her husband have a vasectomy if he wishes her to carry the fetus to term; but the right must be allocated if bargaining is to take place in a reasonable fashion.

In the conflict concerning health care, if the government decided that health care should be provided as equally as possible, then a redistributive policy would appear most suitable. In this case, some form of socialized medicine would be the likely outcome. The doctors might charge the same fee for each patient and bill the government. It can be observed that this policy would also be regulatory in certain aspects since it would regulate the fees of every doctor, as well as the manner in which they charge for their services. The greatest impact, however, would be upon the redistribution of health care among income classes.

In the conflict over the right to geographic mobility and the right

to restrict growth, just as in the abortion issue, a regulatory policy
is needed to determine who has the right to impose costs on others.
A distributive policy paying citizens not to move or cities not to restrict growth would be exceptionally difficult to enforce because the
government would have no way of knowing ahead of time which
citizens actually desired to move or which cities wished to restrict
growth. If, for example, the government decided to employ a distributive policy that paid persons wishing to move not to do so, persons having no desire to move might state that they wished to do so
in order to receive a payment. If the government decided to pay
cities not to restrict growth, each locality would have an incentive
to announce an intention to restrict growth so that it could receive
compensation for not being able to carry out its wishes. In situations such as these where it is difficult to know an individual's or a
group's true preferences, regulatory measures are preferable to distributive or redistributive policies.

In the final example cited on page 229 (the issue of inheritance),
if the state and federal governments were to change their position
and either not allow individuals to transfer wealth to others after
their death or allow an even greater portion of wealth to be transferred than is currently possible, a redistributive policy would be
involved. To disallow inheritance would benefit the economically
disadvantaged at the expense of the advantaged, while allowing
larger amounts of resources to be passed on would benefit the advantaged at the expense of those who have lower accumulated savings. Given the matrix defining our definition of social justice, presumably those policies that benefit the poor at the expense of the
rich would be preferable.

Conflicts Between Individuals and Society

These problems arise when rights are structured so that what is in
the interest of the individual is not in the interest of society. In his
article, ''The Tragedy of Commons,'' Hardin used the analogy of
the English Commons to show how it would always be in the immediate self-interest of a sheep herder to add another sheep to the
Commons, even though the Commons might already be deterio-
rating through overgrazing. This is true because if there were 100

sheep herders with approximately equal numbers of sheep there, each time a herder adds a sheep to the Commons he only experiences one one-hundredth of the costs, while he reaps 100 percent of the benefits. As Beryl Crowe indicated in his reply to Hardin, "The Tragedy of Commons Revisited," situations in which individual and social interests are at odds are ubiquitous in society (22). Problems such as overfishing and overharvesting of whales, many types of air pollution, and most issues involving collective and public goods exhibit the characteristics of the Commons. A collective good is one that when supplied to one person cannot be denied to others. A public good has the same characteristic and in addition, one person's consumption of the good does not reduce the level of consumption available to others. An example of a public good is national defense (23).

Examples of population problems that are commons problems include:

(a) when at the family level it is in the family's interest to have many children because the benefits (economic and/or non-economic) outweigh the costs, but at the societal level rapid population growth creates higher costs than benefits;

(b) when the occupants of automobiles perceive that the negative utility of wearing seat belts is higher than the positive utility, but the costs to society in terms of health care, loss of human capital, and insurance premiums are higher than the benefits of allowing unrestrained occupants;

(c) and when individuals wish to live in single-family units on five-acre lots, but the costs of urban sprawl, created by this settlement pattern, are quite high to the society in the provision of public services, the loss of agricultural land, and the creation of urban slums.

In these situations where individual and social interests conflict, the solution requires a change in the incentive structures surrounding the individual's choice so that the incentives involved would lead him or her to make a choice compatible with the social interest. The incentives could be changed by redistributive policies or regulatory policies. For example, society might tax the young to provide old-age security for the less advantaged in society so that parents would no longer need a larger number of children to secure their welfare after they could no longer work. This would be a redistributive policy. A regulatory policy to achieve the same outcome might be to require either the mother or father to be sterilized after the birth of the second child. Whether a redistributive or a regulatory policy should be chosen depends on a large number of factors, many of which are situation-specific. In Chapter 7, where we will examine several conflicts between individual and social interests, we will explore the possible bases for making this choice.

SUMMARY

In Chapter 6 we have provided a framework for suggesting and evaluating specific population policy alternatives. To accomplish this goal we began with a discussion of the basic dimensions of equity. Then, in order to make the conception of social justice useful for evaluating public policy options, we specified a measure of social justice that could be operationalized and used when dealing with categories of people. After this step has been accomplished, the various criteria for evaluating public policies can be weighted in a consistent manner so that policy X can be said to be preferable to policy Y. In order to help in making policy suggestions, we next set forth a policy typology based on the process of public decision making rather than on a particular substantive area, such as fertility or mortality. This makes it possible to use policy categories across substantive areas rather than to treat each substantive area or issue as a unique case. These policy categories include distributive, redistributive, self-regulatory, and regulatory types. In the discussion, these four categories are then combined with three types of issues: those arising from ineffective decisions; those arising from conflicts between competing individuals or groups; and those arising from conflicts between individual and collective interests. This combination forms a matrix of policies and issues from which alternative actions can be derived. In Chapter 7 we will use this matrix to specify desired population policies.

POTENTIAL POPULATION POLICY ACTIONS

7

In this, the final chapter, we will use the framework which we set up while examining individual psychology, population issues, and governmental policies to suggest both general and specific governmental policy actions that we believe would have beneficial effects on the population problems of the United States. Before so doing, we again remind the reader that our policy suggestions, like all suggestions based on empirical data, go beyond the research findings reported in earlier chapters. We are also constrained by certain ethnocentric and chronocentric biases and, of course, by our own personal values. Our suggestions, therefore, result from the combination of our values and the analytic framework developed in Chapter 6. Readers may wish to apply their own values to our framework for analyzing population regulation and determine where this process would lead them on each of the issues.

In our general approach to population issues, institutions set the general structure of opportunities, incentives, norms, and rights in society, leaving considerable areas of behavior to individual choice. Policies may therefore be directed at changing institutional arrangements or at aiding individuals to make better choices within existing systems. Our own values lead us toward policies that extend individual freedom, encourage greater social equality, and make each individual bear the costs of his or her own decisions. Unfortunately, these three objectives are often in conflict. Our working out of these conflicts reflects our own estimation of the appropriate balance among them for each specific population issue.

In Chapter 6 we found that quite different policy actions were appropriate to the three basic population issues. We then developed a matrix of the interaction between our policy categories and these three issues. As a first step in moving from abstract to specific recommendations, Table 7.1 presents a brief description of general actions appropriate to each type of population problem generated by individual free choice. The general implications of these actions are self-evident, except perhaps for those in Part III (a) of the table. There we assume that certain rights are so basic that they must be

TABLE 7.1

	Problems	Actions
I	Ineffective Decisions	(a) Improve individual capabilities for effective decision making
		(b) Change context of decision making
II	Conflicts between competing interests	(a) Clearly define rights and duties where currently unclear
		(b) Redefine rights and duties where existing rights lead to social injustice
III	Conflicts between individual and social interests	(a) Determine if individual rights are prior to social interests
		(b) Change existing incentives and rights to bring individual interests into congruence with social interests

General policy actions for each of the three basic types of population problems.

protected even when they conflict with short-term social interests. For example, the courts have determined that the right of a pacifist not to fight is prior to society's need even in time of war. The Supreme Court has held that certain portions of the United States Constitution hold a "preferred position," that is, they take precedence over other rights defined by law or custom that conflict with them. Christian Bay discusses how society might determine which rights should hold this preferred position in his book, *The Structure of Freedom* (1).

In the first part of this chapter we will elaborate on the implications of Table 7.1 for the dynamic demographic factor of fertility. Potential population policy actions will be described in more detail, drawing upon the model of decision making developed in Chapters 3 and 4 and that of the four basic policies (distributive, redistributive, self-regulatory, or regulatory) developed in Chapter 6. We will not attempt to be comprehensive in our policy suggestions; rather, we will present and discuss certain key and representative potential policy actions to illustrate various features of our policy model and its application. After examining fertility we will discuss in less detail problems related to choice for the three dynamic demographic factors of mortality, geographic mobility, and status mobility, again drawing upon our decision making and policy models. Finally, the last section will deal with the need for a population bureaucracy.

POTENTIAL FERTILITY POLICIES
FOR INEFFECTIVE DECISIONS

Improving Individual Capabilities for Effective Decision Making
Whether fertility policies should be distributive and self-regulatory (family planning) or redistributive and regulatory (those that go beyond family planning) is the subject of considerable current debate. Distributive and self-regulatory policies include the development of better contraceptive, sterilization, and abortion techniques, media campaigns, and service delivery; on the other hand redistrib-

utive and regulatory policies entail economic development programs for special-need groups, redistributive income plans, and
nonvoluntary restrictions on family size. We will begin by examining some distributive and self-regulatory policies directed at improving the capability of individuals for making effective, fertility-
related decisions. Using the decision model developed in Chapter
3, five conceptually distinct modes of policy action will be discussed.

Informational and Consciousness-raising Programs. These programs include actions designed to provide information and to increase individuals' awareness of their fertility options, to aid them
in becoming cognizant of the social and personal issues these options involve, and to alert them to the possible decision outcome
failures that may follow. Such programs may be developed through
the media, schools, and various other public and private social service organizations. Their purpose is to shift the individual from the
preawareness stage of the decision process to one where issues, options, and outcomes are known and understood, and their personal
relevance recognized. To be effective, therefore, the programs must
affect the individual before ineffective decision making occurs.

Research concerning fertility has identified many of the events or
points in the life-course that are highly associated with ineffective
decision making. For example, in Chapter 3 we indicated that the
probability of an unwanted pregnancy is much higher during eight
recognizable stages of a woman's sexual and reproductive career.
Individual awareness of the earlier vulnerable stages could be acquired through sex education in the public schools prior to the time
when most adolescents become sexually active. Such education
would describe the ways that can be chosen for mastering the challenges and stresses related to sexual career initiation and to adolescent sexual relationships. During later vulnerable stages, other institutions could keep a particular population informed of their own
vulnerabilities in a regular and low-cost manner. For example, the
armed forces could effectively identify and alert persons who might
face an unwanted pregnancy resulting from reunion with their sex-

ual partner after service-related duty, as in the case of the wife of a soldier about to be reunited with her husband after the latter's overseas tour of duty. A pamphlet routinely mailed to her in advance of his return might prepare her for some aspects of his return, including the need for making a decision about contraception, might enumerate the possible choices and the risks and side effects of each method, and might provide her with information as to where contraception could be obtained. Similar policies could be used during the other vulnerable stages. For example, the postpartum period could be, and to some extent is, handled through postpartum family planning programs that prepare women, even before they leave the hospital, for the fertility-control problems they will face during the first few months after delivery (2).

A number of organizations in society could also routinely supply information to persons who are at important transition points in their lives and susceptible to ineffective decision making. The Social Security Administration has records of the age, address, and marital status of most individuals currently working for pay. Ineffective decision making and decision outcome failures in fertility, mortality, and geographic and status mobility are especially associated with changes in age, marital status, occupation, and place of living; and the Social Security Administration could make information available to persons undergoing or about to undergo such changes. We are specially cautious in suggesting such programs because of possible violations of the right to privacy and other abuses. However, these programs could be part of an overall informational service and provided with the necessary precautions to guard individual rights, at the same time making effective use of current research concerning the patterns of ineffective decision making that occur in population-related areas.

An informational policy might be instituted by the Social Security Office selecting certain ages when significant life changes occur. Men and women who reach the age range of forty to forty-five have important life changes in process or, at least, near. If the couple have children, these children may be about to enter college. Geographic mobility becomes more probable as the size of the household is reduced and the parents are no longer concerned with disrupting the social life of their children. The woman may be simultaneously dealing with the "empty nest syndrome" and approaching menopause. She will also be more vulnerable to health problems if using oral contraceptives. To alert individuals to the fertility problems associated with this age period an information packet could be mailed to them. Ideally, the packet would inform individuals not only of their vulnerability to ineffective decision making, but also of the benefits they or their family were eligible for, the services available in their community or region, and where additional information or counseling on reproductive, medical, or occupational concerns could be obtained.

There are, of course, many other public and private organizations that could supply the same information. We are not recommending one organization over another; rather, we are suggesting that use be made of those organizations most appropriate to provide the impetus necessary to move people from a preawareness position to one of recognition both of their vulnerability and of their options.

Educational and Experiential Programs. The second category of programs that can facilitate effective decision making comprises educational and experiential programs designed to improve decision-making skills through practice or practical experience. Informational and consciousness-raising policy actions place the issues surrounding population decisions in a more salient position and provide better information with which to make these decisions, but such policies do not directly help those persons whose decision-making skills are inadequate. As we suggested in Chapter 3, the ego must be capable of integrating competing and conflicting desires in a relatively consistent and long-term, future-oriented way. It must also be able to move skillfully through the stages of decision making. One of the ways that the ego acquires these capabilities and skills is by practice. A decision to get married, to have a baby, to take a serious health risk, to change residences, or to change occupations—all of these, of course, do not lend themselves to repeated trial-and-error learning. Nor are they made with sufficient frequency to teach appropriate decision strategies specific to the unique problems of each. Such decisions also tend to be stressful and produce anxiety, and this places an additional burden on the ego. Finally, these decisions are usually made in conjunction with at least one other person. Each of these characteristics—unknown outcome, infrequency, anxiety, and the involvement of others—makes effective decision making more difficult and the development of decision-making skills more important.

To increase the fertility-related decision-making skills of individuals, we suggest that opportunities for practice be made available. One type of practice occurs in the classroom. A high school in Portland, Oregon, provides an example. In a family-education class students are paired and for several weeks simulate many of the decisions that occur in marriage. Decisions about everyday activities like budgeting and shopping for food are practiced. In addition, students must face common decisions like finding a suitable house or apartment, or coping with an unexpected pregnancy, the loss of employment, and other stress-producing situations. Although this is done in a simulated rather than in a real situation, the students must actually find an available apartment within their community, stay within a budget that reflects average income levels of young married persons in the local area, and change their living patterns to adapt to unexpected setbacks. Because the situation is a simulated one, decisions are not irrevocable and alternative strategies can be employed. It is hoped that this "practice" alerts the students to the potential problems in major life-decision areas and gives them a chance to resolve those issues relevant to themselves in an effective manner; then, if the situation becomes "real," the students should have more of the skills necessary to carefully delineate and evaluate their options.

Other types of practice can occur in nonclassroom, daily activities. For example, adolescents and young adults can gain experience that helps prepare them for their own fertility decisions by working with young children in private homes or in child-care centers. Voluntary associations, labor unions, women's groups, neighborhood associations, welfare organizations, and other existing organizations can be helpful in identifying the unique situations with which their members must deal, and these groups' can provide the appropriate experiences and personal support required to improve decision-making skills prior to a person's facing actual situations.

Anticipatory and Situational Counseling Programs.   Many individuals are involved in one or more community organizations while they are actively working on fertility-related decisions. Schools and colleges, clinics and hospitals, the military services, churches, and corporations all have counselors and counseling services as part of their structure. Policies that support counseling in these contexts, especially counseling that focuses on fertility-related decision making, could substantially increase effective decision making. This would include both situational and anticipatory counseling. Examples include counseling a woman in selecting a contraceptive method, in a contraceptive clinic; counseling a couple about to get married, in a clergyman's office; or counseling a married student dealing with an unplanned pregnancy, in a student counseling program. These are all examples of situational counseling. Counseling becomes anticipatory when it deals with matters that are not current but nonetheless relevant to the counselee's future such as discussing future contraception during abortion counseling or discussing future childbearing during premarital counseling. Emphasis on fertility-related, anticipatory counseling could be achieved in many different organizational settings and could prevent much ineffective decision making before it results in an outcome failure. For example, research on the psychological and behavior antecedents to unwanted pregnancy (3) suggests that counseling programs emphasize:

    (a) the risks of calendar rhythm and withdrawal as methods of contraception;

    (b) the major side effects and undesired consequences of both contraception and pregnancy;

    (c) the psychological mechanisms of suppression and denial including their well-adaptive and maladaptive functions;

    (d) the statistics of conception following random and infrequent sexual intercourse;

    (e) the types of subfecundity and their implications;

(f) the sequences of behavior necessary for adequate contraceptive protection with each contraceptive method;

(g) the psychological factors that may predispose persons to the ineffective use of each contraceptive method;

(h) the motivational psychology of sexual activity;

(i) and the medical, psychological, and ethical aspects of induced abortion.

If these topics were meaningfully covered in clinic, school, and other counseling programs, ineffective decision making would assume less of a role in the production of unwanted pregnancies.

Although a variety of associations exist where anticipatory and situational counseling can take place, in actuality a majority of Americans, excluding those who are students, do not belong to any such voluntary groups or organizations (4). In those associations where counseling could reach the largest numbers of persons, such as in churches, only a relatively small number are prepared to provide the appropriate type of counseling. One means of reaching the remaining portion of the population would be through establishment of community-based Personal and Family Development Centers that would offer a broad range of services, including marriage and family counseling, prenatal care, childbirth training, contraceptive and proceptive information and services, and abortion, sterilization, infertility, and other services related to reproduction. For many individuals, such centers—supported by public funding but contracted out to individuals and small groups in local communities—could provide crucial help in integrating the many aspects of life that relate to union and reproduction. Preferably, such centers would not be organized primarily on the basis of the medical model and would routinely provide informational, educational, and counseling services throughout the sexual, marital, and reproductive career. Optimally, they would also be structured so that they were responsive to the challenges and problems of decision making and adaptation within the other behavior domains discussed throughout this and earlier chapters.

Basic Research Programs.   Although past research has generated significant new knowledge concerning fertility decision making, we are still a long way from identifying the many situational and psychological factors that lead to effective decision making. In addition, we have only scratched the surface in examining the effects of outcome failures upon the decision maker and related others such as the spouse or, if an unplanned pregnancy is carried to term, the child. For instance, what are the psychological consequences of induced abortion for women who have never borne a child, compared with women who have borne one or more? Or, what are the motivational, attitudinal, and belief factors which effect the discontinuation of oral contraceptives? Or, what are the psychological advantages of teenage childbearing or of being a single parent? If the above-suggested informational, educational, and counseling programs are to work effectively, more basic research is required concerning fertility decision making, the consequences of different decisions and of decision-outcome failures, and the effects of the life course and other situational factors on both of these.

Action Research Programs.   A fifth category of actions that can reduce the level of ineffective decision making rests on applied research. This type of research is necessary to determine which institutional and organizational patterns most effectively diminish ineffective decision making and outcome failures. Comparison of the size, location, organization, and other characteristics of existing programs and their success in reaching different target populations is a necessary first step. We also suggest that this research not only compares the effectiveness of each program in increasing successful decision making and reducing decision outcome failures, but also weighs the benefits of these programs against what society must forgo to provide them.

Changing the Context of Decision Making

Our first five sets of policy suggestions have been distributive and self-regulatory policies directed at improving individual decision making through the following actions:

(a) increasing the saliency of potential problems;

(b) providing information necessary to the decision;

(c) helping persons integrate their decisions with each other and with their long-range goals through practice;

(d) providing basic anticipatory and situational counseling services;

(e) and developing and evaluating knowledge of human behavior through basic and applied research.

These policies are aimed at aiding the individual in the making of decisions.

However, as is indicated in Table 7.1, ineffective decisions can also be affected by changing the environment. In fact, it may be cheaper and more effective to change the situation within which the individual makes decisions than to change the individual's decision making ability. To use an example from mortality policy, a great deal of media time and other resources have been devoted to encouraging adults to keep poisons and medications out of the reach of small children. Nevertheless, fatal accidents have continued to occur. To reduce such accidents safety caps have been required on medications and certain dangerous household products. In this way less dependence is placed upon the individual (remembering to place material out of a child's reach after use) and more is placed upon an environment structured to reduce the chance of an accident.

As we indicated in earlier chapters, effective contraceptive practice requires a number of decisions, some of which must be made repeatedly when coitus-dependent contraceptive methods are used. The development of oral contraception reduced environmental constraints since the pills could be taken at any time during the day rather than immediately prior to sexual intercourse. The IUD has further diminished the number of decisions by eliminating the necessity of daily repeating the decision to contracept. The "morning after" pill has eliminated some of the need to plan ahead and aids in dealing with an occasional unanticipated sexual exposure. The development of each of these methods has thus restructured the decision-making context of contraceptive use, and generally reduced the occurrence of decision outcome failures.

But each of these methods has certain negative side effects that make them difficult or risky for some women to use. Additional technological improvements including reversible sterilization, male methods other than sterilization that are coitus-independent, and increases in the safety of oral contraception and IUD's would further encourage more effective contraception. However, if technological improvements in contraception are to reduce the external impediments to effective decision making, serious attention must be given to the individual and cultural factors associated with contraceptive acceptability. This is because it is now widely recognized that different individuals react differently to the behavioral conditions required by each contraceptive method (3) and that different subcultures may require different contraceptive technologies (5, 6).

While personal and cultural factors affect what contraceptive methods are psychologically available, the distribution system for contraception and abortion plays an important role in the methods actually obtainable. For adolescents, the removal of legal restraints on purchasing condoms or other nonprescriptive contraception, the availability of these methods from vending machines, the establishment of Planned Parenthood Teen Clinics, which can distribute information and service at little or no cost, and the legalization of purchasing oral contraceptives by minors without parental consent are policies that would change the opportunity environment of the individual and remove external impediments to effective decision making. For adults as well as adolescents, the legality of induced abortion, especially if it is available in their home community and outside of hospitals, has a strong influence on the options that individuals have for avoiding an unwanted birth.

POTENTIAL FERTILITY POLICIES FOR CONFLICTS BETWEEN COMPETING INTERESTS

Once the issues of providing contraception to minors and making changes in the availability of induced abortion are raised, we move into areas where we are dealing not only with inadequate decision making, but also with conflicts between competing interests. Prior to these two issues the policies outlined represent actions about which there probably would be a high level of consensus. Opinion polls indicate that most people agree that ineffective decision making is a problem, and the polls also show that relatively few persons would see their rights and freedoms threatened by the actions we have suggested for improving individual decision making (7). However, as the public opinion polls conducted for the Commission on Population Growth and the American Future and the minority reports of the Commission show, the provision of contraception to minors and the liberalization of induced abortion laws do constitute issues for which a consensus does not exist, where the current distribution of rights is not clear, and where a significant number of persons perceive that their rights or the rights of others are in jeopardy (7, 8, 9). As we indicated in Chapter 6, at the point where an action *is perceived* as taking from one to give to another, the policy becomes regulatory rather than self-regulatory, if dealing with rights, and redistributive rather than distributive, if dealing with material goods. Therefore, where there are perceived conflicts of interest, whether these conflicts are between one set of individuals and another or between the interest of the individual and the collective interests of society, policies will tend to be regulatory or redistributive. As noted in Chapter 6, political decision makers dislike having to deal with regulatory and redistributive issues because the losers are aware that they are losers and are likely to hold the decision makers accountable. For this reason, although a clarification or redefinition of rights may be desirable from a society-wide point of view, these clarifications and redistributions will not likely receive significant governmental support.

Clarification of Rights

On the issue of induced abortion, the United States Supreme Court moved toward less governmental regulation in its 1973 decision (10). That landmark decision would normally be viewed as a self-regulatory policy, one that is in the interests of the general public and of the individual most directly involved. As we have indicated, however, many saw the policy as a regulatory one because they perceived that it took rights from the fetus and the presumed father and vested them in the pregnant woman. A crucial factor in determining appropriate abortion policies is the status of the fetus. If the fertilized ovum is determined by society to have the status of a human being, with rights and privileges equal to human beings who have already been born, then from the perspective of social justice given in Chapter 6, only when the life of the mother is equally endangered would it be appropriate to consider induced abortion as the legal right of anyone. If, however, the zygote has inferior status, then its inferiority from the point of view of legal rights will determine when the induction of abortion is applicable. If it were decided that the fetus had rights only during the third trimester, widespread availability of legal induced abortion would presumably develop, increasing both the freedom and the equality of those living outside the womb. Induced abortion would increase individuals' ability to choose when they want a child and even to choose the characteristics of that child. Induced abortion, particularly if it were inexpensive and readily available, would also increase the equality of options available to the rich and poor, and to those persons living in different geographic regions. (Currently, even with the court decision, legally induced abortions are far more available to the wealthy and to those persons living in urban areas.) Science cannot resolve the issue of when a zygote becomes a "human being" or what rights the unborn should have. Medical knowledge does tell us, within a certain range, at what stage the fetus is capable of sustaining life outside the womb; but this stage is partially determined by the level of available medical technology and by the different circumstances of each individual. Ultimately each society must determine the rights of the unborn, the pregnant woman, the presumed father, and society. Only when these questions are settled can a set of policies be developed to achieve the highest possible level of social justice.

If, as seems just and desirable to us, the rights of the unborn remain as decided by the Supreme Court in *Roe* v. *Wade*—that is, that only during the final trimester may the state intervene to proscribe an abortion (and the state is not required to do so then)—we would suggest the following set of policies related to abortion.

First, all women should have equal access to induced abortion. This would mean that abortion would be covered by public medical insurance. Second, the state should ensure that induced abortion facilities are available in all major communities. This in turn would mean that communities served by hospitals where induced abortion is forbidden would have alternative facilities. Third, continued research should be devoted to improving the safety of induced abortion and to refining procedures designed to determine fetal characteristics and the prenatal treatment of fetal diseases and defects.

The second issue which involves both the problem of ineffective decision making and conflicts between individuals over rights, depending on individual perceptions, is that of the access of minors to contraceptive information, contraception, and induced abortion. Do minors have the rights to these services without parental consent or do parents have the right to restrict the access of minors for whom they have legal responsibility? As with the issue of induced abortion, the exact distribution of rights remains unclear, and the responsibilities of pharmacists, physicians, and persons who supply these services, as well as the limits on how they may be distributed, varies from state to state. When the Commission on Population Growth and the American Future released its initial policy recommendations, the majority of the Commission supported "affirmative legislation which will permit minors to receive contraceptive and prophylactic information and services in appropriate settings sensitive to their needs." (11) However, several commission members dissented from this recommendation. Dr. Paul Cornely stated that "when we as a society accept the responsibility of giving contraceptive advice and services to those who are minors living in a family unit, then we are striking at the foundation and roots of family life." (11, p. 263) Later, President Nixon sided with the minority recommendation and made a stand against his own commission part of his 1972 political campaign.

One of the reasons the optimal distribution of rights remains unclear is that the effects of one distribution as against another are not known. Presumably the policy maker would have to know the impacts on veneral disease, illegitimacy, early marriages forced by pregnancy, the population growth rate, and other related outcomes for any given distribution of rights. The policy maker would also have to consider the effects on family life, in particular the relationship between parents and their children. Until recently funding for projects of such a sensitive nature has not been available and little direct research has been done on these issues. Presumably this is because political decision makers did not want to have to make decisions on this type of issue.

Although realizing the limitations created by lack of data and by politicians' desire not to act on this issue, we believe that current levels of sexual activity among minor adolescents will not be reduced by preventing their access to contraceptive information and services. Available data show that the majority of sexually active adolescents are not well informed about contraception even though many are involved regularly in unprotected sexual intercourse. We suggest, therefore, that sexually active and potentially sexually active minors be given the legal rights to contraceptive information and services and that parental consent not be required. In addition, the law should be explicit in removing any legal responsibility from physicians, health agencies, and contraceptive suppliers for providing contraception to minors without parental consent. We also recommend that research concerning the effects of contraceptive provision to minors be continued and expanded to examine the effects of these policies on the adolescents and their families, as well as on illegitimacy, venereal disease, and other more directly related phenomena, in order to evaluate and, if appropriate, alter the policy.

Redefinition of Rights

In examining the relationship between the allocation of rights and population issues perhaps no single set of policies is so striking as the "affirmative action" program of the United States Department of Health, Education and Welfare (HEW). Data from the Third World as well as from the economically more advantaged countries clearly indicate that equal opportunities for women and minorities are basic to fertility reduction (12). For example, as we indicated in Chapter 5, numerous demographic, economic, and sociological investigations have documented the many institutional arrangements in society which limit the scope of female participation in the labor force. It has simply not been possible for women to compete equally in the labor market. This limitation encourages higher fertility by reducing alternative career opportunities. Further, in the United States there is substantial evidence that much of the higher fertility rates of blacks can be accounted for by their relatively inferior socioeconomic position (11).

To facilitate equal opportunities for women and minorities, to allow alternatives to parenthood, and to expand social and psychological freedom, rights must be redistributed in society. The list of potential policies that would facilitate such a redistribution is quite long and we cannot hope to cover them all in this chapter. (For the reader interested in this issue we suggest Volumes I and VI of *The Report of the Commission on Population Growth and the American Future* (11).) As a basic first step, however, we would suggest the passage and enforcement of the Equal Rights Amendment. This policy may be largely symbolic, since the Constitution and its Amendments guarantee protection against discrimination on the basis of sex; but symbolic recognition is necessary in order to draw attention to existing discriminatory practices and to ensure that there are no ambiguities. The allocation of greater funds to promote and enforce HEW's affirmative-action policies is a second important step in the encouragement of equality. As a third step, Social Security payments should be changed in order to eliminate the existing disincentives to two-person employment in a family and to part-time employment. For instance, under the existing Social Security structure two families can have the same total taxable income of $28,000, yet the one in which both adults worked would pay social security taxes on all income, while the one in which only one adult worked would pay social security taxes on the first $15,300 solely. In addition, should the wage earner in a single-worker family die, the spouse could draw benefits. On the other hand, in the family where both adults work, if one should die, the survivor could not receive benefits. Thus, the single-worker family pays substantially less into the system, while potentially receiving much more. From an employer's point of view, there are also disincentives for allowing part-time workers or job sharing by husband and wife. If the $28,000 were for a single job position (such as senior accountant for a large firm) and the position is shared by husband and wife, the employer would have to pay social security on all $28,000 plus unemployment payments for both spouses. On the other hand, if only one person occupied the position, social security payments need only be made on the first $15,300 and only half as much must be paid to the state unemployment insurance. In this way, and in many others, society has steered its institutions to favor single-wage earner families and has limited alternatives to the traditional family arrangements.

Our existing institutions have been designed to suit a labor force that is predominantly composed of males and single-wage earners from each family unit. Our society has only recently developed institutions that facilitate alternative roles for women. In spite of the fact that almost one-half of all women of working age are in the labor force and approximately 45 percent of working women are the sole support of a family (11), child-care facilities in the United States are not adequate either in terms of the number of children for which they can provide nor the quality of care available. In the absence of day-care facilities, the woman who has a child may not be able to reenter the labor force. This means that the costs (both monetary and psychological) of an additional child will be lower than would be the case if day-care facilities were available. We would suggest, therefore, that government-subsidized day care be provided for low-income families and that day-care expenses be allowable as a business expense for all other families, without imposing a ceiling on the family income from which child-care expenses may be deducted.

Each of the above policy suggestions—increased availability of induced abortion and contraceptive services to minors, passage of the ERA, increased enforcement of affirmative-action guidelines, changes in the tax laws, changes in institutional structures to facilitate alternative roles, and increased availability of day-care centers—is based on the presumption that women, minorities, and the poor occupy an inferior position with respect to rights. For this reason a redistribution of rights and income is also necessary from a social-justice perspective. However, independent of that perspective, we believe that these policies will generally reduce population-growth rates. These policies are designed to redistribute rights and/or income from males to females, from parents to adolescent children, from families with a single male wage earner to families where both adults work or where the woman is the major provider of income, and from whites to nonwhites. Because the "losers" in this redistribution are likely to perceive their losses and use their influence to resist them, these proposals have received, and will continue to receive, significant political opposition.

POTENTIAL FERTILITY POLICIES FOR CONFLICTS BETWEEN INDIVIDUAL AND SOCIAL INTERESTS

The final set of issues related to fertility arises from the conflict between individual and social interests. If the United States is overpopulated or is approaching the point where further increases in population will lower the quality of life in society, then policies must lead to a congruence between individual and social interests. This means that existing incentives for having children must be reduced or the disincentives for having them increased, or both of these actions must be undertaken. These changes in the perceived benefits and costs of children can be achieved through a redistribution of rights or through regulation. The policies we have previously suggested for the resolution of conflicts between individuals, between individuals and groups, or between groups would tend to increase social justice while at the same time reducing fertility. In moving beyond these policies, we will continue to keep social justice and population reduction policies compatible.

In Chapters 1 and 5 we discussed an important aspect of resolving commons-type issues—the development of a sense of community and belongingness among the users of the commons. This sense of community tends to decrease as the size of social units increases unless structured changes are made to decentralize administrative and political decision making. In addition to the problems created by the sheer size of a "community," the lack of equality in that community may decrease the probability that a sense of community can be developed. It is noteworthy that in Hardin's article, "The Tragedy of Commons," he completely omitted the issue of equality. In the historical instance Hardin used as his example, that of the English Commons, only when the "commons" was used by both nobles and peasants, rather than by only one or the other of the two classes, did the tragedy occur (13, 14). When the users of the commons had equal status, the commons was not overgrazed. Recent research on population growth rates in developing countries has found that when a comparison is made between countries of similar per capita GNP, literacy, energy consumption, and other standard indices of economic development, those with greater social equality have significantly lower birthrates (15). It would seem that one of the keys to the commons problem is the absence of trust and cooperation among the members of the commons (15, 16, 17), especially when it is associated with inequality.

Redistributive and Regulatory Policies

The benefits and costs of having children can be changed either by redistributive or regulatory policies. Educational policies provide one important source of potential redistribution. Currently, the public subsidizes education to a high degree. The rationale for this subsidy rests on the belief that both the individual who receives the education and society as a whole benefit from individual education, as well as on the belief that education is close to being an inalienable right. The subsidy, however, reduces the costs to parents of educating their children, and redistributes income from persons who do not have children in school to persons who do, and from the present to future generations. It is difficult to judge the differential effect of this subsidy across income classes at the primary and secondary-school levels. The reason for this is that education is financed within the states largely through a regressive property tax. This means that the poor pay a higher proportion of their income than do the rich. However, they also have a higher probability of benefit since in the absence of public education at the primary and secondary levels any chance for the less advantaged to become upwardly mobile would be significantly reduced (18). At the postsecondary level, however, there can be little doubt that public education redistributes wealth from the less-advantaged to the more-advantaged citizens (19, 20). Tpis is particularly true at four-year public colleges, where the vast majority of students come from families with incomes well above the median family income and a good number of families with incomes in the top 5 percent. Given the regressive nature of taxation at the state level, the poor are paying to maintain the advantages of the wealthy. One policy for internalizing costs (i.e., making the benefactors pay), in this complex arrangement might be to have the student or his family pay the full cost of public postsecondary education. To insure that the poor were not excluded, loans could be made available that could be repaid from future earnings, or tuition packages could be developed where any individual could attend and then pay a percentage of all future income to the university.

Another means of internalizing the costs of having children would be to structure fringe benefits so that employees with larger numbers of children would pay more for insurance programs than childless employees and those with smaller families. The added increment could be determined by actuarial tables from different-sized families. Benefit packages could also be changed to eliminate maternity benefits or to make them optional, so that income would not be transferred from people without children to people with them.

A comparison of the two policies described above—alteration of the costs of postsecondary education and manipulation of health-benefit packages—indicates how the social-justice matrix in Chapter 6 can be used to evaluate policy alternatives. There is a chance that the rise in cost of health insurance for larger families would mean that children from economically less-advantaged large families would not receive adequate health care, while children from more-advantaged large families would continue to receive proper health care. Since we have included health service in our social-justice matrix and have suggested that these services should not be associated with parental income, we would not offer this policy as a desirable option, since it would increase rather than decrease the association between health and the economic wealth of parents. In contrast, because the poor are currently subsidizing the college education of the children of the wealthy, we expect that the internalization of costs through the education policy which has been suggested would reduce the association between education and parents' wealth. However, the probability that children from the less-advantaged sector of society would not attend college might be increased, since payment of the full cost of their education through loans or liens on their future income might discourage them; whereas children from more-advantaged families, who have their education paid for by their parents, would not be discouraged. For this reason, the actual effects of such a policy would need to be evaluated empirically, and, if necessary, adjustments made to ensure that both fertility and the correlation between parents' income and children's education were reduced.

In Chapter 6 we suggested that regulatory policies might also be appropriate for the resolution of conflicts between individuals and collective interests. Regulatory policies have the effect of increasing the cost of an action that society has determined to be undesirable. For example, almost all societies deem murder and theft undesirable under most conditions and they therefore regulate it. Murder of the "enemy" is acceptable in war, but after the cessation of conflict, the same action becomes a punishable offense. By setting and enforcing a punishment, society raises the cost of such actions for individuals. Automobile speed on highways is regulated because it has been determined that certain speeds create costs, or have a probability of creating costs, for other members of society. Therefore, if an individual exceeds the speed limit, the subjectively estimated cost of his action is increased by the expected punishment multiplied by the estimated probability of being caught. (The cost of the action may also be affected by whether the individual values the risk and breaking the law positively or negatively.)

Regulatory policies have an appeal in that they appear simple (the sanctions for breaking the rule are generally quite clear) and seem to treat everyone equally. They also tend to be perceived as more effective than other policies (21). If the state attempts to change behavior through distributive, self-regulatory, or redistributive policies, there remains some measure of voluntary compliance or noncompliance. Such policies can be aimed at steering the statistical aggregate of individual decisions to achieve the desired fertility level. What any one individual decides is not important as long as the aggregate effect approximates to the desired level. To accomplish this approximation, these policy types depend on the government's having a reasonably accurate estimation of the incentive or disincentive necessary to achieve the appropriate aggregate effects. A regulatory policy would work in an entirely different way. It would say, for example, that each individual can have no more than one child (or two per couple). It would rely on governmental enforcement and punishment rather than on the market, to reach the desired fertility goal.

Regulatory policies concerned with family size might be perceived as more equitable than other policy types because they are designed to treat all persons equally (just as the speed limit for everyone is the same), but this appearance of equity is usually highly misleading. Differences in financial situation and differences in preference often mean that policies that have the same behavior consequences for everyone do not coerce equally. The degree of coercion that individuals experience as a result of any policy is equal to the value of the difference between what those individuals would do in the absence of the governmental policy and what they do given the policy (22). If two persons, one with an income of $100.00 a week and another with an income of $1,000.00 a week each received a $25.00 fine for speeding, the punishment is hardly felt equally. Similarly, if you prefer five children and I prefer one, a regulation limiting every couple to two children would coerce you but not me.

Choosing a Policy for the Commons:
Coercion and Social Justice

If either a redistributive or a regulatory policy can resolve conflicts between individual and social interest, when should one type be chosen over another? Although we cannot say that one would always be preferable since the economic, administrative, and technical feasibility of each would vary, we can offer certain guidelines. The redistributive policies most consistently suggested for reducing fertility are taxation and monetary policies. Examples include the allowing of income-tax deductions for only the first two children in a family and monetary payments for persons who have two or less children. Elimination of the income-tax deductions has been criticized as creating a disincentive too small to be effective for most of the population, placing the heaviest financial burden on those income groups who make enough to pay some taxes but not enough to make the disincentive meaningless, and not affecting the high-fertility segment of the population that does not earn a taxable income. Incentives that encourage small families have been used outside the United States (23, 24), but reaction to these redistributive policies has been that they are highly coercive and discriminate against the poor (11, 25, 26). The alternatives usually suggested are regulatory policies such as one setting a limit of two children per family with appropriate sanctions to encourage compliance or, more frequently, self-regulatory ones stressing educational and propaganda programs that encourage couples to "voluntarily" reduce their family size.

From the point of view of the poor or on the basis of social justice, we believe that the incentive program is better than either a regulation requiring all persons to have only a specified number of children, or an educational and propaganda program directed at changing preferences for family size. Why? The regulatory policy has at least three major drawbacks. First, presumably there is some social value in having a range of family sizes (11). Second, as we indicated in connection with speed limits, if the sanctions for breaking the regulation are monetary, the fine is likely to seem greater to the less economically advantaged than to the more advantaged. In addition, regardless of the sanction, the higher-income and better-educated families tend to use their advantages to reduce the imposed penalty. (This tendency has been well documented (27) and was very clear in connection with the use of the death penalty (28).) Third, because persons have different family-size preferences, the policy coerces only those whose size preferences are larger than the approved one.

In the case of education and propaganda programs to change family-size preferences, there are two shortcomings that have been generally ignored. First, if the appeal to reduce family size is made on the basis that reduction of the fertility rate is beneficial to society, then those persons who comply for the sake of society provide benefits to those who do not do so. Second, the persons who change their preferences presumably first valued a large family for certain benefits that it provided. If these benefits were economic in nature (for example in the developing countries where children may provide needed labor and security in old age), then these benefits are forgone without economic compensation. Since the less advantaged in society are more inclined to have children for economic and related reasons, they suffer a net loss if they reduce their family size.

In the case of the redistributive policy, where monetary incentives are given to persons who have smaller families, individuals and couples will not be worse off on an absolute basis if they decide not to take the incentive; and presumably if they do keep their family size small in order to obtain the incentive, the family has determined that it would be more advantageous to have the incentive than additional children. In other words, nothing has been taken from the family; rather they have been given an additional choice. To illustrate, imagine yourself asking those families, which have limited resources and want a larger number of children than society regards as acceptable, what policy they would prefer:

(a) to be subject to penalties if they exceed the number of children that society desires;

(b) to go through a propaganda program to change their preference patterns;

(c) or to have the option of maintaining their current intentions or receiving a payment for having fewer children.

We believe that the last option would have the greatest support and we suggest that it would increase social justice by making income transfers from the more to the less wealthy. Since incentives as well as disincentives may have a coercive effect, if one wished to ensure that the less wealthy in society were not coerced more than the more wealthy, a combination of incentives and disincentives could be used. For those persons with incomes above the median, progressively higher taxes could be levied for each child over the limit of two; for those persons with incomes below the median, monetary incentives could be given for each child under the limit of two, with larger incentives given to individuals with lower incomes. What we are suggesting is that a redistributive policy could simultaneously steer the fertility rate toward the socially desired level, allow persons within the population to have a range of family sizes, and facilitate economic equality across income classes.

Individual Rights and the Social Interest

We have argued that society has an interest in achieving a given fertility rate and simultaneously allowing individual family size to vary according to individual preference. In other situations, however, society does not wish to allow individual variations, and in these cases, regulatory policies are preferred. Such situations are of two basic types. The first is where the individual action, rather than the statistical aggregate of individual actions, creates a social evil. Although highways have both maximum and minimum speed limits their purpose is not to achieve an average speed. Rather these limits are set to promote traffic safety by creating a relatively smooth flow of traffic. If even one individual drives faster or slower than the limit, his actions create a hazard for himself and other drivers on the road. The second situation in which regulatory rather than redistributive policies are preferred concerns those areas where society wishes to eliminate any differences in the distribution of a particular good or right, *regardless of individual preference*. This occurs when society decides that some good or right should be equally distributed and therefore creates social rules to eliminate any individual's ability to choose not to have the right or to trade it for some other right or material good (29). Examples of these rights or goods include voting, exposure to death during war, and child labor. In all states it is illegal to buy or sell a vote and severe sanctions are applicable to both buyer and seller. During the Vietnam War, selective-service laws were changed so that all males within a given age cohort (with certain exceptions such as conscientious objectors) were equally subject to being drafted. This was a significant change and a radically different policy from previous eras when a rich person could purchase a replacement. Child-labor laws were instituted to prevent children (and their parents) from selling their own services. Each of these cases represents a situation where individuals collectively decided that certain rights or goods are not to be bought or sold. Such policies represent the collective preference of a population about the structure of its society. Similar arguments have been made concerning the right to a specified level of medical care, prohibition of abortion, education, and job opportunities. If society were to decide that parenthood was such a right then our previous argument for redistribution rather than regulatory policies would not apply, or at the very least no incentives could be given for remaining childless.

As a conclusion to this section on fertility, Table 7.2 presents a summary matrix of policy types and free-decision issues for fertility. As can be seen, a number of policies do not fit neatly into just one cell in the matrix. This reflects the fact that two different groups may perceive a policy quite differently. Although we have included in Table 7.2 policies that are designed to eliminate commons-type issues, we do not believe that in the United States the current population size and rate of natural increase justify such coercive policies as fines and incentives or mandatory limitations on the number of children. Certainly at the present time they are not politically feasible. We believe that governmental efforts should be concentrated on reducing ineffective decisions and inequities in access to fertility-related services and equal-employment opportunities for minorities and women. These policies may well be sufficient to reduce the rate of natural increase to achieve population stabilization and prevent the statistical aggregate of individual decisions coming into conflict with the social interest.

TABLE 7.2
A Matrix of Decision Issues and Policy Types Applied to the Substantive Area of Fertility

Category of Decision Issue	Policy Types			
	A. Distributive	B. Redistributive	C. Regulatory	D. Self-regulatory
I Ineffective decisions	Subsidize: (a) informational and consciousness-raising programs (b) programs to provide practice for improving decision skills (c) anticipatory and situational counseling (d) basic behavioral research (e) applied behavioral research (f) development of new contraceptive technology		Give children right to receive sex education in the schools Give certain minors right to contraceptive services without parental permission	Give adults right to information concerning contraceptive use and vulnerable stages, and to determination of fetal characteristics Remove legal restraints on contraceptive distribution for adults

II Conflicts between individuals and/or groups	Change social-security payments and tax laws	Pass and enforce affirmative-action laws
	Subsidize abortion services	Give women right to abortion without consent of the presumed father
	Subsidize day care	Pass Equal Rights Amendment
III Conflicts between individuals and collective interests	(a) eliminate public subsidies for higher education (b) fine more wealthy for having more than 2 children, pay less wealthy for having less than 2 children (c) eliminate maternity benefits (d) change health-benefit packages so that persons with larger families pay more	limit all couples to a maximum of 2 children

POTENTIAL MORTALITY POLICIES

Almost all contemporary societies and most earlier ones have had mortality policies. These generally aim at decreasing the deathrate and increasing the length of life. Because of the wide agreement on the aim of decreasing deaths, coercive policies have been more acceptable politically in mortality regulation than in the regulation of other population factors. In particular, conflicts between individual and social interests are resolved in favor of the latter more frequently when mortality is concerned than when fertility or mobility are. However, medical technology has increased to the point where it is as difficult to identify when life ends as when it begins. As the health regulations extend into more areas of the individual's life, the consensus over the direction of further governmental intervention has weakened. Currently some social critics argue that intervention by combined medical and governmental institutions may be creating more illness than it is preventing and that the right to die is as fundamental as the right to live (30).

As indicated in Chapters 3 and 4, the decision to die or to compromise one's health may vary in its rationality and degree of intention. Health-compromising behavior, like sexual behavior leading to conception, may be the result of effective or ineffective decision making; in the latter case, it may stem from a lack of knowledge, the influence of external factors such as drugs or stress, motivational conflict, or inadequate decision skills. However, health-compromising behavior often is a result of effective decision making. Recognition of this is important in any discussion of policy since the resources by which society can increase health care are not unlimited and their costs must be balanced against the benefits attainable if the resources were allocated elsewhere. Individuals and societies have always put a price on human life whether or not they wish to admit to it. Each of us compromises our health to some degree to attain other goals that make life worth living. The individual purchasing a car can choose a Volvo at a cost of $10,000 or a Volkswagen at a cost of $4,000 and may rationally choose the Volkswagen even though he knows the Volvo offers greater safety.

Similarly, the public does not demand a highway constructed at the highest level of safety since highway safety, like most other under-takings, is subject to diminishing marginal returns. For example, the safest possible highway might have a mortality rate of one per ten-million passenger miles, while a highway that cost one tenth as much would have a rate of two deaths per ten-million passenger miles. At a cost of fifty million dollars per mile of construction for the safest versus five million for the next, society might well choose the lower level and spend the savings elsewhere. In this way, through a deliberate choice society allows a deathrate higher than the minimum possible. Thus, decisions to compromise health and safety can be rational at both the individual and social level.

Ineffective Decisions

Each year thousands of persons die as a direct result of or in con-nection with behaviors that compromised their health. These behav-iors include cigarette smoking, consuming foods high in animal fats, not wearing seat belts, driving while intoxicated, and self-ex-posure to high-risk situations such as hang-gliding. Some of these behaviors are not the product of ineffective decision making but of intentional and fully rational choices. However, ineffective decision making does produce many of these behaviors. We suggest that policies analogous to the five basic sets of actions aimed at improv-ing individual decision making in fertility would also be useful for reducing unwanted mortality. Briefly these include:

(a) informational and consciousness-raising programs that in-crease awareness of the health- and mortality-related conse-quences of behavior and of the social and personal issues in-volved in such consequences, and that establish alertness to the possible sources of disease and death. These programs, like those related to fertility, may be developed through ex-isting or new social organizations;

(b) Educational programs that provide decision skills through classroom and practical experience. For example, schools may give courses that simulate the conditions and typical sit-uational influences in effect when people make decisions

about using drugs, riding with an intoxicated driver, or seeking medical care;

(c) anticipatory and situational counseling programs that provide
personal guidance for future and present situations related to
mortality. As with fertility counseling, the location and ex-
tensiveness of such counseling would carry with the specific
organizational context;

(d) basic research concerning health behavior and periods of
special vulnerability to ineffective decision making;

(e) and action research that seeks new programs to moderate
mortality-related behavior and also evaluates new or existing
programs.

In a previous section we cited the example of safety caps on
medication bottles as a policy designed to make effective decisions
more likely by altering the environment rather than improving individual decision skills. There are, of course, numerous other safety
regulations in building, highway construction, and pollution-emis-
sion codes, that similarly exemplify this type of environmental
change. Many of these are relatively inexpensive, involve either no
inconveniences to the public or quite small ones, and are accepted
as appropriate by the majority of society. However, there are other
widely utilized environmental modifications also designed to increase effective decision making and reduce decision-outcome failures, which are much more intrusive and less uniformly accepted.
One of these is the auto safety-belt program.

When research indicated the value of seat belts a public information campaign urging people to use them was subsidized by the
government—a typical self-regulatory policy to encourage effective
decision making. There was little or no opposition to this campaign, and the car buyer could pay for the belts and their installation. In spite of their safety value, few persons purchased the belts.
In a move to make health-maintenance behavior more likely, the
government removed the option of not buying the belts and made
them mandatory on all new cars. Still, only a minority of persons
with cars equipped with safety belts used them. Later the government required cars to be manufactured that would not start unless

the belts were buckled and that made irritating noises if they were unbuckled while the engine was running. Not to be outdone, people found ways to disengage the system. Because only a minority of passengers use the belts after more than a decade of availability, the government may decide to require that a passive restraint system such as air bags be installed in all new cars.

Given the lengths to which persons go not to wear seat belts we can assume that their health-compromising behavior is intentional. Since the passive-restraint system will be much more costly at the same time that its safety is not much greater than the lap-and-shoulder belt system, the government is imposing a significant cost on both the persons who use the belts and those who do not, while providing additional safety only to the latter. In some respects then, benefits are being redistributed from those who use the currently available safety mechanisms to those persons who intentionally do not use them. We suggest that this redistribution violates the concept of fairness and externalizes, rather than internalizes, costs. Persons arguing for air bags could also argue that in the long run the costs to everyone will become lower by reducing premiums for automobile and accident insurance, by saving medical resources, and by protecting the investments society has made in individuals. However, several alternative policies could accomplish these same objectives. Air bags could be made optional equipment, injury claims of persons not using either belts or passive restraints could be disallowed (as are deaths by suicide under many insurance policies), and, if necessary, not using at least one of the two safety systems could be made illegal, thereby adding additional incentives for safety.

Conflicts between Competing Interests

There are important mortality issues related to the competition between groups over who has the right to protection from death and how the costs of safety and health should be allocated. To illustrate these conflicts we will examine some issues related to driving under the influence of drugs, and to cigarette advertising and smoking. Both of these matters involve the government's allocation of rights and duties between competing groups, which ultimately will affect either who has a greater right to life or who should bear the costs of protecting life and health.

Automobile accidents involving intoxicated drivers cause thousands of deaths each year and even more injuries. We suggest that people can and do intentionally decide to drive while intoxicated. Prior to a social gathering where alcohol will be served or before entering a bar, individuals can, and most probably do, anticipate that their ability to drive after drinking will be significantly reduced and their chances of being in an accident significantly increased. Nevertheless, just as a person may decide to take a chance with unprotected sexual intercourse, a driver may decide that the pleasure of drinking makes it worth the risk of an automobile accident. The driver is not, however, the only individual who bears the cost of the decision. Many other persons must share the cost of higher insurance premiums, police regulation, and the risk of being injured by the intoxicated driver.

A number of partial solutions have been developed for this conflict. Information campaigns have been used to alert persons to the risk. If the problem is one of ineffective decision making, these self-regulatory solutions may be helpful. However, given the continuing high rates of driving while intoxicated, it would appear that either the information programs are not correctly designed and/or a large number of individuals will not respond to this information. In an effort to increase the cost to the driver of drunken driving, criminal penalties for driving while intoxicated have been established in all states. The offender, however, is rarely sentenced to prison and the damage caused is covered in large part by insurance. In some states it is a criminal activity for a tavern or other licensed seller of alcoholic beverages to sell such beverages to persons who have reached a level of intoxication where continuence would endanger the drinker or others. This law is, however, rarely enforced.

One method of dealing with the problem would be to change the environment so that the intoxicated person could not drive. This might be done through the installation of a mechanism that interlocks with the ignition system and requires a driver to perform a delicate task in starting his or her car, one that would be too difficult for most intoxicated drivers. A shortcoming of this policy is that if this equipment were required on all cars, then nondrinking drivers would also have to pay for the device. In other words, the costs would be externalized from the drinker to the nondrinker. This shortcoming could be overcome by having the cost of the ignition mechanism financed through a sales tax on alcoholic beverages, with the amount of the tax proportional to the quantity of alcohol rather than the price of the beverage. Assuming that the level of alcohol consumption was highly associated with driving while intoxicated, the costs of the prevention would be largely internalized to those who drive while intoxicated.

The smoking of cigarettes, the regulation of their sales and advertisements, and the increasing regulation of where persons may smoke, bring together in a complex manner the issues of ineffective decision making and competing interests. Nonsmokers have always found it a disagreeable experience to be in the same area as smokers. Nevertheless, the right of the individual to smoke has generally taken precedence over the rights of nonsmokers. After the Surgeon General determined that cigarette smoking could be harmful to health, the rights of all parties became less clear. Questions concerning the appropriate distribution of rights included: do the cigarette companies have the right to advertise a product that injures the health of others? Does the "public" have a right to equal information concerning the harmful effects of smoking in order to counteract the effect of the millions of dollars spent to convince persons that smoking is a desirable activity? Do nonsmokers have the right to prohibit smoking in order to prevent their being near a smoker and paying higher costs for insurance? The existing answers to these questions indicate both how difficult it can be to reach acceptable policies when regulating rights, and how difficult it can be to regulate an industry as large and powerful as the manufacturers of tobacco products.

The competing rights of the industry to advertise a product injurious to health and of the public to know of the potential danger was decided by the addition of warning notices to advertisement and packaging and by the removal of cigarette advertising from radio and television (while allowing its continuation in the printed media). In view of the difficulties of regulating large and cohesive groups such as the tobacco industry successfully, this particular resolution of the "appropriate" distribution of rights is not surprising. The report of the Surgeon General created two major difficulties for the tobacco industry: liability to suit for health damage and a reduction in sales. The reduction in sales could be primarily traced to the antismoking campaign, which was largely financed through the equal-time requirements on radio and television. The warning notice on packages and advertising relieved the industry of legal liability. At the same time the elimination of the advertising removed the free time given to opponents of smoking. Recent studies of the effects of this elimination suggest that the industry correctly perceived that the radio and television antismoking campaign had been reducing consumer demand as much as the advertising increased it (31).

The Surgeon General's report may have had more impact on the reallocation of rights between smokers and nonsmokers than that between the tobacco industry and the public. Theaters, restaurants, airplanes, and other public places have increasingly recognized the right of nonsmokers to be free from close exposure to smokers by designating certain areas as no-smoking zones. Smoking in many public places has been legally banned. This regulation is mainly symbolic, however, as its enforcement is left to nonsmokers rather than to the authorities. Finally, the Surgeon General's report justified greater taxation on tobacco. This has partially returned the costs of reduced health and safety to the smokers. We suggest that further actions to return the costs of smoking to smokers would be appropriate. An example of such an action would be to require insurance companies and pension plans to have different rates for smokers and nonsmokers that would reflect their respective actuarial tables for sickness and life expectancy.

Conflicts between Individual and Social Interests

One of the more interesting aspects of mortality policies concerns government's willingness to force persons against their wishes to be healthy and not to compromise their health. The United States and other countries have for some time required inoculations for health reasons. Particularly in the case of international travel, smallpox and other inoculations have been used to reduce the spread of contagious diseases. Currently, many school systems require children to have inoculations for measles, mumps, smallpox, diphtheria, and other contagious diseases. Even persons whose religion forbids such inoculations have not been exempted. These policies are generally justified on the basis of the threat to others, rather than because the individual can be required to be healthy (32). That is, they are regulatory policies designed to resolve conflicts between individual and social interests, with the right of society to protect the lives of all citizens holding precedence over individual preferences.

One of the issues that has reached the political agenda and consistently stayed there is the "appropriate" distribution of medical care. Since most individuals want the best possible health care for themselves, even at a high cost to common resources, a conflict between individual and social interests lies at the heart of this issue. For more than three decades public opinion polls have indicated that a majority of American adults favored some form of government-subsidized medical care. Yet national health-insurance plans remain on the agenda of the second session of the Ninety-fourth Congress, with the high probability that they will be on the agenda of the Ninety-fifth Congress as well. Although the United States has significantly more doctors per capita than any other country in North America or northern and western Europe, its infant-mortality rate is surpassed by only two of the sixteen countries in this group; and life expectancy in the United States is lower than in fourteen of the other fifteen countries (33, 34, 35, 36). Although infant-mortality rates and life expectancy are influenced by many factors other than the level of medical care, examination of the distribution of deathrates among ethnic and economic groupings in the United States indicates that life expectancy and infant mortality depend upon the manner in which health care is distributed, and that this distribution is quite skewed in favor of the economically advantaged (35).

As we have indicated in Chapter 6, our own conception of social justice requires that access to medical care be unrelated to class, ethnicity, and sex. Although the specification of a particular distribution and payment plan is beyond the scope of this book, we do suggest that two particular attributes of existing medical services should be changed. We believe that these changes would have the effect of redistributing resources. First, preventive health care should be emphasized to a much greater degree. Existing federal legislation makes it extremely difficult for community-based Health Maintenance Organizations (HMOs) to provide services (33, 37). HMOs consistently outperform other means of medical insurance, whether lower cost or better health of the insured is used as the criterion of comparison (38). Preventive health care requires a planning orientation to one's own health. It also depends upon cooperation between the deliverer of the service and the consumers in order that the latter learn how their own actions influence their health and the cost of their care. For these reasons, HMOs offer services that include not only the usual care for the ill, but also instruction in health-related decision making.

Our second suggestion for changing the provision of health care concerns the technological- and capital-intensive character of health care in the United States. The existing incentive structure encourages the development and use of extremely expensive care for a few people rather than less expensive but more widely available care for many people. Current problems with malpractice suits and insurance further encourages practitioners to prescribe many tests that they know have a relatively low probability of showing positive results, because failure to make these tests leaves them open to malpractice suits. Similarly, the medical profession and federal requirements discourage the use of paramedical personnel for quite routine care that could be provided at a reasonable standard by persons who have not had the years of training necessary to be certified as M.D.'s. Finally, even though we set a price on life when making decisions concerning road safety, building codes, and pollution emissions, in the arena of medical services the presumption is often made that life is priceless. This has meant that extremely expensive services such as kidney machines and extraordinary measures to prolong life are provided for the few who have ready access to the medical arena, while less attention is given to general services for everyone.

Hospitals, doctor-patient relationships, and other institutions and roles surrounding medical care have been removed from the economic market in the sense that the hospital and the doctor are not expected to consider the cost of a service but to provide the very best available. This means that medical institutions discourage calculations concerning what must be forgone in terms of service to others in order to service the patient at hand. This removal of economic calculations may be a valuable attribute at the individual patient level because it allows the doctor to concentrate on curing the patient and encourages trust between doctor and patient (39). However, calculations concerning the distribution of health services must be made if society is to avoid wasting scarce resources. We believe that the existing structure of medical institutions does encourage the waste of resources and the distribution of services in a manner that violates social justice. If a better distribution system is to be developed the government should look to plans that make less intensive care and preventive care more available and more intensive care less available. In this way the medical practitioner could continue to prescribe the best medical care that was available, but what was available would be services and distribution patterns that were less discriminatory.

One final commons-type problem involves the right to die. At present the state generally withholds that right from individuals. This is best indicated by the numerous state laws which proscribe suicide, laws that are largely symbolic because of their nonenforceability. To some extent the right to die is withheld because of religious and moral convictions. It is also withheld because choosing to die is regarded as ineffective decision making. Finally, it is withheld because the individual's wish to die conflicts with social interests in the sense that society has an investment in the individual through his or her productive capacity and inherent worth. We have argued that individuals do, in fact, make effective decisions to die. We also believe that the individual's interest in dying does, in certain circumstances, outweigh the social interest. Therefore, we suggest that the right to die should be vested in the individual to a greater degree than is currently the case.

POTENTIAL GEOGRAPHIC MOBILITY POLICIES

Geographic mobility, like mortality, presents issues concerning rights that are currently undergoing rather extensive changes. The right to travel is part of Anglo-American legal tradition. The Supreme Court has alluded to this right in many cases but has never stated that it is a preferred right nor, necessarily, a right protected by the Constitution (40). However, geographic mobility is necessary from an economic standpoint to assure that the demand and supply of labor will be reasonably balanced. In addition, geographic mobility is closely associated with—and probably a necessary requirement for—social mobility. This association is particularly strong for ethnic minorities (41, 42, 43, 44, 45). At the same time that individuals may believe they have the right to move and our economy requires mobility, many towns and cities believe that they have the right to control their size and their distribution pattern, even if it disrupts the regional economy and denies persons the right of entry into their community. At the individual and family level, the potential of migration for increasing stress and family and social disruption is being recognized more and more. However, geographic mobility also provides important benefits. The family typically improves its economic and social status by moving (46), an improvement which is especially important for blacks (47).

Ineffective Decisions

We indicated in Chapter 4 that the United States is highly mobile compared to other countries. Vocational and other life course decision points are associated with geographic mobility. In spite of these considerations, recent evidence indicates the following:

    (a) one-third of all persons who move across county lines report that they began thinking seriously about moving only a month before they actually departed (11);

(b) two thirds consider no other destination than the place to which they move (11);

(c) six out of ten migrants rely on only one source of information—typically a friend or relative—to explore job opportunities in a new place (11);

(d) and unemployed and underemployed persons living in areas with large labor-force surpluses incorrectly perceive local employment opportunities to be as good as or better than elsewhere (47).

These findings indicate that the types of programs suggested for improving effective decision making in fertility and mortality would be equally appropriate to geographic mobility. The failures of past manpower training and relocation programs show that occupational training and information are, by themselves, not sufficient to achieve success. They must be combined with mobility programs that prepare individuals and families for the adjustments that geographic mobility require. Therefore, we believe that in addition to informational and consciousness-raising programs, other programs that provide decision practice and counseling both before and after moving would be particularly useful in connection with geographic mobility.

Conflicts between Interests and Land-Use Policy

Among the recent societal developments that have enjoyed the attention of research foundations, academic disciplines, and governmental institutions, land-use planning stands high on the list. It has been called the "new mood in America" by a special task force sponsored by the Rockefeller Brothers Fund (48). Land-use planning involves a number of techniques to guide and control the "who," "how many," and "doing what" of a community. The most typical of these techniques is zoning, which covers an almost endless variety of regulations with different rules and procedures. Zoning not only influences large land-use patterns such as whether an area will be industrial, commercial, residential, agricultural, or open space; it can also influence whether the industry will be light or heavy, whether the commerce will be banking and insurance or taverns and prostitution, or whether fences will be three- or four-feet high. In addition to zoning, other popular land-use techniques include private covenants, building codes, subdivision ordinances, transfer-development rights, conservation easements, and moratoria on building permits (40). In brief, land-use planning and controls offer state and local governments one of their most powerful tools to shape and control population growth, distribution, and composition (49). At the same time they offer state and local officials a means of excluding the blacks, poor, large families, and many other categories of persons that the community considers undesirable (50). Because of the powerful potential of land-use planning and policy, and because of the complexity of its issues, we will use it to illustrate both conflicts between competing interests and conflicts between individual and social interests in the area of geographic mobility.

Although most persons would not accept the right of communities to zone out persons on the basis of their ethnic background or their income, and although the courts have determined that such zoning is unconstitutional in that it violates equal protection and due process (40, 50), zoning is legally allowed for the purposes of protecting the health, safety, and general welfare of the community (51). Quite obviously the determination of when zoning is protecting the general welfare and when it is excluding can be difficult and subject to entirely different interpretations. The citizens of a community may see their general welfare best protected by implementing land-use controls either to eliminate or reduce population growth—particularly when it would increase the probability that persons with different ethnic or cultural backgrounds might move into the community. However, geographic mobility is an important means by which persons, particularly minorities, can obtain social and occupational mobility. If communities near locations of expanding employment opportunities limit the number of dwelling units that can be built, it is difficult for geographic mobility to take place. Persons currently living in the inner cities or in rural areas of declining employment may thus be denied the opportunity to move to locations where employment can be found. Zoning can limit mobility not only by limiting the number of dwelling units available, but also by substantially increasing the cost of housing. Previous studies of the impacts of zoning and other land-use controls indicate that they increase the cost of housing well beyond that reflected in the quality of the housing units (50, 52, 53).

Although land-use plans that limit the growth of a community may have negative effects on individuals outside the community and upon the region and nation as a whole, the argument that communities should have the right to limit their own growth also has considerable validity. Communities that grow extremely rapidly may suffer extensive costs in terms of having to cope with the social dislocations that the growth causes, such as extensive public investment in schools, roads, and sewage treatment. Since it normally requires several years for these services to catch up to growth, school children and others dependent on these services may suffer from temporary shortages. Farmers located at the urban fringe may be forced to change their occupations as the taxes on their lands skyrocket. Growth often increases pollution, noise, crime, and other undesired effects. Individuals who retire into what was a small, pleasant community may find themselves ten years later in an inner city surrounded by persons unlike themselves, subjected to higher taxes than they can afford, but unable to move out because of the increased price of housing in other parts of the community. Certainly cities and towns need to plan to minimize the unsightly and extremely energy-wasting urban sprawl that unplanned growth creates. Beyond these justifications for limiting growth, many would argue that citizens of a town *should* have the right to decide what type of community they want and either to encourage or restrict growth to obtain their desires. Finally, the provision of open space and the preservation of prime agricultural lands, scenic beauty, and historical sites provide grounds for land-use planning that are certainly reasonable objectives for health, safety, and the general welfare.

An examination of the goals and guidelines that land-use plans typically include indicates that the provision of environmental amenities, low-cost housing, and geographic mobility need not be logically contradictory (54). In practice, however, a conflict usually arises at the exact point where the needs and preferences of the more-advantaged local citizens are at odds with those of the less-advantaged (55, 56, 57, 58, 59). The conflict is perhaps best illustrated by the case of Petaluma, California, a community in the San Francisco Bay region whose land-use laws are among the most controversial in the history of land-use planning. Petaluma enacted a plan that limited new housing starts to approximately 6 percent of the existing housing stock each year. The district court deciding the case determined that the following consequences would occur if the plan were to spread to similar communities in the San Francisco region. There would be:

(a) a significant shortage in needed housing;
(b) interstate, intrastate, and foreign travel would be seriously inhibited;
(c) the cost of regional housing would increase;
(d) old and substandard housing would remain in the regional housing market without decrease in rent;
(e) and persons of lower income would be unable to move into the better housing left by mobile persons of higher income (60).

In a study of the state land-use plans in Hawaii, Vermont, Florida, and Oregon, the four states with possibly the greatest amount of land-use planning at the state rather than at the local level, it was found that the most probable outcomes of these plans would be to exclude low- and moderate-income families from home ownership, to reduce geographic mobility (particularly for the less wealthy), and to increase the power of governments to exclude low-income persons and ethnic minorities (58). The study also indicated that the basic forces that influence land-use planning, at either the state or the local level, are the regulatory nature of the policy tool and the complexity of the zoning process. As noted in Chapter 6, regulatory policies often end in stalemates among the organized interests involved. When this occurs, policies move from regulatory to distributive and benefits are portioned out among the competing organized groups with costs falling on the unorganized. A process as complex as zoning with its R-1, R-2, R-3, I-1, C-2 classifications* as well as numerous special variances, specifications, and procedural rules does not attract and involve citizens who do not have substantial educational and financial resources and the ability either to interpret the language of zoning or to hire someone who can do so. "Public notice" of zoning changes are typically carried in the small print of the classified pages. These and related barriers to citizen participation have meant that the planning process is usually done by developers, speculators, real-estate brokers, savings-and-loan officers, agricultural groups, representatives from conservation groups (if the land-use planning is at the state or regional level) and, if the zoning action affects a single-family residential area, persons from that neighborhood (52). Noticeably absent from these public hearings are renters, low-income persons, and, of course, persons from other areas who might move to the community if housing were available (58).

Given the types of participants, conflicts over land-use planning usually occur between a developer or property owner who wishes to change a zone from lower to higher density use and the residents of adjoining properties who wish to maintain the open space or the "character of the neighborhood." Other conflicts may involve the developer and the conservationist struggling over the use of open space, agricultural land, or wilderness areas. These conflicts tend to be resolved by allowing the developer to build houses similar to those nearby, by giving "tax relief" to farmers so that they can keep their land in agriculture, and by preserving some open space while allowing other portions to be zoned in large lots for single-family units. The results give developers something to develop, farmers tax subsidies, conservationists some open space, agricultural land, and wilderness, and allows neighborhood groups to surround themselves with other upper middle-class persons. All these actions restrict the supply of housing and the restrictions apply most

---

* R, C, and I designate residential, commercial and industrial use. The numbers indicate the density and intensity allowed within each category. I-1 would be light industry while I-4 would be heavy industry. The meanings of "light" and "heavy" might, however, vary extensively from one town to another.

onerously to the provision of low-cost housing in suburban areas (50, 55).

The distribution of benefits to the developers, conservationists, neighborhood groups, and farmers costs the public money. Some of these costs are quite direct, as in the case of tax relief to farmers and the purchase of open space and wilderness areas. Less obvious are the costs of zoning for large lots and for single-family units which, when compared with higher-density uses and multiple-family units, substantially increase the costs of providing public services such as roads, water and sewage, police and fire protection, and school transportation. These increased costs remain, even after they are balanced against property tax and other forms of local government income (59, 61, 62). Given the regressive nature of taxation at the state and local level (19), it seems that lower-income groups may actually be paying in many instances to be excluded from access to housing and to geographical and social mobility.

Our review of current land-use plans that limit growth combined with our conception of social justice lead to the conclusion that the right to geographic mobility should take precedence over the right to restrict growth. The desire to restrict growth may arise from the desire to prevent persons of certain income or race from entering a community, it may also arise from the desire to reduce noise, water and air pollution, traffic congestion, housing patterns conducive to crime, and other undesirable effects that tend to accompany growth. While we believe the first justification for restricting growth is incompatible with social justice, the second justification may not be. If land-use techniques were based not on zoning but on performance standards, then the right to exclude would be replaced by the right to a certain level of freedom from the negative effects often associated with growth, but not from growth itself. The use of residential, commercial, and industrial zoning classifications were originally justified on the need to separate incompatible uses of land in order to promote health and safety (e.g., to keep schools and houses from being adjacent to a cement factory because of the noise, air pollution, and traffic associated with the factory). However, when zoning by classification is used, it is often not possible to determine whether a community is discriminating against the poor or enhancing safety and health. If, on the other hand, certain standards such as traffic flow, number of decibels, and water quality were used to determine whether a particular amount and type of construction could occur, and if these standards were based on health and safety requirements established through research, then a builder could construct either multiple-family units or single-family units as long as the construction met the specified health and safety standards. These standards would not only facilitate the elimination of arbitrary and capricious zoning, but would also facilitate the improvement of technology related to construction and pollution (63). In this way the quality of life could be maintained and improved, while simultaneously geographic mobility would be allowed.

POTENTIAL STATUS-MOBILITY POLICIES

In our discussion of policy actions related to fertility, mortality, and geographic mobility we have included a number of policies that affect status mobility as well. For example, the movement of women into and between occupations is affected by day-care facilities and women's rights. However, many additional policies affect the principal forms of status mobility more specifically. For example, divorce laws affect the movement of individuals out of the status of marriage, and scholarship programs affect educational mobility. A complete discussion of status-mobility policies is well beyond the scope of this book. Therefore, we will limit ourselves to briefly indicating the relevance of the decision and policy models we have developed to the substantive area of status mobility, using occupational mobility as an example.

As we have indicated on Chapter 4, the United States is a country of high occupational mobility. Many individuals have more than ten stable jobs during the course of their careers, and often these jobs involve a geographic move. Effective occupational decision making is therefore a key to job satisfaction. Since work has such a central role in the entire life course, it may be a key to many other satisfactions as well. Individuals need accurate and full information regarding available jobs. They need to be alerted to job opportunities that may be especially meaningful to them. They need practice in making occupational decisions. Finally, they need support and guidance, frequently in the form of counseling, in making these occupational decisions. We believe in the importance of policies that help people with occupational decision making through programs that meet these needs.

The current incentive structure influencing occupational choice leads to a number of conflicts between competing groups and/or individuals and between individual and social interests. One of the most important of these is sex and minority discrimination in occupational hiring and promotional practices. However, equal opportunity policies clearly give every individual the right to equal consideration for an available job, and we support the strengthening of these policies. Another important issue is unemployment: do individuals have the right to a job? Should public resources be spent in order to provide a job to everyone who wants one or, at least, to provide financial support to the unemployed? We support current policies that provide financial support during periods of unemployment and we believe that the individual's right to have a job should be further strengthened by additional policy actions.

IS THERE A NEED FOR A POPULATION BUREAUCRACY?

Throughout this book we have emphasized the interaction of population issues with each other and with many other issues outside the population field. These interactive features have been embodied in our general systems approach to the subject and by our development of the concept of a population regulation system. Therefore, as a final step in our discussion of potential population policies, it is fitting that we examine the need for a governmental population bureaucracy that could oversee the many problems and coordinate the many activities within the population field, as well as at the interfaces between the population field and other substantive areas. The characteristics of such a bureaucracy have already been well outlined by the Commission on Population Growth and the American Future (11), which recommended the following:

(a) that the federal government improve its capacity to develop and implement population-related programs and to evaluate the interaction between public policies, programs, and population trends;

(b) that the Department of Health, Education, and Welfare substantially increase the staff of the Office of Population Affairs and augment its role of leadership;

(c) that a National Institute of Population Sciences be established within the National Institutes of Health to provide an institutional framework for a greatly expanded program of population research;

(d) that a Department of Community Development be established that would include all of the Department of Housing and Urban Development, some programs from the Departments of Transportation, Agriculture, and Commerce, and some programs from the Office of Economic Opportunity, for the purpose of consolidating and coordinating those programs of assistance for the physical and institutional development of communities;

(e) that an Office of Population Growth and Distribution be set up within the Executive Office of the President;

(f) that additional personnel with demographic expertise be assigned to the Council of Economic Advisors, the Domestic Council, the Council of Environmental Quality, and the Office of Science and Technology;

(g) that a joint Congressional Committee be assigned responsibility for regular review of the population area;

(h) and that state governments reorganize or expand their own agencies in a corresponding fashion in order to give more attention to and take better account of the problems of population.

Although we believe that much greater attention must be given to population issues, we doubt that the establishment of large population bureaus and offices would achieve sufficient benefits to warrant the costs. Population issues must not be thought of as separate ones in need of separate institutions. Indeed the current institutional arrangement in which demographic components exist within each of the major bureaus such as HEW and HUD appears to us to have a greater potential for effecting change. Therefore, we suggest that using these existing components, each bureau be required to prepare a "population impact statement" for its new programs. The appropriate impact statement would accompany every bureau's appropriation request to Congress for each program. Through this process it appears that population issues would become better publicized and would be integrated with, rather than separated from, other government programs.

In addition to impact statements, we suggest that a greater percentage of the public sector funds being devoted to the resolution of population problems and issues be used to develop programs at the local level. The rationale for this suggestion is embodied in our concept of community-based Personal and Family Development Centers, which was discussed earlier in this chapter.

CONCLUSION

In this book we have described our understanding of the complex and dynamic way in which one society—that of the United States of America—regulates its population. In Chapter 1 we introduced a general model of the population regulation system in this society, one which was composed of elements from three main levels of analysis: the level of the individual person; the institutional level; and the aggregate or collective level. In Chapter 2 we discussed how population-regulation systems were vital to the adaptation and survival of all living species and how they were distinct and characteristic for each single species, including humans. We also gave a general description of the three population regulation systems that were associated with three different stages of human social and technological development. In Chapters 3 and 4 we focused on the individual level of the current United States population regulation system and on the linkages of that level to the aggregate level. In these chapters our discussion was primarily in terms of individual decision making and adaptation. In Chapter 5 we focused on the institutional level, discussing each of the institutions of major importance for the current United States population regulation system. In Chapter 6 we discussed in greater detail the specific institution of government and its effects upon the population regulation system through the processes of collective decision making and policy formation. Finally, in this chapter we have suggested specific policies which, given our values and our assumptions about how the population regulation system in the United States actually works, appear to us to deserve the highest priority. In suggesting these specific policies, we have attempted not so much to be comprehensive and systematic as to illustrate the process of identifying and selecting those public policies that will be most effective and appropriate for the United States.

Given the population regulation system as we have described it for this society, we would like to conclude by raising two questions of fundamental importance. First, how adaptive is the system? In other words, how well does it function to preserve the society and its members. Second, how compatible is it with individual happiness and social justice. In other words, does it function in a way that allows all individuals to develop their potential and achieve their personal goals equitably? These questions are general and value-laden and therefore elusive of definitive answers. Nevertheless they are crucial and must be confronted directly. Although we can only offer tentative and speculative conclusions, our analysis leads us to be generally optimistic.

One of the most frustrating aspects of population issues is the realization that those policies that tend to be most effective are the least acceptable to political decision makers. To resolve conflicts between individual and social interests typically requires a redistribution of rights and incentives. In the case of conflicts between individuals with competing interests, social justice typically requires a redistribution from the most advantaged to the least advantaged. Yet, as we have indicated, these redistributions will not be welcomed by political decision makers in a democratic political system. Other authors who have recognized this difficulty have reluctantly concluded that "the eventual rise of 'iron governments,' probably of a military-socialist cast, seems part of the prospect that must be faced." (64) Or, as another suggested in the title of his work, the choice is between "Leviathan or Oblivion." (65) However, the more authoritarian governments have not been more successful than the more democratically oriented governments in making "life less solitary, poor, nasty, and brutish" (66); nor have these governments better resolved conflicts between individual and social interests (67, 68). The logic of collective dilemmas necessitates "mutual coercion mutually agreed upon"; but as we have seen, coercion is compatible with democratic government as long as it is *mutually agreed upon*. In fact, a recent examination of commons-type problems has indicated that from a purely deductive perspective, democracy offers a better solution than despotism (69).

In spite of its shortcomings, it seems to us that a democracy of rational, self-interested individuals is a highly workable form of population regulation, with effective mechanisms for maintaining social evolution and for achieving social justice. However, this optimism is based upon assumptions about the presence of certain qualities in a society and its members. It is based upon the assumption that most individuals can develop strong, integrated egos which, within an appropriately supportive social environment, will enable individuals to make effective decisions and adapt to circumstances in a successful and satisfying way. It is further based upon the assumption that social institutions will function to encourage and support individual efficacy and rational action, to maintain a clear and just set of expectations, rights, and duties, and to keep individual and social interests congruent. It is finally based on the assumption that all individuals can participate actively in the process of collective decision making and self-government at the local and national levels.

In conclusion, we suggest that the fundamental features of our social system require expansion rather than reduction in the freedom of individual and family choice with respect to the issues of population; but freedom can only have meaning in the social context where it is understood that social rights imply social obligations. Under these conditions, it appears to us that the self-regulatory population mechanisms within the United States will work in the short term to preserve society without compromising principles of individual liberty and social justice. But with what effect upon other societies outside of the United States? And what of the long term? Ultimately, then, our two fundamental questions about the adaptiveness of the system and its compatibility with social justice lead us not only to examine our own system, but to look beyond it to other population regulation systems and to future times.

SUMMARY

In this chapter we propose and then discuss a series of public policies that we believe would be effective with respect to the problems of population, and we use several of the analytic frameworks introduced in earlier chapters. The problems of population are considered as resulting from ineffective decisions, from conflicts between competing interests, and from conflicts between individual and social interests. We suggest several general types of policy action that will be responsive to the problems in each of these categories. These actions include: improving individual capabilities for effective decision making; changing the context of decision making; clarifying current rights and duties; redefining certain rights and duties; determining where individual rights are prior to social interests; and making individual interests congruent with social interests. We then proceed to a discussion of specific policy actions of potential use in each of the four substantive areas of fertility, mortality, geographic mobility, and status mobility, utilizing the fourfold policy typology presented in Chapter 6. We next turn to a consideration of the need for a population bureaucracy. The chapter concludes with a general review of the book and with a discussion of the future adaptiveness of the United States population-regulation system for society and its members and the future compatibility of that system with individual happiness and social justice.

NOTES

CHAPTER 1

1. P. Ehrlich. *The Population Bomb*. N.Y.: Ballantine Books, 1968.
2. *The Report of the Commission on Population Growth and the American Future*, Library of Congress, U.S. Government Printing Office, Washington, D.C., 1972.
3. K. E. Boulding. The Economics of the Coming Spaceship Earth. In G. Hardin, ed., *Population, Evolution and Birth Control: A Collage of Controversial Ideas*, 2nd Ed. San Francisco: W. H. Freeman, 1969.
4. P. M. Hauser. World Population: Retrospect and Prospect. In *Rapid Population Growth*, prepared by a Study Committee of the Office of the Foreign Secretary, National Academy of Sciences. Baltimore: John Hopkins Press, 1971. Pp. 103–122.
5. P. M. Hauser. The Population of the United States: Retrospect and Prospect. In .P. M. Hauser, Ed., *Population Dilemma*, 2nd Ed. Englewood Cliffs, N.J.: Prentice-Hall, 1969. Pp. 85–105.
6. Population Growth, Chap. 2, in *The Report of the Commission on Population Growth and the American Future*, Library of Congress, U.S. Government Printing Office, Washington, D.C., 1972. Pp. 9–21.
7. U.S. Bureau of the Census, *Current Population Reports* Series P-25, No. 448. Projections of the Population of the United States by Age and Sex (interim Rev.): 1970 to 2020. U.S. Government Printing Office, Washington, D.C., April 16, 1971.
8. M. Mesarovic and E. Pestel. *Mankind at the Turning Point*. N.Y.: E. P. Dutton, 1974.

9. World Population Estimates. Washington, D.C.: The Environmental Fund, 1974.

10. J. Simon. Science Does Not Show That There Is Overpopulation in the U.S.—or Elsewhere. In E. Pohlman, Ed., *Population: A Clash of Prophets*, N.Y.: Signet, 1973. Pp. 48–62.

11. E. Pohlman. *Population: A Clash of Prophets*. N.Y.: Signet, 1973.

12. P. K. Whelpton and C. V. Kiser. Social and Psychological Factors Affecting Fertility. *Eugenics Review*, 1959, *1*, 35–42.

13. N. B. Ryder. The Recent Decline in the American Birth Rate. In E. Pohlman, Ed., *Population: A Clash of Prophets*. N.Y.: Signet, 1973. Pp. 86–91.

14. J. Sklar and B. Berkov. The American Birth Rate: Evidences of a Coming Rise. *Science*, 1975, *189*, 693–699.

15. U.S. Population in 2000—Zero Growth or Not? *Population Bulletin*, Vol. 30, (5) (Population Reference Bureau, Inc., Washington, D.C., 1975).

16. L. F. Schnore. Social Mobility in Demographic Perspective. *American Sociological Review*, 1961, *26*, 407–423.

17. L. von Bertalanffy. *General System Theory: Foundations, Development, Applications*. N.Y.: Braziller, 1968.

18. J. G. Miller. Living Systems: Basic Concepts. *Behavioral Science*, 1965, *10*, 193–237.

19. J. G. Miller. *Living Systems*. N.Y.: John Wiley & Sons, 1972.

20. R. R. Grinker, Ed. *Toward a Unified Theory of Human Behavior: An Introduction to General Systems Theory*. N.Y.: Basic Books, 1967.

21. M. Edel. *Economies and the Environment*. Englewood Cliffs, N.J.: Prentice-Hall, 1973.

22. M. Olson and H. Landsberg, Eds. *The No-Growth Society*. N.Y.: W. W. Norton and Co. 1973. Pp. 1–13, 89–101.

23. H. Daly, Ed. *The Economics of the Steady State*. San Francisco: W. H. Freeman, 1972.

24. E. S. Lee. Migration in Relation to Education, Intellect, and Social Structure. *Population Index*, 1970, *36*, 437–443.

25. C. V. Willie. A Perspective from the Black Community: A Position Paper. In E. Pohlman. *Population: A Clash of Prophets*. N.Y.: Signet, 1973. Pp. 444–451.

26. A. J. Coale. Man and His Environment. *Science*, 1970, *170*, 132–136.

27. Resources and the Environment, Chapter 5, in *The Report of the Commission on Population Growth and the American Future*, Library of Congress, U.S. Government Printing Office, Washington, D.C., 1972. Pp. 55–76.

28. J. T. Fawcett. *Psychology and Population*. N.Y.: The Population Council, 1970.

29. J. M. Stycos. Some Dimensions of Population and Family Planning: Goals and Means. *Journal of Social Issues*, 1974, *30*, 1–30.

30. J. Blake. Population Policy for Americans: Is the Government Being Misled? *Science,* 1969, *164,* 522–529.

31. O. Harkavy, F. S. Jaffe, S. M. Wishik. Family Planning and Public Policy: Who is Misleading Whom? *Science,* 1969, *165,* 367–373.

32. K. E. Boulding. *The Meaning of the 20th Century.* N.Y.: Harper & Row, 1964.

33. P. A. Morrison. *Population Movements: Where the Public Interest and Private Interests Conflict.* R-987-CPG. Santa Monica: Rand, August, 1972.

34. P. A. Morrison. *Population Movements and the Shape of Urban Growth: Implications for Public Policy.* R-1072-CPG. Santa Monica: Rand, August, 1972.

35. National Institute of Education. Request for Proposal #R-76-0004.

36. J. Parsons. *Population Versus Liberty.* London: Pemberton Books, 1971.

37. R. L. Heilbroner. *An Inquiry Into Human Prospect.* N.Y.: Norton, 1974.

38. C. Bay. *The Structure of Freedom.* Stanford: Stanford University Press, 1961.

39. G. Hardin. *Population, Evolution and Birth Control: A Collage of Controversial Ideas,* 2nd Ed. San Francisco: W. H. Freeman, 1964.

40. J. Rawls. *A Theory of Justice.* Cambridge, Mass.: Harvard University Press, 1971.

41. T. Lowi. American Business, Public Policy, Case Studies, and Political Science. *World Politics,* 1964, *16,* 677–715.

42. R. Salisbury and J. Heinz. A Theory of Policy Analysis and Some Preliminary Applications. A Paper presented to the American Political Science Association Convention, Washington, D.C., Sept., 1968. Reprinted in I. Sharkansky, Ed., *Policy Analysis in Political Science.* San Francisco: Markham Publishing Co., 1970. Pp. 39–60.

43. T. Lowi. Population Policies and the American Political System. In R. Clinton, W. S. Flash, and R. K. Godwin, Eds., *Political Science in Population Studies.* Lexington, Mass.: Lexington Books, 1972. Pp. 25–54.

44. B. Berelson. Beyond Family Planning. *Science,* 1969, *163,* 533–543.

CHAPTER 2

1. G. G. Simpson, C. S. Pittendrigh, L. H. Tiffany. *Life: An Introduction to Biology.* N.Y.: Harcourt, Brace and World, Inc., 1957.

2. D. A. Dewsbury. Diversity and Adaptation in Rodent Copulatory Behavior. *Science,* 1975, *190,* 947–954.

3. B. C. R. Bertram. The Social System of Lions. *Scientific American,* 1975, *232,* 54–65.

4. R. A. Hinde. *The Biological Bases of Human Social Behavior.* N.Y. and London: McGraw-Hill, 1974.

5. A. E. Emerson. The Evolution of Adaptation in Population Systems. In S. Tax, Ed., *The Evolution of Life: Its Origin, History, and Future, Volume I: Evolution after Darwin.* Chicago: University of Chicago Press, 1960. Pp. 307–348.

6. J. A. King. Behavioral Modification of the Gene Pool. In J. Hirsch, Ed., *Behavior-Genetic Analysis*. N.Y.: McGraw-Hill, 1967, Pp. 22–34.

7. C. Darwin. *The Origin of Species*. London: Murray, 1859. (Quoted from 6th Ed., 1872.)

8. A. J. Nicholson. The Role of Population Dynamics in Natural Selection. In S. Tax, Ed., *The Evolution of Life: Its Origin, History, and Future, Volume I: Evolution after Darwin*. Chicago: University of Chicago Press, 1960. Pp. 477–522.

9. M. E. Solomon. *Population Dynamics*. London: Edward Arnold Ltd., 1971.

10. M. Williamson. *The Analysis of Biological Populations*. London: Edward Arnold, Ltd., 1972.

11. J. J. Christian and D. E. Davis. Endocrines, Behavior, and Population. In I. A. McLaren, Ed., *Natural Regulation of Animal Populations*. N.Y.: Atherton Press, 1971. Pp. 69–98.

12. D. H. Stott. Cultural and Natural Checks on Population Growth. In A. P. Vayda, Ed., *Environment and Cultural Behavior*. Garden City, N.Y.: Natural History Press, 1969. Pp. 90–120.

13. V. C. Wynne-Edwards. Self-Regulating Systems in Populations of Animals. In I. A. McLaren, Ed., *Natural Regulation of Animal Populations*. N.Y.: Atherton Press, 1971. Pp. 99–115.

14. J. A. Weins. On Group Selection and Wynne-Edwards' Hypothesis. In I. A. McLaren, Ed., *Natural Regulation of Animal Populations*. N.Y.: Atherton Press, 1971. Pp. 116–135.

15. S. L. Washburn and D. A. Hamburg. The Implications of Primate Research. In I. DeVore, Ed., *Primate Behavior: Field Studies of Monkeys and Apes*. N.Y.: Holt, Rinehart and Winston, 1965. Pp. 607–622.

16. P. Jay. Field Studies. In A. M. Schrier, H. F. Harlow, and F. Stollnitz, Eds., *Behavior of Nonhuman Primates: Modern Research Studies*. N.Y.: Academic Press, 1965. Pp. 525–592.

17. P. Dolhinow. Primate Patterns. In P. Dolhinow, Ed., *Primate Patterns*. Holt, Rinehart and Winston, 1972. Pp. 352–392.

18. H. Kummer. Social Organization of Hamadryas Baboons: A Field Study. *Bibliotheca Primatologica*, 1968, *6*, 1–189.

19. H. Kummer. *Primate Societies*. N.Y.: Aldine, 1971.

20. W. A. Mason. Use of Space by Callicebus Groups. In P. C. Jay, Ed., *Primates: Studies in Adaptation and Variability*. N.Y.: Holt, Rinehart and Winston, 1968. Pp. 200–216.

21. K. R. L. Hall and I. DeVore. Baboon Social Behavior. In P. Dolhinow, Ed., *Primate Patterns*. N.Y.: Holt, Rinehart and Winston, 1972. Pp. 125–180.

22. G. B. Schaller. The Behavior of the Mountain Gorilla. In P. Dolhinow, Ed., *Primate Patterns*. N.Y.: Holt, Rinehart and Winston, 1972. Pp. 85–124.

23. J. D. Goss-Custard, R. I. M. Dunbar, and F. P. G. Aldrich-Blake. Survival,

Mating and Rearing Strategies in the Evolution of Primate Social Structure. *Folia Primat,* 1972, *17,* 1–19.

24. A. Jolly. *The Evolution of Primate Behavior.* N.Y.: Macmillan Co., 1972.

25. H. F. Harlow and M. K. Harlow. The Affectional Systems. In A. M. Schrier, H. F. Harlow, and F. Stollnitz, Eds., *Behavior of Nonhuman Primates: Modern Research Studies.* N.Y.: Academic Press, 1965. Pp. 287–334.

26. T. Rowell. *The Social Behavior of Monkeys.* Kingsport, Tenn.: Penguin Books, 1972.

27. G. B. Schaller. *The Mountain Gorilla: Ecology and Behavior.* Chicago: University of Chicago Press, 1963.

28. J. Ellegson. Territorial Behavior in the Common White-Handed Gibbon. In P. C. Jay, Ed., *Primates: Studies in Adaptation and Variability.* N.Y.: Holt, Rinehart and Winston, 1968.

29. J. MacKinnan. Reproductive Behavior in Wild Orang-Utan Populations. Presented at Burg Wartenstein Symposium No. 62, *The Behavior of Great Apes,* New York, July 20–28, 1974.

30. B. Galdikas-Brindamour. Orangutan Adaptation at Tanjung Puting Reserve: Mating and Ecology. In D. Hamburg, J. Goodall, and McGowan, Eds., *Perspectives of Human Evolution and Behavior of Great Apes.* Menlo Park, Cal.: Benjamin Press, forthcoming.

31. V. Reynolds and F. Reynolds. Chimpanzees of the Budango Forest. In I. DeVore, Ed., *Primate Behavior: Field Studies of Monkeys and Apes.* N.Y.: Holt, Rinehart and Winston, 1965. Pp. 368–424.

32. J. Goodall. Chimpanzees of the Gombe Stream Reserve. In I. DeVore, Ed., *Primate Behavior: Field Studies of Monkeys and Apes.* N.Y.: Holt, Rinehart and Winston, 1965. Pp. 425–474.

33. H. M. McHenry. Fossils and the Mosaic Nature of Evolution. *Science,* 1975, *190,* 425–430.

34. S. L. Washburn and J. Shirek. Human Evolution. In J. Hirsch, Ed., *Behavior-Genetic Analysis.* N.Y.: McGraw-Hill, 1967. Pp. 10–21.

35. E. R. Service. *Origins of the State and Civilization: The Process of Cultural Evolution.* N.Y.: W. W. Norton, 1975.

36. R. B. Lee and I. DeVore, Eds. *Man the Hunter.* Chicago: Aldine Publishing Co., 1968.

37. A. Zihlman, Motherhood in Transition: From Ape to Human. In W. B. Miller, and L. Newman, Eds. *The First Child and Family Formation,* Chapel Hill, N.C.: Carolina Population Center, forthcoming.

38. J. B. Birdsell. Some Predictions for the Pleistocene Based on Equilibrium Systems Among Recent Hunter-Gatherers. In R. B. Lee and I. DeVore, Eds., *Man the Hunter.* Chicago: Aldine Publishing Co., 1968. Pp. 229–240.

39. S. L. Washburn and C. S. Lancaster. The Evolution of Hunting. In R. B. Lee and I. DeVore, Eds., *Man the Hunter.* Chicago: Aldine Publishing Co., 1968. Pp. 293–303.

40. C. G. Darwin. Can Man Control His Numbers? In S. Tax, Ed., *Evolution after Darwin;* Volume II: *The Evolution of Man.* Chicago: University of Chicago Press, 1960. Pp. 463–473.

41. L. Z. Freedman and A. Roe. Evolution and Human Behavior. In A. Roe and G. G. Simpson, Eds., *Behavior and Evolution.* New Haven: Yale University Press, 1958. Pp. 455–479.

42. J. Cawte. Psychosexual and Cultural Determinants of Fertility Choice Behavior. *American Journal of Psychiatry,* 1975, *132,* 750–753.

43. W. N. Stephens. *The Family in Cross-Cultural Perspective.* N.Y.: Holt, Rinehart and Winston, 1963.

44. Harlow, H. F. *Learning to Love.* San Francisco: Albion, 1971.

45. J. Bowlby. *Attachment and Loss.* Volume I. *Attachment.* N.Y.: Basic Books, 1969.

46. W. Peterson. A General Typology of Migration. *American Sociological Review,* 1958, *23,* 256–266.

47. K. Davis. the Migrations of Human Populations. *Scientific American,* 1974, *231,* 92–105.

48. R. M. Adams. The Evolutionary Process in Early Civilizations. In S. Tax, Ed., *Evolution after Darwin* Volume II. *The Evolution of Man.* Chicago: University of Chicago Press, 1960. Pp. 153–168.

49. J. D. Durand. The Modern Expansion of World Population. Proceedings of the American Philosophical Society, 1967, 111, 136–145.

50. A. J. Coale. The History of the Human Population. *Scientific American,* 1974, *231,* 40–51.

51. S. Polgar. Population History and Population Policies from an Anthropological Perspective. *Current Anthropology,* 1972, *13,* 203–211.

52. *Culture and Population Change.* American Association for the Advancement of Science, Washington, D.C., August 1974.

53. G. L. Cowgill. On Causes and Consequences of Ancient and Modern Population Changes. *American Anthropologist,* 1975, *77,* 505–525.

54. D. E. Dumond. The Limitation of Human Population: A Natural History. *Science,* 1975, *187,* 713–721.

55. L. Henry. Some Data on Natural Fertility. *Eugenics Quarterly,* 1961, *8,* 81–91.

56. F. Rosa. Family Planning and Breast Feeding. PAG *Bulletin,* Protein-Calorie Advisory Group of the United Nations, Sept. 1975.

57. G. Devereaux. *A Study of Abortion in Primitive Societies* N.Y.: Julian Press, 1955.

58. N. Howell. The Population of Dobe Area !Kung. In R. B. Lee and I. DeVore, Eds., *Kalahari Hunter-Gatherers.* Cambridge, Mass.: Harvard University Press, 1976.

59. E. Boserup. Environment, Population, and Technology in Primitive Societies. *Population and Development Review,* 1976, *2,* 21–36.

60. S. Polgar. Evolution and the Ills of Mankind. In S. Tax, Ed., *Horizons of Anthropology,* Chicago: Aldine Publishing Co., 1964. Pp. 200–211.

61. G. Sjoberg. *The Preindustrial Society: Past and Present.* N.Y.: The Free Press, 1960.

62. S. Polgar. Cultural Development, Population and the Family. Paper presented at World Population Conference, 1974, Symposium on Population and the Family, Honolulu, August 6–15, 1973.

63. N. E. Himes. *The Medical History of Contraception.* N.Y.: Gamut Press, 1963.

64. W. L. Langer. Checks on Population Growth: 1750–1850. *Scientific American,* 1972, *226,* 92–99.

65. D. O. Cowgill. Transition Theory as General Population Theory. In T. R. Ford and G. F. DeJong, Eds., *Social Demography,* Englewood Cliffs, N.J.: Prentice-Hall, 1970. Pp. 627–632.

66. A. J. Coale. Demographic Transition. In *International Population Conference,* Volume I. Liège, Belgium, 1973, Pp. 53–72.

67. D. Kirk. A New Demographic Transition? In *Rapid Population Growth: Consequence and Policy Implications.* Prepared by a Study Committee of the Office of the Foreign Secretary, National Academy of Sciences. Baltimore: Johns Hopkins Press, 1971. Pp. 123–147.

68. M. S. Teitelbaum. Relevance of Demographic Transition Theory for Developing Countries. *Science,* 1975, *188.* Pp. 420–425.

CHAPTER 3

1. G. A. Davis. *Psychology of Problem Solving: Theory and Practice.* N.Y.: Basic Books, 1973.

2. R. W. White. Strategies of Adaptation: An Attempt at Systematic Description. In G. V. Coelho, D. A. Hamburg, and J. E. Adams, Eds., *Coping and Adaptation.* N.Y.: Basic Books, 1974. Pp. 47–68.

3. W. B. Miller. Conception Mastery: Ego Control of the Psychological and Behavioral Antecedents to Conception. *Comments on Contemporary Psychiatry,* 1973, 1, 157–177.

4. J. Cohen. *Behavior in Uncertainty and Its Social Implications.* N.Y.: Basic Books, 1964.

5. N. Kogan and M. A. Wallach. *Risk Taking: A Study in Cognition and Personality.* N.Y.: Holt, Rinehart, and Winston, 1964.

6. R. D. Luce. Psychological Studies of Risky Decision Making. In W. Edwards and A. Tversky, Eds., *Decision Making.* London: Penguin, 1967. Pp. 334–352.

7. A. Tversky and D. Kahneman. Judgment Under Uncertainty: Heuristics and Biases. *Science,* 1974, *185,* 1124–1131.

8. W. B. Miller, and A. E. Weisz: Psychosocial Aspects of Unwanted Pregnancy: A Controlled Study. Paper presented at the Dana Research Lecture Series, Insti-

tute of Psychiatry and Human Behavior, Department of Psychiatry, University of Maryland School of Medicine, April 3, 1971.

9. W. B. Miller. Sexual and Contraceptive Behavior in Young Unmarried Women. *Primary Care*, Sept. 1976, *3*, 427–453.

10. K. Luker. *Taking Chances: Abortion and the Decision Not to Contracept.* Berkeley: University of California Press, 1975.

11. W. Lee. *Decision Theory and Human Behavior.* N.Y.: John Wiley and Sons, 1971.

12. W. B. Miller. A Survey of Psychological Antecedents to Conception Among Abortion Seekers. *Western Journal of Medicine*, 1975, *122*, 12–19.

13. H. B. Gelatt, Decision Making: A Conceptual Frame of Reference for Counseling. *Journal of Counseling Psychology*, 1962, *9*, 240–245.

14. W. Edwards. The Theory of Decision Making. *Psychology Bulletin*, 1954, *51*, 380–417.

15. J. R. Udry. *The Social Context of Marriage.* Philadelphia: J. B. Lippincott, 1966.

16. C. A. Insko, et al. Attitude Toward Birth Control and Cognitive Consistency: Theoretical and Practical Implications of Survey Data. *Journal of Personality and Social Psychology*, 1970, *16*, 228–237.

17. H. Triandis, et al. *The Analysis of Subjective Culture.* N.Y.: Wiley, 1972.

18. M. Fishbein and J. Jaccard. Theoretical and Methodological Considerations in the Prediction of Family Planning Intentions and Behavior. *Representative Research in Social Psychology*, 1973, *4*, 37–51.

19. T. J. Crawford. Theories of Attitude Change and the "Beyond Family Planning" Debate: The Case for the Persuasion Approach in Population Policy. *Journal of Social Issues*, 1974, *30*, 211–233.

20. D. J. Bogue and V. S. Heiskanen. *How to Improve Written Communications for Birth Control.* Chicago: University of Chicago Family Study Center, and New York: National Committee on Maternal Health, Inc., 1963.

21. N. Lin and R. Hingson. Diffusion of Family Planning Innovations: Theoretical and Practical Issues. *Studies in Family Planning*, 1974, *5*, 189–194.

22. J. F. Marshall. A Conceptual Framework for Viewing Responses to Family Planning Programs. *Journal of Cross-Cultural Psychology*, 1972, *3*, 1–21.

23. J. T. Fawcett. Psychological Determinants of Nuptiality. International Union for the Scientific Study of Population. *International Population Conference*, Liège, 1973, Vol. 2, 1973. Reprinted by East-West Population Institute, No. 43.

24. E. S. Lee. A Theory of Migration. *Demography*, 1966, *24*, 47–57.

25. M. H. Becker, Ed., *The Health Belief Model and Personal Health Behavior.* Health Education Monographs, 1974, *2*.

26. P. M. Blau, et al. Occupational Choice Participation and Social Mobility. In N. J. Smelser and W. T. Smelser, Eds., *Personality and Social Systems.* N.Y.: Wiley, 1963. Pp. 559–570.

27. P. H. Haas, Wanted and Unwanted Pregnancies: A Fertility Decision-Making Model. *Journal of Social Issues,* 1974, *30,* 125–165.
28. E. S. Shneidman. Orientation Towards Death: A Vital Aspect of the Study of Lives. In R. W. White, Ed., *The Study of Lives.* N.Y.: Atherton Press, 1964.
29. W. B. Miller. Relationships Between the Intendedness of Conception and the Wantedness of Pregnancy. *Journal of Nervous and Mental Disorders,* 1974, *159,* 396–406.
30. W. B. Miller. The Intendedness and Wantedness of the First Child. In W. B. Miller and L. F. Newman, Eds., *The First Child and Family Formation,* Chapel Hill, N.C.: Carolina Population Center, forthcoming.
31. W. B. Miller. Psychosocial Aspects of Surgical Sterilization in Women. Paper presented at conference on Research on the Behavioral Aspects of Surgical Contraception, Center for Population Research, NICHD, Bethesda, Md., June 18–19, 1973, Lexington Books, forthcoming.
32. E. H. Erikson. Identity and the Life Cycle. *Psychological Issues,* 1959, *1,* 1–171.
33. D. J. Levinson, et al. The Psychosocial Development of Men in Early Adulthood and the Mid-Life Transition. In D. F. Ricks, A. Thomas, and M. Roff, Eds., *Life History Research in Psychopathology,* Vol. 3. Minneapolis: University of Minnesota Press, 1974.
34. H. Feldman and M. Feldman. The Family Life Cycle: Some Suggestions For Recycling. *Journal of Marriage and the Family,* 1975, *37,* 277–286.
35. W. B. Miller. Personality and Ego Factors Relative to Family Planning and Population Control. In *Proceedings of the Conference on Psychological Measurement in the Study of Population Problems,* held under the joint auspices of the Institute of Personality Assessment and Research, University of California, Berkeley, and the APA Task Force on Psychology, Family Planning and Population Policy, Feb. 26–27, 1971.
36. W. B. Miller. Psychological Vulnerability to Unwanted Pregnancy. *Family Planning Perspectives,* 1973, *5,* 199–201.
37. T. H. Holmes and R. H. Rahe. The Social Readjustment Rating Scale. *Journal of Psychosomatic Research,* 1967, *11,* 213–218.
38. T. H. Holmes and M. Masuda. Life Change and Illness Susceptibility. In J. P. Scott and E. C. Senay, Eds., *Separation and Depression.* Washington, D.C.: American Association for the Advancement of Science, 1973. Pp. 161–186.
39. G. V. Coelho, D. A. Hamburg, J. E. Adams, Eds. *Coping and Adaptation.* N.Y.: Basic Books, 1974.
40. R. S. Lazarus. *Psychological Stress and the Coping Process.* N.Y.: McGraw-Hill, 1966.
41. R. S. Lazarus, J. R. Averill, and E. M. Opton, Jr. The Psychology of Coping: Issues of Research Assessment. In G. V. Coelho, D. A. Hamburg, and J. E. Adams, Eds., *Coping and Adaptation.* N.Y.: Basic Books, 1974. Pp. 249–315.
42. D. A. Hamburg, G. V. Coelho, and J. E. Adams. Coping and Adaptation:

Steps Toward a Synthesis of Biological and Social Perspectives. In G. V. Coelho, D. A. Hamburg, J. E. Adams, Eds., *Coping and Adaptation*. N.Y.: Basic Books, 1974. Pp. 403–440.

CHAPTER 4

1. U.S. Bureau of the Census, Current Population Reports, Series P-23, No. 49, *Population of the United States, Trends and Prospects: 1950–1990*, U.S. Government Printing Office, Washington, D.C. 1974.

2. R. A. Lewis. A Longitudinal Test of a Developmental Framework for Pre-marital Dyadic Formation. *Journal of Marriage and the Family*, 1973, *35*, 16–25.

3. J. T. Fawcett. Psychological Determinants of Nuptiality. International Union for the Scientific Study of Population. *International Population Conference*, Liège 1973, Vol. 2, No. 43. 1973. Reprinted by East-West Population Institute.

4. L. W. Hoffman and M. L. Hoffman. The Value of Children to Parents. In J. T. Fawcett, Ed., *Psychological Perspectives on Population*. N.Y.: Basic Books, 1973. Pp. 19–76.

5. J. T. Fawcett. *The Value of Children in Asia and the United States. Comparative Perspectives*. Papers of the East-West Population Institute, No. 32, July 1974.

6. B. D. Townes, et al. An Application of Decision Theory to the Study of Birth Planning. Paper presented at the American Psychological Association Meeting, New Orleans, Aug. 1974.

7. J. J. Jaccard and A. R. Davidson. Toward an Understanding of Family Planning Behaviors: An Initial Investigation. *Journal of Applied Social Psychology*, 1972, *2*, 228–235.

8. L. J. Beckman. Motivations, Roles and Family Planning of Women. Unpublished report for Center for Population Research, NIH, Grant HD-07323, Jan. 1976.

9. L. Bumpass and C. F. Westoff. The "Perfect Contraceptive" Population. *Science*, 1970, *169*, 1177–1182.

10. W. B. Miller. Relationships Between the Intendedness of Conception and the Wantedness of Pregnancy. *Journal of Nervous Mental Disorders*, 1974, *159*, 396–406.

11. W. B. Miller. Conception Mastery: Ego Control of the Psychological and Behavioral Antecedents to Conception. *Comments on Contemporary Psychiatry*, 1973, *1*, 157–177.

12. W. B. Miller. Sexual and Contraceptive Behavior in Young Unmarried Women. *Primary Care*, Sept. 1976, *3*, 427–453.

13. J. Bardwick. Psychological Factors in the Acceptance and Use of Oral Contraceptives. In J. T. Fawcett, Ed., *Psychological Perspectives on Population*. N.Y.: Basic Books, 1973. Pp. 274–305.

14. H. P. David. Psychological Studies in Abortion. In J. T. Fawcett, Ed., *Psychological Perspectives on Population*. N.Y.: Basic Books, 1973. Pp. 241–273.

15. W. B. Miller. Psychological and Psychiatric Aspects of Population Problems. In S. Arieti, Ed., *American Handbook of Psychiatry*, Vol. 6. N.Y.: Basic Books, 1976. Pp. 977–1019.

16. W. B. Miller. A Survey of Psychological Antecedents to Conception Among Abortion Seekers. *Western Journal of Medicine*, 1975, *122*, 12–19.

17. K. L. Cannon and R. Long. Premarital Sexual Behavior in the Sixties. *Journal of Marriage and the Family*, 1971, *33*, 36–49.

18. C. F. Westoff. The Yield of the Imperfect: The 1970 National Fertility Study. *Demography*, 1975, *12*, 573–580.

19. P. C. Glick. Some Recent Changes in American Families. *Current Population Reports* P-23 No. 52. U.S. Department of Commerce, Bureau of the Census, 1975.

20. P. C. Glick. Updating the Life Cycle of the Family. Paper presented at the annual meeting of the Population Association of America, Montreal, April 1976.

21. P. J. Stein. Singlehood: An Alternative to Marriage. In M. B. Sussman, Ed. *The Family Coordinator: Special Issues on the Second Experience: Variant Family Forms and Life Styles*. Minneapolis: National Council on Family Relations, Vol. 24, 1975. Pp. 489–504.

22. J. E. Veevers. The Moral Careers of Voluntarily Childless Wives: Notes on the Defense of a Variant World View. *The Family Coordinator*, 1975, *24*, 473–487.

23. A. S. Rossi. Transition to Parenthood. *Journal of Marriage and the Family*, 1968, *30*, 26–39.

24. J. C. Ridley. The Changing Position of American Women: Education, Labor Force Participation, and Fertility. In Fogarty International Center Proceedings, No. 3, *The Family in Transition*. Washington, D.C.: U.S. Government Printing Office, Nov. 3–6, 1969. Pp. 199–236.

25. P. K. Whelpton, A. A. Campbell, and J. E. Patterson. *Fertility and Family Planning in the United States*. Princeton, N.J.: Princeton University Press, 1966.

26. C. F. Westoff, et al. *Family Growth in Metropolitan America*. Princeton, N.J.: Princeton University Press, 1961.

27. C. F. Westoff, et al. *The Third Child*, Princeton, N.J.: Princeton University Press, 1963.

28. L. Bumpass and C. F. Westoff. *The Later Years of Childbearing*. Princeton, N.J.: Princeton University Press, 1970.

29. V. D. Thompson. Family Size: Implicit Policies and Assumed Psychological Outcomes. *The Journal of Social Issues*, 1974, *30*, 93–124.

30. K. W. Terhune. *A Review of the Actual and Expected Consequences of Family Size*. U.S. Department of Health, Education and Welfare, Public Health Ser-

vice, National Institutes of Health, Publication No. (NIH) 75-779, July 1974.

31. R. B. Zajonc. Family Configuration and Intelligence. *Science*, 1976, *192*, 227–236.

32. B. K. Trimble and J. H. Doughty. The Amount of Hereditary Disease in Human Populations. *Annual of Human Genetics*. London, 1974, *38*, 199–209.

33. C. J. Epstein, et al. The Center-Satellite System for the Wide-Scale Distribution of Genetic Counseling Services. *American Journal of Human Genetics*, 1975, *27*, 322–332.

34. A. G. Motulsky. Brave New World? *Science*, 1974, *185*, 653–663.

35. J. H. Pearn. Patient's Subjective Interpretation of Risks Offered in Genetic Counseling. *Journal of Medical Genetics*, 1973, *10*, 129–134.

36. *Population Reports*. Sex Preselection—Not Yet Practical. Washington, D.C., George Washington University, 1975, Series 1, No. 2.

37. W. B. Miller. Letter: Reproduction, Technology and the Behavioral Sciences. *Science* 1974, *183*, 149.

38. C. F. Westoff and R. R. Rindfuss. Sex Preselection in the United States: Some Implications. *Science*, 1974, *184*, 633–636.

39. J. Lederberg. Biological Innovation and Genetic Intervention. In J. A. Behnke, Ed. *Challenging Biological Problems, Directions toward Their Solution*. N.Y.: Oxford University Press, 1972. Pp. 7–27.

40. C. F. Westoff. The Decline of Unplanned Births in the United States. *Science*, 1976, *191*, 38–42.

41. U.S. Bureau of the Census. *Current Population Reports*. Series P-25, No. 448, Fertility Indicators, 1970. U.S. Government Printing Office, Washington, D.C. April 16, 1971.

42. P. Cutright. Illegitimacy: Myths, Causes and Cures. *Family Planning Perspectives*, 1971, *3* (1), 25–48.

43. C. Tietze. Therapeutic Abortions in the United States. *American Journal of Obstetrics and Gynecology*, 1968, *101*, 784.

44. Center for Disease Control: *Abortion Surveillance* (1974). Issued April, 1976.

45. W. B. Miller. The Intendedness and Wantedness of the First Child. In W. B. Miller and L. F. Newman, Eds., *The First Child and Family Formation*, Chapel Hill, N.C.: Carolina Population Center, forthcoming.

46. L. C. Coombs, et al. Premarital Pregnancy and Status before and after Marriage. *American Journal of Sociology*, 1970, *75*, 800–820.

47. L. C. Coombs and Z. Zumeta. Correlates of Marital Dissolution in a Prospective Fertility Study: A Research Note. *Social Problems*, 1970, *18*, 92–102.

48. G. Vadies and R. Pomeroy. Out-of-Wedlock Pregnancy Among American Teenagers. *Journal of Clinical Child Psychology*, 1974, *3* (3), 27–29.

49. H. B. Presser and L. L. Bumpass. The Acceptability of Contraceptive Sterilization among U.S. Couples: 1970. *Family Planning Perspectives*, 1972, *4* (4), 18–26.

50. J. Blake. Abortion and Public Opinion. *Science*, 1971, *171*, 540–549.

Notes

299

51. G. Lipson and D. Wolman. Polling Americans on Birth Control and Population. *Family Planning Perspectives*, 1972, *4*, 39.
52. R. Athanasiou, et al. Psychiatric Sequelae to Term Birth and Induced Early and Late Abortion: A Longitudinal Study. *Family Planning Perspectives*, 1973, *5*, 227–231.
53. J. D. Osofsky, H. J. Osofsky, and R. Rajan. Psychological Effects of Abortion: With Emphasis Upon Immediate Reactions and Followup. In H. J. Osofsky and J. D. Osofsky, Eds., *The Abortion Experience*. New York: Harper and Row, 1973. Pp. 188–205.
54. C. Tieteze. The Effect of Legalization of Abortion on Population Growth and Public Health. *Family Planning Perspectives*, 1975, *3*, 123–127.
55. M. J. Kramer. Legal Abortion Among New York City Residents: An Analysis According to Socioeconomic and Demographic Characteristics. *Family Planning Perspectives*, 1975, *7*, 128–137.
56. A. Margolis, et al. Contraception after Abortion. *Family Planning Perspectives*, 1974, *6*, 56–60.
57. C. Tietze. The "Problem" of Repeat Abortion. *Family Planning Perspectives*, 1974, *6*, 148–150.
58. M. S. Frankel. *The Public Policy Dimensions of Artificial Insemination and Human-Semen Cyrobanking*. Program of Policy Studies in Science and Technology, George Washington University, Washington, D.C. Monograph #18, December 1973.
59. U.S. National Center for Health Statistics, *Vital Statistics of the United States*, 1972.
60. D. J. Bogue. *Principles of Demography*. N.Y.: John Wiley and Sons, 1969.
61. R. Dubois. *Mirage of Health*. Garden City, N.Y.: Doubleday, 1959.
62. D. Mechanic. *Medical Sociology*. N.Y.: Free Press, 1968.
63. J. Aronson. *The Right to Die: Decision and Decision Makers*. N.Y.: Group for the Advancement of Psychiatry, 1973.
64. W. B. Miller. Psychiatry and Physical Illness: The Psychosomatic Interface. In C. P. Rosenbaum and J. E. Beebe, Eds., *An Introduction to Psychiatric Treatment: Crisis, Clinic and Consultation*. N.Y.: McGraw-Hill, 1975. Pp. 475–495.
65. W. Haddon, E. Suchman, and D. Klein. *Accident Research and Approaches*. N.Y.: Harper and Row, 1964.
66. E. Tanay. Psychiatric Aspects of Homicide Prevention. *American Journal of Psychiatry*, 1972, *128*, 815–818.
67. L. Beall. The Dynamics of Suicide: A Review of the Literature, 1897–1965. *Bulletin of Suicidology*, 1969, *2*, 2–16.
68. N. Maccoby and J. W. Farquhar. Communication for Health: Unselling Heart Disease. *Journal of Communication*, 1975, *25*, 114–126.
69. M. Lalonde. *A New Perspective on the Health of Canadians*. Information Canada, Ottawa, 1974.
70. R. E. Markland and D. E. Durand. An Investigation of Socio-Psychological

Factors Affecting Infant Immunization. *American Journal of Public Health*, 1976, *66*, 168–170.

71. G. V. Stimson. Obeying Doctor's Orders: A View from the Other Side. *Social Science and Medicine*, 1974, *8*, 97–104.

72. R. F. Gillum and A. J. Barsky. Diagnosis and Management of Patient Noncompliance. *Journal of the American Medical Association*, 1974, *228*, 1563–1567.

73. M. H. Becker and L. A. Maiman. Sociobehavioral Determinants of Compliance with Health and Medical Care Recommendations. *Medical Care*, 1975, *13*, 10–24.

74. M. Kohl, Ed. *Beneficent Euthanasia*. Buffalo, N.Y.: Prometheus Books, 1975.

75. B. J. Culliton. The Haemmerli Affair: Is Passive Euthanasia Murder? *Science*, 1975, *190*, 1271–1275.

76. G. H. Gallup. *The Gallup Poll: Public Opinion, 1935–1971*, Vol. 1: 1935–1948. N.Y.: Random House, 1972. P. 656.

77. G. H. Gallup. *The Gallup Poll: Public Opinion 1935–1971*, Vol. 2: 1949–1958. N.Y.: Random House, 1972. Pp. 887–888.

78. *Gallup Opinion Index*, Report No. 98. Majority of Americans Now Say Doctors Should Be Able to Practice Euthanasia. Princeton, N.J., August 1973. Pp. 35–37.

79. *Gallup Opinion Index*, Report No. 122. Public Opposes ''Right-To-Die'' Even in Hopeless Situations. Princeton, N.J., August 1975. Pp. 20–24.

80. R. Barker. *Ecological Psychology*. Stanford, Cal.: Stanford University Press, 1968.

81. S. Milgram. The Experience of Living in Cities. *Science*, 1970, *167*, 1461–1468.

82. *Interchange*, Vol. 5, No. 2, 1776–1976: Populating a Nation. Washington, D.C.: Population Reference Bureau Inc., March 1976.

83. *Population Bulletin*, 1971, *27*.

84. D. J. Bogue, H. S. Shyrock, Jr., and S. A. Hoermann. *Streams of Migration Between Subregions, Vol. IX*. Oxford, Ohio: Scripps Foundation for Research in Population Problems, Miami of Ohio University, 1953.

85. P. M. Hauser. The Census of 1970. *Scientific American*, 1971, *225*, 17–25.

86. T. Srole, et al. *Mental Health in the Metropolis: The Midtown Manhattan Study*. N.Y.: McGraw-Hill, 1962.

87. G. Wilbur. Migration Expectancy in the United States. *Journal of the American Statistical Association*, 1963, *58*, 444–453.

88. O. R. Galle, W. R. Grove, and J. M. McPherson. Population Density and Pathology: What Are the Relations for Man? *Science*, 1972, *176*, 23–30.

89. D. M. Heer and J. W. Boyton. A Multivariate Regression Analysis of Differences in Fertility of U.S. Counties. *Social Biology*, 1970, *17*, 180–194.

90. H. J. Gans. *People and Plans*. N.Y.: Basic Books. 1968.

91. J. Cassel. Health Consequences of Population Density and Crowding. In *Rapid*

Population Growth, prepared by Study Committee of the Office of the Foreign Secretary, National Academy of Sciences. Baltimore: Johns Hopkins Press, 1971. Pp. 462–478.

92. M. J. Horowitz, D. F. Duff, and L. O. Stratton. Personal Space and the Body-Buffer Zone. *Archives of General Psychiatry,* 1964, *11,* 651–656.

93. E. T. Hall. *The Hidden Dimension.* Garden City, N.Y.: Doubleday and Co., Inc., 1966.

94. H. M. Choldin. Population Density and Social Relations. Presented at meetings of the Population Association of America, Toronto, April 14, 1972.

95. J. L. Freedman. The Effects of Population Density on Humans. In J. T. Fawcett, *Psychological Perspectives on Population.* N.Y.: Basic Books, 1973. Pp. 209–240.

96. P. A. Morrison. *Dimensions of the Population Problem in the United States.* Prepared for the Commission on Population Growth and the American Future. Santa Monica, Cal.: Rand, August 1972.

97. W. Peterson. *Population.* London: Macmillan & Co., 1969.

98. R. P. Shaw. *Migration Theory and Fact.* Bibliography Series Number Five. Philadelphia: Regional Science Research Institute, 1975.

99. D. J. Bogue, M. J. Hagood, and G. K. Bowles. *Differential Migration in the Corn and Cotton Belt.* Vol. II. Oxford, Ohio: Scripps Foundation for Research in Population Problems, Miami of Ohio University, 1957.

100. P. H. Rossi. *Why Families Move.* Glencoe, Ill.: The Free Press, 1955.

101. G. R. Leslie and A. H. Richardson. Life-Cycle, Career Pattern and the Decision to Move. *American Sociological Review,* 1961, *26,* 894–902.

102. P. A. Morrison. The Role of Migration in California's Growth. In K. Davis and F. G. Styles, Eds., *California's Twenty Million: Research Contributions to Population Policy.* Berkeley: Institute of International Studies, 1971.

103. R. Gutman. Population Mobility in the Middle Class. In L. J. Duhl, Ed., *The Urban Condition.* N.Y.: Basic Books, 1963. Pp. 172–183.

104. D. M. Wilner and R. P. Walkley. Effects of Housing on Health and Performance. In L. J. Duhl, Ed., *The Urban Condition.* N.Y.: Basic Books, 1963. Pp. 215–228.

105. E. B. Brody. Preventive Planning and Strategies of Intervention: An Overview. In E. G. Brody, Ed., *Behavior in New Environments.* Beverly Hills, Cal.: Sage Publications, 1969. Pp. 437–443.

106. L. F. Schnore. Social Mobility in Demographic Perspective. *American Sociological Review,* 1961, *26,* 407–423.

107. H. V. Muhsam. The Marriage Squeeze. *Demography,* 1974, *11,* 291–300.

108. E. Shanas and P. M. Hauser. Zero Population Growth and the Family Life of Old People. *Journal of Social Issues,* 1974, *30,* 79–92.

109. *Population Bulletin:* Family Size and the Black American. Washington, D.C.: Population Reference Bureau, Vol. 30, No. 4, 1975.

110. U.S. Bureau of the Census. *Current Population Reports,* Series P-20, No. 286. School Enrollment—Social and Economic Characteristics of Students: October 1974. U.S. Government Printing Office, Washington, D.C., 1975.

111. U.S. Bureau of the Census, *Current Population Reports,* Series P-20, No. 270. College Plans of High School Seniors: October 1973. U.S. Government Printing Office, Washington, D.C., 1974.

112. P. M. Blau and O. D. Duncan. *The American Occupational Structure.* N.Y.: John Wiley and Sons, 1967.

113. R. A. Van Dusen and E. B. Sheldon. The Changing Status of American Women. *American Psychologist,* 1976, *31,* 106–116.

CHAPTER 5

1. R. W. Williams, Jr. *American Society,* 2nd ed. N.Y.: Knopf, 1960. P. 22.

2. W. Albig. *Modern Public Opinion.* N.Y.: McGraw-Hill, 1956. P. 74.

3. M. E. Olsen. *The Process of Social Organization.* N.Y.: Holt, Rinehart, and Winston, 1968.

4. E. Fromm. *Escape from Freedom.* N.Y.: Rinehard, 1941.

5. J. R. Commons. *The Economics of Collective Action.* K. H. Parsons, Ed. Madison: University of Wisconsin Press, 1970.

6. A. Etzioni. *The Active Society: A Theory of Societal and Political Processes.* N.Y.: The Free Press, 1968.

7. K. Davis and J. Blake. Social Structure and Fertility: An Analytic Framework. *Economic Development and Cultural Change,* 1956, *4,* 211–235.

8. M. Levy, Jr. *The Family Revolution in Modern China.* Cambridge: Cambridge University Press, 1949. Pp. 168–170.

9. R. L. Coser, Ed. *The Family: Its Structure and Functions,* 2nd ed. N.Y.: St. Martin's Press, 1974.

10. R. Udry. *The Social Context of Marriage,* 2nd ed. Philadelphia: Lippincott, 1971.

11. L. Rainwater. *And the Poor Get Children.* Chicago: Quadrangle Books, 1960. Pp. 60–167.

12. J. M. Beshers. *Population Processes in Social Systems.* N.Y.: The Free Press, 1967. Pp. 96–100.

13. T. W. Schultz. The Value of Children: An Economic Perspective. *Journal of Political Economy,* 1973, *81* (2), S2-14.

14. T. W. Schultz. The High Value of Human Time: Population Equilibrium. *Journal of Political Economy,* 1974, *82* (2), S2-10.

15. D. N. DeTray. Child Quality and the Demand for Children. *Journal of Political Economy,* 1973, *81* (2), S70-95.

16. J. Blake. Are Babies Consumer Durables? A Critique of the Economic Theory of Reproduction Motivation. *Population Studies,* 1968, *22,* 5–25.

17. R. W. Willis. A New Approach to the Economic Theory of Fertility Behavior. *Journal of Political Economy,* 1974, *82* (2), S14-64.

18. J. Mincer and S. Polacheck. Family Investments in Human Capital: Earnings of Women. *Journal of Political Economy,* 1974, *82* (2), S76–108.

19. P. A. Samuelson. *Economics,* 8th ed. N.Y.: McGraw-Hill, 1970. Pp. 449–450.

20. R. B. Zajonc. Family Configuration and Intelligence. *Science,* 1976, *192,* 227–236.

21. C. O. Carter. Family Planning and Population Quality. In H. B. Parry, Ed. *Population and Its Problems: A Plain Man's Guide.* Oxford: Clarendon Press, 1974. Pp. 250–256.

22. A. Leibowitz. Home Investments in Children. *Journal of Political Economy,* 1974, *82* (2), S111–31.

23. P. Uhlenberg. Demographic Correlates of Group Achievement: Contrasting Patterns of Mexican-Americans and Japanese-Americans. *Demography,* 1972, *9,* 119–128.

24. M. Komorovsky. Thirty Years Later: The Masculine Case. In J. Huber, Ed. *Changing Women in a Changing Society.* Chicago: University of Chicago Press, 1973. Pp. 11–122.

25. C. F. Epstein. Reconciliation of Woman's Roles. In R. Coser, Ed. *The Family: Its Structure and Functions,* 2nd ed. N.Y.: St. Martin's Press, 1974. Pp. 473–489.

26. R. L. Coser and G. Rokoff. Women in the Occupational World: Social Disruption and Conflict. In Coser, Ed. *The Family, op. cit.*

27. W. B. Shepard and A. Holden. Family Characteristics and Spatial Mobility: An Empirical Inquiry into the Nature of Households and the Probability of Moving. A paper presented at the Annual Meetings of the Pacific Sociological Association, Victoria, British Columbia, April, 1975.

28. S. S. Sandell. The Economics of Family Migration. In H. S. Parnes et al., *Dual Careers: A Longitudinal Analysis of Labor Force Experiences of Women,* Vol. 4. Columbus, Ohio: Center for Human Resource Research, The Ohio State University Press, 1974. Pp. 141–160.

29. L. H. Long. Women's Labor Force Participation and the Residential Mobility of Families. *Social Forces,* 1974, *52,* 342–349.

30. R. Seidenberg. *Corporate Wives—Corporate Casualties.* N.Y.: Doubleday, 1975.

31. W. F. Ilchman. Population Knowledge and Population Policies. In R. K. Godwin, Ed. *Comparative Policy Analysis.* Lexington, Mass.: D. C. Heath and Co., 1975. Pp. 232–237.

32. W. Peterson. *Population,* 3rd ed. N.Y.: Macmillan, 1974, Chap. 8.

33. A. Inkeles and D. H. Smith. *Becoming Modern: Individual Change in Six Developing Countries.* Cambridge, Mass.: Harvard University Press, 1974. Pp. 133–147.

34. J. Freeman, Ed. *Women: A Feminist Perspective*. Palo Alto, Cal.: Mayfield Publishing Co., 1975.

35. R. Lakoff. *Language and Woman's Place*. N.Y.: Harper and Row, 1975.

36. I. Illich. *Deschooling Society*. N.Y.: Harper and Row, 1970.

37. B. Berelson. KAP Studies in Fertility. In B. Berelson, Ed. *Family Planning and Population Programs*. Chicago: University of Chicago Press, 1965. Pp. 655–668.

38. F. Furstenberg et al. Birth Control Knowledge and Attitudes Among Unmarried Pregnant Adolescents: A Preliminary Report. *Journal of Marriage and the Family*, 1969, *31*, 34–42.

39. G. C. Wright, Jr. Population Attitudes of the Poor in North Carolina: Implications for Family Planning Programs in the South. In R. L. Clinton and R. K. Godwin, Eds. *Research in the Politics of Population*. Lexington, Mass.: D. C. Heath, 1972. Pp. 135–152.

40. G. D. Ness. Methodological Issues in Population and Politics: A Comment. In R. Clinton, Ed. *Population and Politics: New Directions in Political Science Research*. Lexington, Mass.: D. C. Heath, 1973.

41. P. Bachrach and E. Bergman. *Power and Choice: The Formulation of American Population Policy*. Lexington, Mass.: D. C. Heath, 1973.

42. J. R. Udry. *The Media and Family Planning*. Cambridge, Mass.: Ballinger Publishing Co., 1974.

43. M. T. O'Keefe. The Anti-Smoking Commercials: A Study of Television's Impacts on Behavior. *Public Opinion Quarterly*, 1971, *33*, 241–248.

44. P. Schiller. Effects of Mass Media on Sexual Behavior of Adolescent Females. In *Technical Reports of the Commission on Obscenity and Pornography*, Vol. 1. Washington, D.C.: U.S. Government Printing Office, 1971. Pp. 191–195.

45. A. Yarrow. Effects on Contraceptive Practices of a Scottish Saturation Project on Family Planning. *Community Medicine*, 1972, *7*, 281–283.

46. N. Maccoby and J. W. Farquhar. Communication for Health: Unselling Heart Disease. *Journal of Communication*, 1975, *25*, 114–126.

47. R. Freedman and J. Y. Takeshita. *Family Planning in Taiwan, An Experiment in Social Change*. Princeton, N.J.: Princeton University Press, 1969.

48. F. Fromm-Reichman. *Principles of Intensive Psychotherapy*. Chicago: University of Chicago Press, 1950.

49. L. M. Brammer and E. L. Shostrom. *Therapeutic Psychology*. Englewood Cliffs, N.J.: Prentice-Hall, 1960.

50. E. B. Brody. Preventive Planning and Strategies of Intervention: An Overview. In E. B. Brody, Ed. *Behavior in New Environments*. Beverly Hills, Calif.: Sage Publications, 1970. Pp. 437–446.

51. M. Edelman. *Politics as Symbolic Action: Mass Arousal and Quiescence*. Chicago: Markham, 1970.

52. B. H. Siegan. *Land Use Without Zoning*. Lexington, Mass.: D. C. Heath, 1972.

53. R. G. Barker. *The Definition of Ecological Psychology.* Stanford, Cal.: Stanford University Press, 1968.

54. E. P. Willems. Forces toward Participation in Behavior Settings. In R. G. Barker and P. V. Gump, Eds. *Big School, Small School: High School Size and Student Behavior.* Stanford, Cal.: Stanford University Press, 1964.

55. A. W. Wicker. Undermanning, Performances, and Students. Subjective Experiences in Behavior Settings of Large and Small High Schools. *Journal of Personality and Social Psychology,* 1968, *13,* 255–261.

56. A. W. Wicker. Size of Church Membership and Members' Support of Church Behavior Settings. *Journal of Personality and Social Psychology,* 1969, *13,* 278–288.

57. S. Verba and N. Nie. *Participation in America: Political Democracy and Social Equality.* N.Y.: Harper and Row, 1972. Pp. 174–247.

58. L. W. Porter and E. E. Lawler. Properties of Organizational Structure in Relation to Job Attitudes and Job Behavior. *Psychological Bulletin,* 1965, *64,* 23–51.

59. C. G. Benello and D. Rousopoulos. *The Case for Participatory Democracy.* N.Y.: Viking Press, 1971. Pp. 3–11.

60. M. Olson, Jr. *The Logic of Collective Action: Public Goods and the Theory of Groups.* N.Y.: Schocken Press, 1965.

61. R. W. Maddox and R. F. Fuguay. *State and Local Government,* 3rd ed. New York: Van Nostrand, 1975. Pp. 478–499.

62. J. Gillespie. Toward Freedom in Work. In C. G. Benello and D. Rousopoulos, *The Case for Participatory Democracy.* N.Y.: Viking Press, 1971. Pp. 72–94.

63. W. Z. Hirsch. Expenditure Implications of Metropolitan Growth and Consolidation. *Review of Economics and Statistics,* 1959. Pp. 232–241.

64. E. Ostrom, R. Parks, and G. Whittiker. Do We Really Want to Consolidate Urban Police Forces? *Public Administration Review,* 1973, *33,* 423–432.

CHAPTER 6

1. T. R. Dye. *Understanding Public Policy.* Englewood Cliffs, N.J.: Prentice-Hall, 1972. P. 1.

2. Roe v. Wade, 410 U.S. 113; 93 S.Ct. 705 (1973).

3. A. A. Schmid. The Economics of Property Rights: A Review Article. *Journal of Economic Issues,* March 1976, 159–168.

4. B. Berelson. Beyond Family Planning. *Studies in Family Planning,* 1969, *38,* 1–16.

5. E. Furubotn and S. Pejovich, Eds. *The Economics of Property Rights.* Cambridge, Mass.: Ballinger Publishing Co., 1974.

6. C. Bay. *The Structure of Freedom.* N.Y.: Atheneum, 1965.

7. A. E. Kier Nash. Going Beyond John Locke? Influencing American Population Growth. *Milbank Memorial Fund Quarterly,* 1971, *49,* 3–31.

8. G. Hardin. The Tragedy of Commons. *Science,* 1968, *162,* 1243–1248.

9. R. Solow. The Economist's Approach to Pollution and Its Control. *Science,* 1971, *173,* 998–1003.

10. J. Rawls. *A Theory of Justice.* Cambridge, Mass.: Harvard University Press, 1971.

11. D. Ervin, et al. *Evaluating Land Use Controls: Economic and Political Effects.* Cambridge, Mass.: Ballinger, Publishing Co., 1977. Chapter 3.

12. D. Berry and G. Steiker. *The Concept of Justice in Regional Planning: Some Policy Implications.* RSRI Discussion paper No. 69, Philadelphia, Regional Science Research Institute, 1973.

13. L. Lipsitz. Political Philosophy and Population Policy: Insights and Blindspots of a Tradition. In R. Clinton, W. Flash, and K. Godwin, Eds., *Political Science in Population Studies.* Lexington, Mass.: D. C. Heath and Co., 1972. P. 131.

14. R. K. Godwin and W. B. Shepard. State Population Policies: Conflict and Choice. A paper presented at the 1974 annual meetings of the Population Association of America, New York, April 1974.

15. K. Boulding. Social Justice and Social Dynamics. In R. Brandt, Ed. *Social Justice.* Englewood Cliffs, N.J.: Prentice-Hall, 1971. Pp. 73–92.

16. A. Maslow. A Theory of Human Motivation. In P. L. Harriman, Ed., *Twentieth Century Psychology.* N.Y.: The Philosophical Library, 1946. Pp. 24–28.

17. T. Lowi. American Business, Public Policy, Case Studies, and Political Science. *World Politics,* 1964, *16,* 677–715.

18. T. Lowi. Population Policies and the American Political System. In R. Clinton, W. Flash, and K. Godwin, Eds., *Political Science and Population Studies.* Lexington, Mass.: D. C. Heath, 1972. Pp. 25–54.

19. R. Salisbury and J. Heinz. A Theory of Policy Analysis and Some Preliminary Applications. In I. Sharkansky, Ed., *Policy Analysis in Political Science.* Chicago: Markham, 1972. Pp. 39–60.

20. R. K. Godwin. *Population Policies Available to the State of Oregon.* Corvallis, Ore.: Oregon State University Press, August 1973, summarized in *Family Planning Digest,* January 1975.

21. R. K. Godwin and W. B. Shepard. State Land Use Policies: Winners and Losers. *Environmental Law Review,* 1975, *5,* 703–726.

22. B. Crowe. The Tragedy of Commons Revisited. *Science,* 1969, *166,* 1103–1107.

23. M. Olson Jr. *The Logic of Collective Action: Public Goods and the Theory of Groups,* rev. ed. Cambridge, Mass.: Harvard University Press, 1971. Pp. 12–16.

CHAPTER 7

1. C. Bay. *The Structure of Freedom.* N.Y.: Atheneum Press, 1965.

2. G. I. Zatuchni. *Post-Partum Family Planning.* N.Y.: McGraw-Hill, 1970.

3. W. B. Miller. Psychological Antecedents to Conception Among Abortion Seekers. *Western Journal of Medicine,* 1959, *122,* 12–19.

4. S. Verba and N. Nie. *Participation in America: Political Democracy and Social Equality.* N.Y.: Harper and Row, 1972. Pp. 173–176.

5. S. Polgar, Ed. *Culture and Population: A Collection of Current Studies.* Chapel Hill, N.C.: Carolina Population Center, 1968.

6. A. Davidson and J. Jaccard. Population Psychology: A New Look at an Old Problem. *Journal of Personality and Social Psychology,* 1975, *31,* 1073–1082.

7. C. C. Hetrick, A. E. K. Nash, and A. J. Wyner. Population and Politics: Information, Concern, and Policy Support Among the American Public. In A. E. K. Nash, Ed., *Governance and Population,* Vol. 4 of the Research Reports Prepared for the Commission on Population Growth and the American Future. Washington, D.C.: Government Printing Office, 1972. Pp. 301–302.

8. J. N. Erlenborn. Separate Statement. *The Report of the Commission on Population Growth and the American Future.* N.Y.: Signet, 1972. Pp. 291–298.

9. G. Olivarez. Separate Statement. *The Report of the Commission on Population Growth and the American Future.* N.Y.: Signet, 1972. Pp. 291–298.

10. Roe v. Wade, 410 U.S. 113; 93 S.Ct. 705 (1973).

11. *The Report of the Commission on Population Growth and the American Future.* N.Y.: Signet, 1972.

12. W. P. McGreevey. *The Policy Relevance of Recent Social Science Research on Fertility.* Washington, D.C.: Interdisciplinary Communications Programs of the Smithsonian Institution, 1974. Pp. 1–42.

13. G. Hardin. The Tragedy of Commons. *Science,* 1968, *162,* 1243.

14. D. S. Kleinman. *Human Adaptation and Population Growth.* Ann Arbor, Mich.: School of Public Health, 1976.

15. T. King. *Population Policies and Economic Development.* Baltimore: Johns Hopkins University Press, 1974. Pp. 41–148.

16. B. L. Crowe. The Tragedy of Commons Revisited. *Science,* 1969, *166,* 1103–1107.

17. M. Olsen, Jr. *The Logic of Collective Action: Public Goods and the Theory of Groups.* N.Y.: Schocken Press, 1965.

18. J. S. Coleman, et al. *Equality of Educational Opportunity.* Washington, D.C.: U.S. Government Printing Office, 1966.

19. *Tax Burdens and Benefits of Government Expenditures by Income Class, 1961 and 1965.* N.Y.: Tax Foundation Inc., 1967.

20. H. S. Wilensky. *The Welfare State and Equality: Structural and Ideological Roots of Public Expenditures.* Berkeley, Cal.: University of California Press, 1975.

21. T. J. Lowi. Population Policies and the American Political System. In R. L. Clinton, W. S. Flash, and R. K. Godwin, Eds., *Political Science in Population Studies.* Lexington, Mass.: D. C. Heath and Company, 1972. Pp. 39–41.

22. A. Breton. *The Economic Theory of Representative Government*. Chicago: Aldine, 1974. P. 56.

23. O. D. Finnigan and T. H. Sun. Planning, Starting, and Operating an Educational Incentives Project. *Studies in Family Planning*, 1972, *3*, 1–7.

24. L. W. Kangas. Integrated Incentives for Fertility Control. *Science*, 1970, *169*, 1278–1283.

25. B. Berelson. Beyond Family Planning. *Studies in Family Planning*, 1969, *38*, 1–16.

26. A. J. Dyck. Population Policies and Ethical Acceptability. In National Academy of Science, *Rapid Population Growth: Consequences and Policy Implications*. Baltimore: Johns Hopkins Press, 1971. Pp. 618–638.

27. J. M. Mitchell and W. C. Mitchell. *Policy Analysis and Public Policy*. Chicago: Rand McNally, 1969. Pp. 207–250.

28. Furman v. Georgia, 409 U.S. 902, 93; S.Ct. 902 (1975).

29. L. C. Thurow. Toward a Definition of Economic Justice. *The Public Interest*, 1973, *31*, 56–80.

30. I. Illich. *The Morbid Society*. N.Y.: Pantheon Books, 1976.

31. M. T. O'Keefe. The Anti-Smoking Commercials: A study of Television's Impact on Behavior. *Public Opinion Quarterly*, 1971, *33*, 241–248.

32. R. L. Crain, E. Katz, and D. B. Rosenthal. *The Politics of Community Conflict: The Fluoridation Decision*. N.Y.: Bobbs-Merrill, 1969.

33. N. Glazer. Perspectives on Health Care. *The Public Interest*, 1973, *31*, 110–125.

34. O. Anderson. *Health Care: Can There Be Equality? The United States, Sweden, and England*. N.Y.: John Wiley, 1972.

35. H. Schwartz. *The Case for American Medicine: A Realistic Look at Our Heath Care System*. N.Y.: David McKay, 1972.

36. Population Reference Bureau. *1975 World Population Data Sheet*. Washington, D.C.: Population Reference Bureau, 1975.

37. *Congressional Quarterly, Weekly Report, 1975*. Pp. 2471 and 2856.

38. A. R. Somers. *Health Care in Transition: Directions for the Future*. Chicago: Hospital Research and Educational Trust, 1971.

39. P. Singer. Freedom and Utilities in the Provision of Health Care. A paper presented at the conference "Markets and Morals" sponsored by the Battelle Memorial Institute, Seattle, Wash., May 1974.

40. V. J. Evans. Legal Aspects of Migration. A paper presented at the Annual Meetings of the Population Association of America, Montréal, April 1976.

41. S. Thernstrom. Migration and Social Mobility, 1870–1970. The Boston Case and the American Pattern. A paper prepared for the Conference on Social Mobility in Past Societies. Princeton, N.J.: Institute for Advanced Study, June 1972.

42. E. P. Hutchinson. *Immigrants and Their Children*. N.Y.: John Wiley and Sons, 1956.

43. P. Blau and O. D. Duncan. *The American Occupational Structure*. N.Y.: John Wiley, 1967.

44. S. M. Lipset. Social Mobility and Equal Opportunity. *The Public Interest*, 1972, *29*, 90–108.

45. P. A. Morrison. Population Movements and the Shape of Urban Growth: Implications for Policy. In *Population Distribution and Policy, The Commission on Population Growth and the American Future*, 5, Washington, D.C.: U.S. Government Printing Office, 1972.

46. S. S. Sandell. The Economics of Family Migration. In H. S. Parnes, et al., *Dual Careers: A Longitudinal Analysis of Labor Force Experiences of Women*, Volume 4. Columbus, Ohio: Center for Human Resource Research, 1974.

47. P. A. Morrison. *How Population Movements Shape National Growth*. Rand Paper Series, 1973. P. 5007.

48. W. K. Reilly, Ed. *The Use of Land: A Citizen's Guide to Urban Growth*. N.Y.: Thomas Y. Crowell Company, 1973.

49. R. K. Godwin. Population Policies Available to the State of Oregon. *Family Planning Digest*, 1975.

50. E. M. Bergman. *Eliminating Exclusionary Zoning*. Cambridge, Mass.: Ballinger, 1974. Pp. 1–32.

51. Village of Euclid v. Amber Realty, 272 U.S. 365 (1926).

52. B. H. Siegan. *Land without Zoning*. Lexington, Mass.: Lexington Books, 1972.

53. D. Falk and H. Granklin. *In-Zoning*. Washington, D.C.: The Potomac Institute, 1975.

54. Oregon Land Conservation and Development Commission. *Statewide Goals and Guidelines for Comprehensive Land Use Plans*. Salem, Ore.: The Oregon Government Printing Office, 1975.

55. R. F. Babcock. *The Zoning Game: Municipal Practices and Policies*. Madison, Wis.: University of Wisconsin Press, 1966.

56. R. F. Babcock and F. P. Bosselman. *Exclusionary Zoning: Land Use Regulation and Housing in the 1970's*. N.Y.: Praeger, 1973.

57. L. Sagalyn and G. Sternlieb. *Zoning and Housing Costs: The Impact of Land Use Controls on Housing Price*. Center for Urban Policy Research, New Brunswick, N.J.: Rutgers University, 1973.

58. R. K. Godwin and W. B. Shepard. State Land Use Planning: Winners and Losers. *Environmental Law Review*, 1975, *5*, 703–726.

59. R. R. Mace and W. J. Wicker. *Do Single Family Homes Pay Their Way?* Washington, D.C.: Urban Land Institute, 1968.

60. Petaluma District Court Case 375 F. Supp. 580 (1975).

61. Massachusetts State Department of Commerce and the Massachusetts Institute of Technology, Urban and Regional Services Section. *The Effects of Large Lot Size on Residential Development*. Washington, D.C.: Urban Land Institute, 1958.

62. C. J. Gibbs. An Economic Study of Sewage Transmission and Land Use. Cor-

vallis, Ore.: unpublished Ph.D. dissertation, Oregon State University, 1973.

63. J. R. Pease. *Performance Standards: A Technique for Controlling Land Use.* Corvallis, Ore.: Oregon State University Extension Service, 1974.

64. R. Heilbroner. *An Inquiry into the Human Prospect.* N.Y.: W. W. Norton, 1974. p. 39.

65. W. Olphus. Leviathan or Oblivion. In H. Daly, Ed. *Toward a Steady State Economy.* San Francisco: W. H. Freeman, 1973. Pp. 215–230.

66. T. Hobbes, *Leviathan.* London, 1657; rpt. 1947. P. 65.

67. J. Orbell and B. Rutherford. Can Leviathan Make the Life of Man Less Solitary, Poor, Nasty, Brutish and Short? *British Journal of Political Science,* 1973, *3,* 383–407.

68. J. Orbell and B. Rutherford, Social Peace as a Collective Good. *British Journal of Political Science,* 1974, *4,* 501–510.

69. J. Orbell and L. Wilson. Democracy and the Tragic Commons. *American Political Science Review,* 1978, in press.

SUGGESTED READINGS

The list of articles and books below represents readings that should give the interested reader an opportunity to delve more deeply into topics covered in this book. They include pieces we believe to be closely related to the book, standard references in different substantive topics, and materials that are germane to the issues discussed in this book but could not be given extensive treatment. We have divided the readings into eight headings.

I. GLOBAL POPULATION AND THE ENVIRONMENT

Crowe, B. The Tragedy of Commons Revisited. *Science,* 1969, *166,* 1103–1107.

Daly, H., Ed. *The Economics of Steady State.* San Francisco: W. H. Freeman, 1972.

Hardin, G. The Tragedy of Commons. *Science,* 1968, *162,* 1243–1248.

Hauser, P. M., Ed. *Population Dilemma,* 2nd ed. Englewood Cliffs, N.J.: Prentice-Hall, 1969.

Mesarovic, M., and E. Pestel. *Mankind at The Turning Point.* N.Y.: E. P. Dutton, 1974.

The National Academy of Science. *Rapid Population Growth: Consequences and Policy Implications.* Baltimore: The Johns Hopkins University Press, 1971.

Olson, M. *The Logic of Collective Action: Public Goods and the Theory of Groups.* N.Y.: Schocken Press, 1965.

Olson, M., and H. Landsberg, Eds. *The No-Growth Society.* N.Y.: W. W. Norton and Co., 1973.

Pohlman, E. *Population: A Clash of Prophets.* N.Y.: Signet, 1973.

The Population Reference Bureau, Inc. *World Population Growth and Response 1965–1975—A Decade of Global Action.* Washington, D.C., April, 1976.

The Report of the Commission on Population Growth and the American Future. N.Y.: Signet, 1972.

II. EVOLUTIONARY AND HISTORICAL PERSPECTIVES

Boserup, E. Environment, Population, and Technology in Primitive Societies. *Population and Development Review,* 1976, *2,* 21–36.

DeVore, I., Ed. *Primate Behavior: Field Studies of Monkeys and Apes.* N.Y.: Holt, Rinehart and Winston, 1965.

Dolhinow, P., Ed. *Primate Patterns.* N.Y.: Holt, Rinehart and Winston, 1972.

Henry, L. Some Data on Natural Fertility. *Eugenics Quarterly,* 1961, *8,* 81–91.

Himes, N. E. *The Medical History of Contraception.* N.Y.: Gamut Press, 1963.

Hinde, R. A. *The Biological Bases of Human Social Behavior.* N.Y. and London: McGraw-Hill, 1974.

Lederberg, J. Biological Innovation and Genetic Intervention. In J. A. Behnke, Ed., *Challenging Biological Problems: Directions Toward Their Solution.* N.Y.: Oxford University Press, 1972. Pp. 7–27.

Lee, R. B., and I. DeVore, Eds. *Man the Hunter.* Chicago: Aldine Publishing Co., 1968.

McLaren, I. A., Ed. *Natural Regulation of Animal Populations.* N.Y.: Atherton Press, 1971.

Polgar, S. Population History and Population Policies From an Anthropological Perspective. *Current Anthropology,* 1972, *13,* 203–211.

Tanner, N., and A. Zihlman. Women in Evolution. Part I: Innovation and Selection in Human Origins. *Signs: Journal of Women in Culture and Society,* 1976, *1,* (3), Pt. 1.

Tax, S., Ed. *The Evolution of Life: Its Origin, History, and Future. Evolution After Darwin.* Chicago: University of Chicago Press, 1960. Vols. I–III.

III. THE DECISION-MAKING AND ADAPTATIONAL PROCESS

Becker, M. H. *The Health Belief Model and Personal Health Behavior.* Health Education Monographs, 1974, *2.*

Coelho, G. V., D. A. Hamburg, and J. E. Adams, Eds. *Coping and Adaptation.* N.Y.: Basic Books, 1974.

Gelatt, H. B. Decision Making: A Conceptual Frame of References for Counseling. *Journal of Counseling Psychology,* 1962, *9,* 240–245.

Luce, R. D. Psychological Studies of Risky Decision Making. In W. Edwards and A. Tversky, Eds., *Decision Making.* London: Penguin, 1967. Pp. 334–352.

Tversky, A., and D. Kahneman. Judgement Under Uncertainty: Heuristics and Biases. *Science*, 1974, *185*, 1124–1131.

IV. INDIVIDUAL PSYCHOLOGY AND POPULATION

Blake, J. Are Babies Consumer Durables? A Critique of the Economic Theory of Reproduction Motivation. *Population Studies*, 1968, *22*, 5–25.

Blau, P. M., et al. Occupational Choice Participation and Social Mobility. In N. J. Smelser and W. T. Smelser, Eds., *Personality and Social Systems*. N.Y.: Wiley, 1963. Pp. 559–570.

Bumpass, L., and C. F. Westoff. The "Perfect Contraceptive" Population. *Science*, 1970, *169*, 1177–1182.

Calderone, M. S., Ed. *Manual of Family Planning and Contraceptive Practice*. Baltimore: The Williams and Wilkins Co., 1970.

Fawcett, J. T. *Psychology and Population*. N.Y.: The Population Council, 1970.

Fawcett, J. T., Ed. *Psychological Perspectives on Population*. N.Y.: Basic Books, 1973. Pp. 19–76.

Freedman R., and J. Y. Takeshita. *Family Planning in Taiwan. An Experiment in Social Change*. Princeton, N.J.: Princeton University Press, 1969.

Galle, O. R., W. R. Grove, and J. M. McPherson. Population Density and Pathology: What are the Relations for Man? *Science*, 1972, *176*, 23–30.

Group for the Advancement of Psychiatry. *Humane Reproduction*. Volume III, Report no. 85. N.Y.: August, 1973.

Haas, P. H. Wanted and Unwanted Pregnancies: A Fertility Decision Making Model. *Journal of Social Issues*, 1974, *30*, 125–165.

Jaccard, J. J., and A. R. Davidson. The Relation of Psychological, Social, and Economic Variables to Fertility-Related Decisions. *Demography*, August, 1976, *13*, (3), 329–338.

Legalized Abortion and the Public Health. Report of a study, Washington, D.C.: National Academy of Sciences, Institute of Medicine, May, 1975.

Luker, K. *Taking Chances: Abortion and the Decision Not to Contracept*. Berkeley: University of California Press, 1975.

Milgram, S. The Experience of Living in Cities. *Science*, 1970, *167*, 1461–1468.

Miller, W. B. Relationships Between the Intendedness of Contraception and the Wantedness of Pregnancy. *Journal of Nervous Mental Disorders*, 1974, *159*, 396–406.

Miller, W. B. A Survey of Psychological Antecedents to Contraception Among Abortion Seekers. *Western Journal of Medicine*, 1975, *122*, 12–19.

Miller, W. B. Sexual and Contraceptive Behavior in Young Unmarried Women. *Primary Care*, Sept. 1976, *3*, 427–453.

Miller, W. B., and L. Newman, Eds. *The First Child and Family Formation, op. cit.*

Moore-Cavar, E. C. *International Inventory of Information on Induced Abortion*.

Columbia University, N.Y.: International Institute for the Study of Human Reproduction, Division of Social and Administrative Sciences, 1974.

Osofsky, H. J., and J. D. Osofsky, Eds. *The Abortion Experience.* Hagerstown,
Maryland: Harper and Row, 1973.

Pohlman, E. *The Psychology of Birth Planning.* Cambridge, Mass.: Schenkman
Publishing Co., 1969.

Schultz. T. W. The Value of Children: An Economic Perspective. *Journal of Political Economy,* 1973, *81,* (2), S2–14.

Wicker, A. W. Undermanning, Performances, and Students. Subjective Experiences
in Behavior Settings of Large and Small High Schools. *Journal of Personality and
Social Psychology,* 1968, *13,* 255–261.

V. CULTURAL AND SOCIAL INFLUENCES AND POPULATION

Arnold, F., et al. *The Value of Children, A Cross-National Study,* Volume I. Honolulu, Hawaii: East West Population Institute, East-West Center, 1975.

Blau, P., and O. D. Duncan. *The American Occupational Structure.* N.Y.: John
Wiley and Sons, 1967.

Brody, E. G., Ed. *Behavior in New Environments.* Beverly Hills, Cal.: Sage
Publications, 1969. Pp. 437–443.

Cowgill, D. O. Transition Theory as General Population Theory. In T. R. Ford and
G. F. DeJong, Eds., *Social Demography.* Englewood Cliffs, N.J.: Prentice-Hall,
1970. Pp. 627–632.

Davis, K., and J. Blake. Social Structure and Fertility: An Analytic Framework.
Economic Development and Cultural Change, 1956, *4,* 211–235.

Furstenberg, Frank F., Jr. The Social Consequences of Teenage Parenthood. *Family
Planning Perspectives,* 1976, *8,* (4), 148–164.

Gebhard, P. H., et al. *Pregnancy, Birth and Abortion.* N.Y.: John Wiley and Sons,
Inc., Science Editions, 1958.

Goldscheider, C. *Population Modernization and Social Structure.* Boston: Little
Brown and Co., 1971.

Kanter, J. F., and M. Zelnik. Contraception and Pregnancy: Experience of Young
Unmarried Women in the United States. *Family Planning Perspectives,* 1973, *5,*
(1), 21–36.

Lalonde, M. *A New Perspective on the Health of Canadians.* Information Canada,
Ottawa, 1974.

Lee, E. S. A Theory of Migration. *Demography,* 1966, *24,* 47–57.

Marshall, J. F. and S. Polgar, Eds. *Culture, Natality, and Family Planning.* University of North Carolina at Chapel Hill: Carolina Population Center, 1976.

Namboodiri, N. K., Ed. Fertility Models and Measurement. *Social Forces,* 1975,
54, (1).

Rainwater, L. *And the Poor Get Children.* Chicago: Quadrangle Books, 1960.

Schnore, L. F. Social Mobility in Demographic Perspective. *American Sociological Review*, 1961, *26*, 407–423.

Shaw, R. Paul. *Migration Theory and Fact*. Bibliography Series Number Five, Philadelphia, Pennsylvania: Regional Science Research Institute, 1975.

Terhune, K. W. *A Review of the Actual and Expected Consequences of Family Size*. United States Department of Health, Education and Welfare, Public Health Service, National Institutes of Health, Publication No. (NIH) 75–779, July, 1974.

Westoff, C. F. The Yield of the Imperfect: The 1970 National Fertility Study. *Demography*, 1975, *12*, 573–580.

Westoff, C. F., et al. *The Third Child*. Princeton, N.J.: Princeton University Press, 1963.

Whelpton, P. K. and C. V. Kiser. Social and Psychological Factors Affecting Fertility. *Eugenics Review*, 1959, *1*, 35–42.

Whelpton, P. K., A. A. Campbell, and J. E. Patterson. *Fertility and Family Planning in the United States*. Princeton, N.J.: Princeton University Press, 1966.

VI. FAMILY STRUCTURE AND POPULATION ISSUES

Coombs, L. C., et al. Premarital Pregnancy and Status Before and After Marriage. *American Journal of Sociology*, 1970, *75*, 800–820.

Coser, R. L., Ed. *The Family: Its Structure and Functions*, 2nd ed. N.Y.: St. Martin's Press, 1974.

Fatherhood. *The Family Coordinator*, Oct. 1976, *25*, (4).

Huber, J., Ed. *Changing Women in a Changing Society*. Chicago: University of Chicago Press, 1973.

Rainwater, L. *Family Design: Marital Sexuality, Family Size, and Family Planning*. Chicago: Aldine, 1965.

Rossi, A. S. Transition to Parenthood. *Journal of Marriage and the Family*, 1968, *30*, 26–39.

Sussman, M. B., Ed. The Second Experience: Variant Family Forms and Life Styles. *The Family Coordinator*, Oct. 1975, *24*, (4).

VanDusen, R. A., and E. B. Sheldon. The Changing Status of American Women. *American Psychologist*, 1976, *31*, 106–116.

Zajonc, R. B. Family Configuration and Intelligence. *Science*, 1976, *192*, 227–236.

VII. POPULATION POLICY

Back, K. W., and J. T. Fawcett. Population Policy and the Person: Congruence or Conflict? *The Journal of Social Issues*, 1974, *30*, (4).

Berelson, B. Beyond Family Planning. *Studies in Family Planning*, 1969, *38*, 1–16.

Berelson, B., Ed. *Population Policy in Developed Countries*. N.Y.: McGraw-Hill, 1974.

Clinton, R. L., Ed. *Population and Politics*. Lexington, Mass.: D. C. Heath and Co., 1973.

Glazer, N. Perspectives on Health Care. *The Public Interest*, 1973, *31*, 110–125.

Godwin, R. K., and W. B. Shepard. State Land Use Policies: Winners and Losers. *Environmental Law Review*, 1975, *5*, 703–726.

Kangas, L. W. Integrated Incentives for Fertility Control. *Science*, 1970, *169*, 1278–1283.

King, T. *Population Policies and Economic Development*. Baltimore: The Johns Hopkins University Press, 1974. Pp. 41–148.

Lipset, S. M. Social Mobility and Equal Opportunity. *The Public Interest*, 1972, *29*, 90–180.

Teitelbaum, M. S. Relevance of Demographic Transition Theory for Developing Countries. *Science*, 1975, *188*, 420–425.

VIII. GENERAL PUBLIC POLICY

Bay, C. *The Structure of Freedom*. Stanford: Stanford University Press, 1961.

Clinton, R., W. Flash, and R. K. Godwin, Eds. *Political Science in Population Studies*. Lexington, Mass.: D. C. Heath and Co., 1972.

Dye, T. *Understanding Public Policy*. Englewood Cliffs, N.J.: Prentice-Hall, 1972.

Edelman, M. *Politics as Symbolic Action: Mass Arousal and Quiescence*. Chicago: Markham, 1970.

Etzioni, A. *The Active Society: A Theory of Societal and Political Processes*. N.Y.: The Free Press, 1968.

Rawls, R. *A Theory of Justice*. Cambridge, Mass.: Harvard University Press, 1971.

Thurow, L. C. Toward A Definition of Economic Justice. *The Public Interest*, Spring, 1973, Pp. 56–80.

Verba, S., and N. Nie. *Participation in America: Political Democracy and Social Equality*. N.Y.: Harper and Row, 1972.

AUTHOR INDEX

Adams, J. E., 111 n. 42
Adams, R. M., 49 n. 48
Albig, W., 171 n. 2
Aldrich-Blake, F.P.G., 41 n. 23
Anderson, O., 269 n. 34
Aronson, J., 147 n. 63
Athanasiou, R., 142 n. 52
Averill, J. R., 111 n. 41

Babcock, R. F., 276 n. 55, 278 n. 55
Bachrach, P., 192 n. 41
Bardwick, J., 129 n. 13
Barker, R. G., 151 n. 80, 202 n. 53
Barsky, A. J., 150 n. 72
Bay, C., 20 n. 38, 209 n. 6, 235 n. 1
Beall, L., 149 n. 67
Becker, M. H., 82 n. 25, 150 n. 73
Beckman, L. J., 125 n. 8
Benello, C. G., 203 n. 59
Berelson, B., 25 n. 44, 190 n. 37, 209 n. 4, 256 n. 25
Bergman, E. M., 192 n. 41, 274 n. 50, 275 n. 50, 278 n. 50
Berkov, B., 8 n. 14
Berry, D., 212 n. 12
Bertram, B.C.R., 35 n. 3

Beshers, J. M., 179 n. 12, 192 n. 12
Birdsell, J. B., 46 n. 38, 51 n. 38, 53 n. 38
Blake, J., 16 n. 30, 141 n. 50, 175 n. 7, 176 n. 7, 181 n. 16
Blau, P. M., 83 n. 26, 168 n. 112, 272 n. 43
Bogue, D. J., 80 n. 20, 144 n. 60, 153 n. 84, 154 n. 60, 162 n. 99
Boserup, E., 54 n. 59
Bosselman, F. P., 276 n. 56
Boulding, K. E., 4 n. 3, 16 n. 32, 214 n. 15
Bowlby, J., 48 n. 45
Bowles, G. K., 162 n. 99
Boyton, J. W., 154 n. 89
Brammer, L. M., 197 n. 49
Breton, A., 255 n. 22
Brody, E. B., 198 n. 50, 163 n. 105
Bumpass, L. L., 127 n. 9, 135 n. 28, 141 n. 49

Cannon, K. L., 132 n. 17
Carter, C. O., 183 n. 21
Cassel, J., 155 n. 91
Cawte, J., 48 n. 42

Choldin, H. M., 157 n. 94
Christian, J. J., 38 n. 11
Coale, A. J., 14 n. 26, 49 n. 50, 60 n. 66
Coelho, G. V., 111 nn. 39, 42
Cohen, J., 70 n. 4
Coleman, J. S., 253 n. 18
Commons, J. R., 174 n. 5, 209
Coombs, L. C., 139 nn. 46, 47
Coser, R. L., 178 n. 9, 186 n. 26, 189 n. 26
Cowgill, D. O., 60 n. 65
Cowgil, G. L., 50 n. 53, 54 n. 53
Crain, R. L., 269 n. 32
Crawford, T. J., 79 n. 19
Crowe, B. L., 231 n. 22, 252 n. 16
Culliton, B. J., 151 n. 75
Cutright, P., 139 n. 42

Daly, H., 13 n. 23
Darwin, C. G., 37 n. 7, 47 n. 40
David, H. P., 129 n. 14
Davidson, A. R., 125 n. 7, 244 n. 6
Davis, D. E., 38 n. 11
Davis, G. A., 65 n. 1
Davis, K., 49 n. 47, 175 n. 7, 176 n. 7
De Tray, D. N., 180 n. 15
Devereaux, G., 53 n. 57
De Vore, I., 46 n. 36, 41 n. 21
Dewsbury, D. A., 34 n. 2
Dolhinow, P., 40 n. 17
Doughty, J. H., 138 n. 32
Dubois, R., 145 n. 61
Duff, D. F., 157 n. 92
Dumond, D. E., 51 n. 54, 54 n. 53
Dunbar, R.I.M., 41 n. 23
Duncan, O. D., 168 n. 112, 272 n. 43
Durand, D. E., 150 n. 70
Durand, J. D., 49 n. 49
Dyck, A. J., 256 n. 26
Dye, T. R., 206 n. 1, 208 n. 1

Edel, M., 13 n. 21
Edelman, M., 201 n. 51
Edwards, W., 74 n. 14
Ellegson, J., 43 n. 28
Emerson, A. E., 36 n. 5
Epstein, C. F., 185 n. 25
Epstein, C. J., 138 n. 33

Erikson, E. H., 101 n. 32
Erlenborn, J. N., 245 n. 8
Erlich, P., 1 n. 1
Ervin, D., 212 n. 11
Etzioni, A., 175 n. 6
Evano, V. J., 272 n. 40, 274 n. 40

Falk, D., 275 n. 53
Farquhar, J. W., 149 n. 68, 195 n. 46
Fawcett, J. T., 16 n. 28, 81 n. 23, 122 n. 3, 125 n. 5
Feldman, H., 101 n. 34, 107 n. 34
Feldman, M., 101 n. 34, 107 n. 34
Finnigan, O. D., 256 n. 23
Fishbein, M., 79 n. 18
Frankel, M. S., 143 n. 58
Freedman, J. L., 158 n. 95
Freedman, L. Z., 47 n. 41
Freedman, R., 195 n. 47
Freeman, J., 189 n. 34
Fromm, E., 174 n. 4
Fromm-Reichman, F., 196 n. 48
Fuquay, R. F., 203 n. 61
Furstenberg, F., 190 n. 38
Furuboth, E., 209 n. 5, 210 n. 5

Galdikas-Brindamour, B., 44 n. 30
Galle, O. R., 154 n. 88
Gallup, G. H., 151 n. 76
Gans, H. J., 155 n. 90
Gelatt, H. B., 72 n. 13
Gibbs, C. T., 278 n. 62
Gillespie, J., 203 n. 62
Gillum, R. F., 150 n. 72
Glazer, N., 269 n. 33, 270 n. 33
Glick, P. C., 132 n. 19, 133 nn. 19, 20
Godwin, R. K., 214 n. 14, 218 n. 20, 223 nn. 20, 21, 224 n. 21, 274 n. 49, 276 n. 58
Goodall, J., 45 n. 32
Goss-Custard, J. D., 41 n. 23
Granklin, H., 275 n. 53
Grinker, R. R., 10 n. 20
Grove, W. R., 154 n. 88
Gutman, R., 162 n. 103

Haas, P. H., 89 n. 27
Haddon, W., 148 n. 65

Hagood, M. J., 162 n. 99
Hall, E. T., 157 n. 93
Hall, K.R.L., 41 n. 21
Hamburg, D. A., 40 n. 15, 111 n. 42
Hardin, G., 21 n. 39, 210 n. 8, 252 n. 13
Harkavy, O., 16 n. 31
Harlow, H. F., 42 n. 25, 48 n. 44
Harlow, M. K., 42 n. 25
Hauser, P. M., 6 nn. 4, 5, 153 n. 85, 159 n. 85, 162 n. 85, 165 n. 108
Heer, D. M., 154 n. 89
Heilbroner, R. L., 19 n. 37, 284 n. 64
Heinz, J., 24 n. 42, 217 n. 19, 218 n. 19, 219 n. 19, 221 n. 19
Heiskanen, V. S., 80 n. 20
Henry, L., 52 n. 55
Hetrick, C. C., 245 n. 7
Himes, N. E., 58 n. 63
Hinde, R. A., 35 n. 4, 42 n. 4
Hingson, R., 80 n. 21
Hirsch, W. Z., 203 n. 63
Hobbes, T., 284 n. 66
Hoermann, S. A., 153 n. 84
Hoffman, L. W., 123 n. 4
Hoffman, M. L., 123 n. 4
Holden, A., 186 n. 27, 189 n. 27
Holmes, T. H., 109 nn. 37, 38
Horowitz, M. J., 157 n. 92
Howell, N., 53 n. 58
Hutchinson, E. P., 272 n. 42

Ilchman, W. F., 189 n. 31
Illich, I., 189 n. 36, 262 n. 30
Inkeles, A., 189 n. 33, 190 n. 33
Insko, C. A., 79 n. 16

Jaccard, J. J., 79 n. 18, 125 n. 7, 244 n. 6
Jaffe, F. S., 16 n. 31
Jay, P., 40 n. 16
Jolly, A., 42 n. 24

Kahneman, D., 70 n. 7
Kangas, L. W., 256 n. 24
Katz, E., 269 n. 32
Kier Nash, A. E., 210 n. 7
King, J. A., 36 n. 6
King, T., 252 n. 15
Kirk, D., 60 n. 67

Kiser, C. V., 8 n. 12
Klein, D., 148 n. 65
Kleinman, D. S., 252 n. 14
Kogan, N., 70 n. 5
Kohl, M., 151 n. 74
Komorovsky, M., 185 n. 24
Kramer, M. J., 142 n. 55
Kummer, H., 41 nn. 18, 19

Lakoff, R., 189 n. 35
Lalonde, M., 150 n. 69
Lancaster, C. S., 46 n. 39, 51 n. 39
Landsberg, H., 13 n. 22
Langer, W. L., 58 n. 64
Lawler, E. E., 203 n. 58
Lazarus, R. S., 111 nn. 40, 41
Lederberg, J., 138 n. 39
Lee, E. S., 14 n. 24, 81 n. 24
Lee, R. B., 46 n. 36
Lee, W., 71 n. 11, 72 n. 11, 74 n. 11
Leibowitz, A., 183 n. 22
Leslie, G. R., 162 n. 101
Levinson, D. J., 101 n. 33
Levy, Jr., M., 177 n. 8
Lewis, R. A., 121 n. 2
Lin, N., 80 n. 20
Lipset, S. M., 272 n. 44
Lipsetz, L., 213 n. 13
Lipson, G., 141 n. 51
Locke, J., 213
Long, R., 132 n. 17
Lowi, T. J., 24 nn. 41, 43, 217 nn. 17, 18, 218 n. 18, 219 n. 18, 220 n. 18, 221 nn. 17, 18, 224 n. 17, 255 n. 21
Luce, R. D., 70 n. 6
Luker, K., 70 n. 10, 89 n. 10

Maccoby, N., 149 n. 68, 195 n. 46
Mace, R. R., 276 n. 59
MacKinnan, J., 44 n. 29
McGreevey, W. P., 248 n. 12
McHenry, H. M., 46 n. 33
McPherson, J. M., 154 n. 88
Maddox, R. W., 203 n. 61
Maiman, L. A., 150 n. 73
Margolis, A., 142 n. 56
Markland, R. E., 150 n. 70
Marshall, J. F., 80 n. 22

Maslow, A., 216 n. 16
Masor, W. A., 41 n. 20
Masuda, M., 109 n. 38
Mechanic, D., 147 n. 62, 148 n. 62
Mesarovic, M., 6 n. 8
Milgram, S., 152 n. 81
Mill, J. S., vii, 214
Miller, J. G., 10 nn. 18, 19
Miller, W. B., 70 nn. 3, 8, 9, 72 nn. 9, 12, 89 n. 9, 94 nn. 29, 30, 95 n. 31, 107 nn. 35, 36, 127 n. 10, 128 n. 11, 129 nn. 12, 15, 16, 138 n. 37, 139 nn. 10, 45, 140 nn. 11, 12, 148 n. 64, 158 n. 15, 240 n. 3, 244 n. 3
Mincer, J., 182 n. 18, 186 n. 18
Mitchell, W. C., 256 n. 27
Mitchell, J. M., 256 n. 27
Morrison, P. A., 17 n. 34, 159 n. 96, 162 n. 102, 272 nn. 45, 47, 273 n. 47
Motilsky, A. G., 138 n. 34
Muhsam, H. V., 164 n. 107

Nash, A.E.K., 245 n. 7
Ness, G. D., 191 n. 40
Nicholson, A. J., 37 n. 8
Nie, N., 203 n. 57, 241 n. 4
Nixon, R. M., 247

O'Keefe, M. T., 193 n. 43, 195 n. 43, 268 n. 31
Olivarez, G., 245 n. 9
Olphus, W., 284 n. 65
Olsen, M. E., 171 n. 3, 173 n. 3
Olson, M., Jr., 13 n. 22, 203 n. 60, 231 n. 23, 252 n. 17
Opton, E. M., Jr., 111 n. 41
Orbell, J., 284 nn. 67, 69
Osofsky, H. J., 142 n. 53
Osofsky, J. D., 142 n. 53
Ostrom, E., 203 n. 64

Parks, R., 203 n. 64
Parsons, J., 18 n. 36
Pearn, J. H., 138 n. 35
Pease, J. R., 279 n. 63
Pejovich, S., 209 n. 5, 210 n. 5
Pestel, E., 6 n. 8

Peterson, W., 49 n. 46, 59 n. 46, 189 n. 32, 159 n. 97
Pittendrigh, C. S., 31 n. 1
Pohlman, E., 7 n. 11, 14 n. 25
Polacheck, S., 182 n. 18
Polgar, S., 244 n. 5, 50 n. 51, 54 n. 51, 55 n. 60, 56 n. 62, 60 nn. 51, 62
Pomeroy, R., 141 n. 48
Porter, L. W., 203 n. 58
Presser, H. B., 141 n. 49

Rahe, R. H., 109 n. 37
Rainwater, L., 179 n. 11
Rajan, R., 142 n. 53
Rawls, J., 22 n. 40, 211 n. 10, 214 n. 10, 245 n. 10
Reilly, W. K., 273 n. 48
Reynolds, F., 45 n. 31
Reynolds, V., 45 n. 31
Richardson, A. H., 162 n. 101
Ridley, J. C., 134 n. 24
Rindfuss, R. R., 138 n. 38
Roe, A., 47 n. 41
Rokoff, G., 186 n. 26, 189 n. 26
Rosa, F., 53 n. 56
Rosenthal, D. B., 269 n. 32
Rossi, A. S., 134 n. 23
Rossi, P. H., 162 n. 100
Rousopoulos, D., 203 n. 59
Rowell, T., 42 n. 26, 48 n. 26
Rutherford, B., 284 n. 68
Ryder, N. B., 8 n. 13

Sagalyn, L., 276 n. 57
Salisbury, R., 24 n. 42, 217 n. 19, 218 n. 19, 219 n. 19, 221 n. 19
Samuelson, P. A., 182 n. 19
Sandell, S. S., 189 n. 28, 272 n. 46
Schaller, G. B., 41 n. 22, 42 n. 27, 45 n. 22
Schiller, P., 194 n. 44
Schmid, A. A., 209 n. 3
Schnore, L. F., 10 n. 16, 163 n. 106
Schultz, T. W., 180 nn. 13, 14, 182 n. 14
Schwartz, H., 269 n. 35
Seidenberg, R., 187 n. 30
Service, E. R., 46 n. 35
Sharas, E., 165 n. 108

Shaw, R. P., 160 n. 98
Shepard, W. B., 186 n. 27, 189 n. 27, 214 n. 14, 223 n. 21, 224 n. 21, 276 n. 58, 277 n. 58
Shirek, J., 46 n. 34
Shneidman, E. S., 93 n. 28
Shostrom, E. L., 197 n. 49
Shyrock, H. S., Jr., 153 n. 84
Siegan, B. H., 201 n. 52, 275 n. 52, 277 n. 52
Simon, J., 7 n. 10
Simpson, G. G., 31 n. 1
Singer, P., 271 n. 39
Sjoberg, G., 56 n. 61
Sklar, J., 8 n. 14
Smith, D. H., 189 n. 33, 190 n. 33
Solomon, M. E., 38 n. 9
Solow, R., 210 n. 9
Somers, A. R., 270 n. 38
Srole, T., 153 n. 86
Steiker, G., 212 n. 12
Stein, P. J., 133 n. 21
Stephens, W. N., 48 n. 43
Sternliel, G., 276 n. 57
Stimson, G. V., 150 n. 71
Stott, D. H., 38 n. 12
Stratton, L. O., 157 n. 92
Stycos, J. M., 16 n. 29
Suchman, E., 148 n. 65
Sun, T. S., 256 n. 23

Takeshita, J. Y., 195 n. 47
Tanay, E., 149 n. 66
Teitelbaum, M. S., 60 n. 68
Terhune, K. W., 136 n. 30
Thernstrom, S., 272 n. 41
Thompson, V. D., 136 n. 29
Thurow, L. C., 258 n. 29
Tietze, C., 139 n. 43, 142 n. 54, 142 n. 57
Tiffany, L. H., 31 n. 1
Townes, B. D., 125 n. 6
Triandis, H., 79 n. 17
Trimble, B. K., 138 n. 32
Tversky, A., 70 n. 7

Udry, J. R., 77 n. 15, 178 n. 10, 180 n. 10, 192 n. 42, 195 n. 42

Uhlenberg, P., 183 n. 23

Vadies, G., 141 n. 48
Van Dusen, R. A., 168 n. 113
Veevers, J. E., 133 n. 22
Verba, S., 203 n. 57, 241 n. 4
von Bertalanffy, L., 10 n. 17

Walkley, R. P., 163 n. 104
Wallach, M. A., 70 n. 5
Washburn, S. L., 40 n. 15, 46 nn. 34, 39, 51 n. 39
Weins, J. A., 39 n. 14
Weisz, A. E., 70 n. 8
Westoff, C. F., 127 n. 9, 132 n. 18, 134 n. 18, 135 nn. 26, 27, 28, 138 n. 38, 139 nn. 9, 40, 143 n. 27
Whelpton, P. K., 8 n. 12, 134 n. 25, 143 n. 25
White, R. W., 65 n. 2
Whittiker, G., 203 n. 64
Wicker, A. W., 202 nn. 55, 56
Wicker, W. J., 276 n. 59, 278 n. 59
Wilbur, G., 154 n. 87
Wilensky, H. S., 253 n. 20
Willems, E. P., 202 n. 54
Willie, C. V., 14 n. 25
Williams, R. W., 171 n. 1
Williamson, M., 38 n. 10, 39 n. 10
Willis, R. W., 181 n. 17
Wilner, D. M., 163 n. 104
Wilson, L., 284 n. 69
Wishik, S. M., 16 n. 31
Wolman, D., 141 n. 51
Wright, Jr., G. C., 190 n. 39
Wyner, A. J., 245 n. 7
Wynne-Edwards, V. C., 39 n. 13

Yarrow, A., 195 n. 45

Zajonc, R. B., 137 n. 31, 183 n. 20
Zatuchni, G. I., 237 n. 2
Zihlman, A., 46 n. 37
Zumeta, Z., 139 n. 47

SUBJECT INDEX

Abortion: as conflict of interest, 22, 228–29; as example of coercion, 208–9; as fetal care behavior, 128; changes in public attitude toward, 141–42; effect of liberalization of, 208–9; government action on morality or rights of, 200; policies related to, 246–47; self-regulating policy and, 245–46; substantive psychological factors influencing, 130; temporal aspect of, in decision making, 69–70; use as means to control birth intervals, 52. *See also* Childbearing; Family
Accident proneness, 148
Active decision making, 75–76; instigating event in, 75–76
Adaptation: as defense against distress, 110; as related to theory of evolution, 31; broad goals of, 109–10; compared with decision making, 109–10; context of, 110–11; coping in, 65; ego in, 110; failure in, 111; hyperadaptiveness in, 37–38; influence of, on population regulation system, 39–40; influence of human culture on, 49–50; influence of human evolution on, 47–49; internal

regulation in, 110; Lazarus model of, 111; maintenance of self-image in, 110; maladaptation and, 110–11; mastery in, 65; positive aspects of, 111–12; process of, 109–10; psychological, 65; regulation of interpersonal relationships in, 110; securing of gratification in, 110; specific goals of, 109; strategy of, used in agricultural society, 53–57; strategy of, used in gathering-hunting society, 51–53; strategy of, used in industrial society, 57–60. *See also* Decision making
Adaptation stage, 98
Adolescents: contraceptive behavior and, 140–41, 222–23, 244–45; density related to delinquency of, 154; in marriage, 134–35; influence of pornography on female, 194. *See also* Child caring; Family
Affirmative Action Program of HEW, 248–49
Age-specific fertility rate, 118
Agricultural society, 53–57
Anticipatory and situational counseling: community-based marriage/family

Anticipatory counseling (*cont.*)
centers, 241; community organization
and, 240. *See also* Distributive policy;
Counseling
Apes: dyad formation of, 40–41; features
that distinguish from other animals, 40;
geographic mobility in, 42; parental
care systems in, 41–42; reproductive
behavior in, 40–42; sexual behavior in,
41; sources of mortality in, 42; unique-
ness of population regulation system
in, 40. *See also* Chimpanzees/Gorillas;
Gibbons; Orangutans
Auto safety-belt program, 264–65. *See
also* Mortality
Awareness stage, 95

Baby boom, 8, 14, 132; effect on fertility,
165; effect on status distribution, 164
Basic and applied research programs: as
measure to prevent ineffective decision
making, 241–42. *See also* Distributive
policy
Behavior domains, 116
Behavioral processes, in reproduction,
34–36. *See also* Chimpanzees/
Gorillas; Gibbons; Orangutans
Belongingness, 202; sense of community
and, 251–52. *See also* Conflicts of
interest
Biological-level policy, 24. *See also* Policy
Birth intervals, 119; four means to control, 52–53; importance in agricultural
society, 54–55; in chimpanzees, 45; in
gathering-hunting society, 52–53; influences determining length of, 135–
36. *See also* Childbearing
Body buffer zone (Horowitz), 155–57
Brown v. Board of Education, 213–14

Child caring, 123; changes brought about
through human evolution, 48–49; importance of, in industrial society, 58;
in agricultural society, 54–55; in
gathering-hunting society, 52–53; in-

vestment of parental time in, 183–85.
See also Parental care system
Childbearing: advantages of early, 134;
alternatives to, 125; behavior domains
in, 127; consequences of, 123–25; disadvantages of early, 134–35; economic
theory of, 180–81; employment competition and, 125; Fawcett's scheme
of, 123–25; Hoffman's scheme of,
123; influence of experience-based decision making on, 133–34; influence of
social ideology changes on, 132–33;
influence of technological/biological
advances on, 132; MAB systems in,
127; psychological factors involved in,
122–25; role of women in, 132, 134;
social structural factors in, 122–25. *See
also* Child caring
Chimpanzees/Gorillas: infant mortality
in, 45; parental care systems in, 45;
social structure of, 45
Choice point, 95, 97
Chronocentrism, problems with, 27
Cigarette smoking, 267–68
Coercion, 207–8
Collective action, 174, 209
Collective good, 202, 231
Commission on Population Growth and
the American Future, 245, 247, 281
Commons conflict: effect of increase in
institutional size on, 202–3; three social conditions of, 22–23. *See also*
Conflicts of interest
Communication: as related to family size,
179; in dyadic decision making, 77
Community: decentralization in, 203–4;
effect of size on, 202–3; influence of
equality on problems of, 251–52; resolving conflict problems in, 202;
rights structure in, 22; sense of, 202;
social level policies and, 24–25
Community context: incentive structure
in, 100–101; normative structure in,
100–101; opportunity structure of,
100–101; rights structure in, 100–101;
role in decision outcome failure,
106–9; role in ineffective decision
making, 106–9

Conception variables, 176
Conflict factor: contradictory roles as, 104; in ineffective decision making, 104; opposition as, 104. *See also* Conflicts of interest
Conflicts of interest: abortion and contraception as, 244–48; commons conflict, 21, 22, 230–32; enforced health care as, 268–69; fertility as, 228–29, 251–52; geographic mobility as, 229–30; government subsidized health care as, 269–72; individual-group, 22–23, 228–30; individual-individual, 22; individual-society, 230-32; mortality as, 228–29, 265–68; relationship to free decision making and, 22–23; social mobility as, 229–30; zoning regulations as, 277–79
Consideration stage, 97
Contraception: access of minors to, 140–41, 244; as element in life-cycle context, 101–2; as risk-taking factor, 105; as self-regulatory policy, 245–48; contraceptive services decision, 222; counseling and, 198; decision-making process involved in, 67; education and, 190–91; goal-directed behavior in, 88–89; in unplanned pregnancy, 128; ineffective decision making and, 226–27; influence on sexual behavior in industrial society, 58; integration of ego in conflicts of, 92; model of, 79; probabilistic aspect of, 70; problems of male, 140; risk involved in, 71–72; substantive psychological factors influencing, 129
Coping: behavior in, 111, 142, 157; in adaptation, 65; integration of ego and, 94; response of, 111
Counseling: difference between psychotherapy and, 197; family planning and, 198–99; geographic mobility and, 198; influence on psychological freedom, 196–97; structure of, 196; types of, 197. *See also* Anticipatory and situational counseling
Crude birthrate, 118
Crude death rate, 144

Crude marriage rate, 118
Culture: influence on individual decision making, 171; Olsen's definition of, 171

Death-producing behavior, 93–94
Death-promoting behavior, 147
Decision making: compared with adaptation, 67–68; compared with problem solving, 65; nonrational factors that influence, 74–75; routinized/habitual vs. unroutinized, 64–65. *See also* Ineffective decision making
Decision-making content, 69
Decision-making context: role in decision outcome failure, 106–9; role in ineffective decision making, 105–9; situational aspects of, 99–103
Decision-making process, 69; sequential contraception-adoption process as, 79–80
Decision-making stages, 95–99
Decision-making strategies: combination strategy, 73–74; safe/miniloss strategy, 74; subjective expected utility in, 73–74; wish/maxigain strategy, 73
Decision-making style, 74; in active/passive decision making, 76
Decision outcome failure, 103; decision-making contexts as elements in, 106–9; vulnerable stages of women and, 107–9
Deme, 31
Demographic transition, 60
Demography: definition, 8–9; research on, in education institutions, 190–91
Demopsychology, 13, 115–16
Density: adaptive psychology to specific conditions of, 155; as regulator of population, 37; Charles Darwin on, 37; community moderation of, 157; crowding and, 38–39; density-dependent mechanisms in population regulation, 37–39; dominance and, 39; effects of, on agricultural society, 55–56; high conditions of, 157; influence on quality of life, 158–59; low conditions of, 159; measurements of, 154; migration and, 39; population potential and, 154; pri-

Density (*continued*)
vacy and, 154; range of, in U.S., 153; required resources and, 38; self-limiting systems in, 37; social isolation and, 154–55; spatial, 154; temporal; 154; use intensity in, 155

Developmental factor, 103

Dialectic tribe, 51

Distributive policy, 236–42; advantages of, 217–18; compared with redistributive policy, 220–21; definition of, 217; examples of, 217–18; feasibility of, 224–25; to correct ineffective decision making. *See also* Policy

Divorce: analogy to migration, 131; counseling and, 198; decision making in, 130–31

Dominance: as factor in population regulation system, 38–39; in dyadic decision making, 77–78; role in dyadic/family context, 99–100. *See also* Chimpanzees/Gorillas; Gibbons; Orangutans

Doubling time, 6

Drunken driving, 265–67

Duties: as constraints on freedom, 174; governmental determination of, 199–200

Dyad, mother-son mating in, 35. *See also* Pair bonding

Dyadic decision making, 76–78

Dyadic or family context: as opposed to individual context, 99; marriage in, 99–100; role in decision-outcome failure, 106–7; role in ineffective decision making, 105–6. *See also* Pair bonding

Dynamic factors, 115–16; as elements of population regulation systems, 10; fertility as, 9; geographic mobility as, 9; mortality as, 9; status mobility as, 9

Economic theory of fertility, 180–81. *See also* Fertility

Economies of scale, 14, 203

Educational experiential programs: ego integration and, 238; in high school, 239; propaganda programs in, 238;

voluntary work and, 239. *See also* Distributive policy

Educational institutions: busing and, 188; demographic research and, 191; effect on freedom, 174, 190–91; functions of, 189–90; influence on social change, 188; specific and general roles of, 188–90

Ego: ambivalence in integration of, 91; contraception and, 92; effect of increase in freedom on, 173–74; goal-achieving adaptive process by, 92–93; integration of conflicts in, 91–92; intention in, 93–95; motives in, 91

Empty nest syndrome, 238. *See also* Role of women

Enclosure movement, 57

Equal Rights Amendment, 249

Equity: allocative, 212; individual vs. collective, 212–13; procedural, 211–12

Estrus cycle, 34–35

Ethnocentrism, problems with, 27

Euthanasia, 150–51. *See also* Rights

Evolution, as related to adaptation, 31. *See also* Adaptation

Exogamy, 51–52

Expectancy–times–evaluation model, 79

Family: children in, 54–55, 179, 182–85; dominance in, 178; economic theory of, 180–82; fertility in, 179; free choice in, 136; marriage in, 54; property inheritance systems and, 55; reciprocal caring and, 180, 187; siblings in, 137, 182–85; size of, 136–37, 178; social stratification or social mobility and, 183–85; structuralist functionalist paradigm and, 178

Family planning: counseling and, 198–99; effect of education on, 189; effect of media on, 194–95; evaluation of, by six categories, 209; family planning decision-making model, 79; life-cycle context and, 101–2; policies and, 217; voluntary nature of, 209

Fecundity, 32–33, 117

Fertility: compared with fecundity, 32; effect of counseling on, 240; effect of equal opportunity for women and minorities on, 248–49; effects of evolution on, 33–34; effective decision making in, 236–37; estrus cycle and, 34–35; self-regulatory and distributive policies of, 236–42; solving problems regarding, 236–37

Fertility rates, 117–18; effect of household economics on, 180–81; effect of institutions on, 175–77; family influence on, 179; media and, 195; status distribution and, 164–65; variables of, 175–76

Fertility variables: Davis/Blake analytic model of, 175; influence of MAB systems on, 175

Fetal care behavior: abortion as, 128; health-development promoting, 128; infanticide as, 128. See also Child caring; Childbearing

Free choice. See Individual free choice

Free riders, 23

Freedom: birth control and, 19–20; coercion of, from nongovernmental sources, 213–14; conflict between equality and, 213–14; definition of, 17–18, 213–14; education and, 188–92; expansion of, through counseling, 196–98; increase or decrease of, in U.S., 19; institutions and, 173; macro/micro, 18–19; media and, 195; potential, 20; qualifying considerations of, 17–18; social, 18; three types of (biological, technological, psychological), 17–18, 200–201

Gathering-hunting society, 51–53

Gender preselection, 138. See also Childbearing

General fertility rate, 118

General marriage rate, 118

Genetic disease, 66, 137–38

Geographic distribution: density in, 154–58; population shifts in U.S. as aspects of, 153; time series data in U.S. for, 152–53

Geographic mobility: as conflict of interest, 22, 229, 273–79; counseling and, 198; ineffective decisions and, 272–73; in human evolution, 49–50; institutions and, 177–78; MAB systems and, 162; migration and, 36, 160; moving in, 159–60; psychological/behavioral problems of, 163; stereotypes of sex roles and, 185–86; stress points in, 162; use of stem family in, 163

Gestation variables, 176

Gibbons, 43

Goal-achieving, adaptive process, 92–93

Goal-directed behavior: contraception in, 88–89; organization of, 86–89

Gorillas. See Chimpanzees

Government institutions: effectiveness in solving population problems, 200–201; function of, in determining social norms, 201–2; influence on biological/technological freedom, 200–201; issues of morality and, 199–200

Government subsidized day care, 250–51. See also Child caring; Health care

Health belief model (Rosenstock/Becker), 82–83

Health care: as conflict of interest, 229; as redistributive policy, 253–54; government enforced, 268–70; technological, capital intensive nature of, 270–71. See also Health Maintenance Organization

Health-compromising behavior: current issues in, 149–50; increased attention in America on, 150; probability in, 147; types of, 147–49

Health-maintenance behavior, 147, 195

Health Maintenance Organizations, 270

Homeostasis, 10

Homicide, 148–49

Household economics: childbearing issues and, 180; definition of, 180; economic theory of fertility and, 180–81; female employment in, 182; influence of time on, 182; opportunity

Household economics (*continued*)
  costs and, 182; social stratification and
  status mobility in, 180
Human evolution: adaptive strategy of,
  46–47; changes in parental care systems due to, 48–49; changes in reproduction due to, 48; changes in sexual
  behavior due to, 47–48; development
  of culture in, 49–50; geographic mobility and, 49; mortality and, 49; population growth in, 50–51. *See also* Agricultural society; Gathering-hunting
  society; Industrial society

Illness behavior, 82, 147–48
Implementation stage, 97–98
Incentive programs, 256–57
Individual free choice: free migration as
  aspect of, 59; growth of, in industrial
  society, 57; increase of, in agricultural
  society, 56–57; increase of, in childbearing, 131–132; increase of, in marriage, 131–32; population problems
  related to, 217; social interests and, 15;
  three problems related to, 217. *See also*
  Freedom
Individualistic fallacy, 172
Industrial society, 57–60
Ineffective decision making: decision-
  making contexts in, 105–9; factors in,
  103–5; free decision making and,
  20–21; influence of lack of skills on,
  21; influence of misinformation on, 21;
  influence of situational factors on, 21;
  use of distributive and self-regulatory
  policies to counteract, 226–27
Infanticide: as means to control birth
  intervals, 53; crowding and, 38–39;
  fetal care behavior and, 128; guppies
  and, 37; primates and, 42, 45. *See also*
  Mortality
Informational/consciousness raising programs, 237. *See also* Distributive
  policy
Instigating factors, 98
Institutional rules, 172–73
Institutionalized roles, 172
Institutions, of society: culture and, 171;

fertility and, 175–76; freedom and,
  173–75; identification of individual
  with, 173; role formation and, 172;
  rules of, 172; size and, 175–76, 202–3
Intention: intendedness scale as aspect of,
  94; role of ego integration in, 92–95
Intercourse variables, 176
Internalization of externalities: 26,
  209–10, 228, 266–67; education and,
  253; health benefit packages as, 253;
  smoking and, 268
Internalized rule, 172
Irish potato famine, 175–76

Laissez-faire individual liberty: definition, 15–16; fertility regulation
  and, 16; geographic mobility and, 17;
  making policy as influenced by, 16;
  occupational mobility and, 17; voluntaristic aspect of, 16
Land use planning and zoning, 273–79;
  conflict of interest over, 277–78; discrimination to low income families,
  276–78. *See also* Geographic mobility
Learning factor. *See* Ineffective decision
  making
Liberty, 213
Life course. *See,* Life cycle context
Life-cycle context: careers in, 101; decision outcome failures and, 107–9;
  Erikson's concepts of, 101; ineffective
  decision making and, 107–9; vulnerable stages of women and, 107–9
Life event context, random, 102–3; role
  in decision outcome failures, 109; role
  in ineffective decision making, 109
Life expectancy, 144
Lion prides, 34–35
Loopholes, 220–21

Marital decision-making model (Fawcett), 81
Marriage: advantages and disadvantages
  of, 133–34; alternatives to, 121–22;
  change in women's role and, 132;
  counseling and, 198; dyadic family
  context in, 99–100; factors influencing
  (Davis/Blake analytic model), 175;

free choice and, 57–58; human evolution and, 48; influence of parents
on children in, 179; influence of
technological/biological changes on,
131–32; MAB systems in, 119; marriage in gathering-hunting society, 51;
norms in, 119; passive decision making
in, 76; proximate substantive factors
affecting decision making in, 119–20;
social structural factors that influence,
122; teenagers and, 134; temporal aspect of, 76
Marriage squeeze, 132, 164
Material policy, 24. *See also* Policy
Media: influence in changing MAB systems, 195; influence on family planning decisions, 195; influence on
health maintenance, 195; influence of
social and psychological freedom on,
194; influence on social change; stage
of awareness and, 195
Microeconomic Theory, 180. *See also*
Household economics
Migration. *See* Geographic Mobility
Migration model (Lee), push-pull factors
in, 81–82
Money: as medium of exchange,
influence on moral issues, 200
Mortality: accident proneness in, 148; as
conflict of interest, 228–30, 265–272;
current issues in, 149–51; homicide
and, 149; human evolution and, 49;
health-compromising behavior and,
145–47, 263; infanticide in, 33, 36, 38,
177–78; infanticide in primates and,
42, 45; institutions and, 177; planned,
144–45; policy in, 243, 262–72; population regulation system and, 38; situational changes and, 243; suicide and,
149; variables of, 177–78

Natural selection: differential reproduction and, 32–33; influence in local
population, 31; longevity and, 36
Niche: hyperadaptiveness and, 38; influence of geographic mobility on, 36
Nondecisions, 207
Nonindustrialized countries, 60

Nuptial age-specific fertility rate, 118
Nuptial general fertility rate, 118
Nuptial total fertility rate, 118
Nuptiality rate, 118

Occupational Choice Model (Blau),
82–83
Occupational status mobility: changing
role of women and, 168; changing
social trends and, 168–69; free choice
in, 169. *See also* Status Mobility
Opportunity costs, 182
Optimum population, achievement of, 39
Orangutans: long call of, 44; parental care
systems in, 44; territoriality in, 44

Pair bonding: in apes, 43–46; in canines,
35; influence in marriage, 48
Parental care system: changes in response
to density, 37, 39; differential fecundity in, 33; in lion prides, 34–35. *See
also* Apes; Chimpanzees/Gorillas;
Gibbons; Orangutans
Passive decision making: by default,
75–76; instigating event in, 75–76
Personal space (Hall), 157
Petaluma, California court case, 207–8,
276
Policy: assessment of, 25–26; at the
biological level, 24; categories of,
216–20; comparison of, 220–23;
criteria for evaluation of, 209–10;
definition of, 206; determination of
equity in, 211; distribution of public
money in, 24; estimates of feasibility
in, 216, 224–25; implementation of,
223; influence of information and
propaganda on, 227–28; material
policies, 24; organized groups and,
223–24; psychological level, 24; regulatory, 24; relationship to free decision making, 23–24; at the social level,
24–25; symbolic, 24. *See also* Distributive policy; Redistributive policy;
Regulatory policy; Self-regulatory policy
Population Bomb (Erlich), 3
Population bureaucracy, 280–82

Population explosion, 4

Population regulation system: adaptation and, 37, 39; Charles Darwin on, 37; community organization and, 14; density as factor in, 37–40; differential mortality in, 38–39; definition of, 10; dominance in, 38–39; economic growth and, 13; group politics and, 14; individual and institutional decisions and, 11–12; migration and, 39; reproductive reserve in, 38; resource-carrying capacity and, 14; size in, 13–14

Population size: Barker's review of, 151; direct effects of, 151; effect of personal experience on perception of, 6–7; history of increase in, 6; indirect effects of, 151–52; limited scientific understanding of, 7–8; Milgram on, 151–52; negative aspects of, 151–52; personal identification in, 152; quality and quantity of life and, 7

Pornography, influence on adolescent females, 194

Potential freedom, 20. See also Freedom

Preawareness stage, 95

Premarital dyad formation, 121

President's Commission on Population Growth and the American Future. See Commission on Population Growth and the American Future

Probability, 70–73

Problems of population: increase of violence and, 4; influence of ecology movement on, 3; influence of fuel and economic crisis on, 4; influence of humanitarian concern and, 4; influence of mass media on, 4; influence of role of women on, 3

Proception: definition, 66; probabilistic aspect of, 70

Proceptive behavior: and probability of conception, 128; lack of information on, 143; subfecundity and sterility in, 143–44

Property (institution), 175–77

Psychodemography, 13, 115–16

Psychological process factors: ego integration of, 89–95; hierarchical and sequential organization of behavior in, 86–89; stages of decision making in, 95–99

Psychotherapy, 197. See also Counseling

Public good, 231

Rationality, as aspect of decision making, 73–74. See also Decision making

Reciprocal caring, 180, 187. See also Family

Redistributive policy: definition of, 208; educational policies and, 252–53; examples of, 218; feasibility of, 225; fertility reduction and, 255–56; health care policies and, 253–54; minorities and, 248–49; monetary incentive and, 257–58; nonsmokers and, 268; women and, 248–51; vs. distributive, 218–21

Regulatory policy, 254–55, 258–61; compared with self-regulatory, 221–23; definition of, 219–20; disadvantages of, 220; education and, 252; examples of, 220; feasibility of, 225; individual and collective interest conflicts in, 254–55; organized interest groups and, 223–24

Replacement level, 8, 164

Reproduction: decision-making process and, 66–67; differential, 32–33; exogamy as regulator of, 52; human evolution and, 48; intendedness of conception in, 94–95; methods of fertilization in, 32–34; nonrandom fecundity and, 32–33; nonrandom mating and, 32; nonrandom survival, 32–33; norms in, 119; reproductive reserve in, 38

Rights: allocation of, by political systems, 211, 216; Civil Rights Legislation, 215–16; definition of, 209; euthanasia as, 200, 271–72; government determination of, 199–200; inequality of educational, 210–11; of adolescents to contraception, 247–48; of fetus, 246; of women and minorities, 248–51; preferred position of, 235; structure of, within community, 22; to own property, 175–76. *See also* Conflict of interest

Risk factors: decision making under conditions of, 71–72; strategies used in, 72–73

Risk figures, 72

Risk-taking factor: calculated risks as, 105; contraception as, 105; in ineffective decision making, 104–5

Roe v. Wade, 246

Role, of women: agricultural society and, 54–55; conflicts in childbearing and, 134; conflicts in marriage and, 134; government subsidized day care and, 250; industrial society and, 58; media and, 194; occupational status mobility and, 167; stereotypes in, 185–86. *See also* Family; Household economics

Roles: consequences of, 172; institutionalized, 172; MAB systems in, 172; social, 172; stereotypes in sex, 185–86. *See also* Culture; Family; Role, of women

Seat belts, 227

Self-regulatory policy, 244–48, 256; advantages of, 219; compared with regulatory policy, 221–23; definition of, 219; examples of, 219; feasibility of, 225; to correct ineffective decision making, 226–27

Separation. *See* Divorce

Sequential contraception-adoption model, 79–80

Sexual behavior: adolescents and, 87–89, 105–6, 139–41; anatomical changes that influence, 34; behavioral processes in, 34; contraception and, 58; counseling and, 198; influence of culture and its institutions on, 175–76; influence of Irish potato famine on, 175–76; innate patterning in, 33; lion prides and, 34–35; monkey troops and, 35; pair bonding in, 35; sexism in textbooks and, 189; substantive psychological factors in, 129

Siblings: influence of numbers on, 182–83; influence of rank on, 137.

See also Childbearing

Sick-role behavior, 82, 147–48

Situational counseling. *See* Anticipatory and situational counseling

Social factors: in primates, 40–42; in reproduction, 34–35

Social interaction, 172

Social justice, 210; definition of, 214–15; inequality in, 214; policies in, 213; propaganda and, 227–28; variables of, 215

Social level policy, 24; and community incentive structure, 25; and community normative structure, 25; and community opportunity structure, 25; and community rights structure, 25. *See also* Community; Policy

Social norms, 171

Social order, 171. *See also* Culture

Social roles, 172. *See also* Roles

Social Security Office, 237; two-person employment and, 249. *See also* Redistributive policy

Social stratification, 183–85. *See also* Status mobility

Somatic condition, 147

Spaceship Earth, 4, 152

Stage of awareness, 195

Status distribution: as capacity concept, 163; effect of baby boom on, 164; fertility rates and, 164; importance of age in, 163; racial status in, 165–66; senior citizens in, 165; zero population growth, influence on, 165

Status mobility: conflict of interests in, 230; descriptive concept of, 163; educational trends in, 166–67; institutions and, 177–78; MAB systems in, 166; occupation mobility as, 167–68, 280–81; women and, 167

Stress, 155; in density conditions, 157

Stress factor. *See* Ineffective decision making

Stress points, 162

Structural factors: as elements of population regulation system, 10; geographic distribution as, 9, 115; population composition as, 9, 115–16; size as, 9,

Structural factors (*continued*)
115–16; status distribution and, 115–16
Structuralist functionalist paradigm, 178. *See also* Family
Structure. *See* Community context; Policy; Rights
Structure of Freedom (Bay), 235
Subjective probabilities, 72
Subsystems, 115–16
Suicide, 93–94; dyadic psychology in, 148–49. *See also* Morality
Supreme Court decision on abortion (1973), 245–46. *See also* Rights
Supreme Court desegregation decision (1954), 4. *See also* Rights
Symbolic policy, 24. *See also* Policy
System: attitudinal, 85; belief, 85; motivational, 85; self-limiting, 38. *See also* Population regulation system

Temporal aspects of decision making, 69–70
Territoriality: birds and, 38; density and, 155–57; marginality in, 36; population regulation system and, 39; social factor in migration and, 36. *See also* Apes; Chimpanzees/Gorillas; Geographic mobility; Gibbons; Orangutans

Total fertility rate, 118
Tragedy of Commons (Hardin), 210, 230–31, 252
"Tragedy of Commons Revisited, The" 231

Uncertainty: decision making under conditions of, 71–72; strategies used in, 72–73
Universal exchange media, 26–27. *See also* Money
Unplanned pregnancy: as self-regulatory policy, 226–27; conceptive behavior and, 128; decision-making process in, 66–67; emphasis in counseling on, 240–41; integration of ego in, 130; MAB systems in, 129–30; as "number failures," 139; probability in, 128; sexual behavior in, 127–28; as timing failures, 139

Vulnerable stages of women, 107–9, 173, 236

Work institution, 177. *See also* Fertility; Institutions, of society
Working rules, 172

Zero Population Growth, 3